# Lecture Notes in Artificial Intelligence 4008

Edited by J. G. Carbonell and J. Siekmann

Subseries of Lecture Notes in Computer Science

Juan Carlos Augusto    Chris D. Nugent (Eds.)

# Designing
# Smart Homes

The Role of Artificial Intelligence

 Springer

Series Editors

Jaime G. Carbonell, Carnegie Mellon University, Pittsburgh, PA, USA
Jörg Siekmann, University of Saarland, Saarbrücken, Germany

Volume Editors

Juan Carlos Augusto
Chris D. Nugent
University of Ulster at Jordanstown
School of Computing, Jordanstown, UK
E-mail: {jc.augusto, cd.nugent}@ulster.ac.uk

Library of Congress Control Number: 2006928047

CR Subject Classification (1998): I.2, H.3.4, H.4-5, J.3-5, K.4, K.6

LNCS Sublibrary: SL 7 – Artificial Intelligence

ISSN        0302-9743
ISBN-10     3-540-35994-X Springer Berlin Heidelberg New York
ISBN-13     978-3-540-35994-4 Springer Berlin Heidelberg New York

Springer is a part of Springer Science+Business Media

springer.com

© Springer-Verlag Berlin Heidelberg 2006
Printed in Germany

Typesetting: Camera-ready by author, data conversion by Scientific Publishing Services, Chennai, India
Printed on acid-free paper      SPIN: 11788485      06/3142      5 4 3 2 1 0

# Preface

The area of smart homes is fast developing as an emergent area attracting the synergy of several areas of science. Here we offer a collection of contributions addressing how artificial intelligence (AI), one of the core areas of computer science, can bring the growing area of smart homes to a higher level of functionality where homes can truly realize the long-standing dream of proactively helping their inhabitants in an intelligent way.

Here we focus on a particular exemplar application scenario (provision of healthcare and safety-related services to increase the quality of life) and we explore the application of specific areas of AI to this scenario. What will be presented is not an exclusive suite of solutions: other AI techniques can also be applied and other problems can be solved with similar approaches. We hope this volume is the spark that ignites further explorations into these possibilities.

The book starts with an introductory section, *Smart Homes Can Be Smarter*, where we describe a smart home scenario and provide some basic terminology which will be used in other sections.

The next contribution, *Spatiotemporal Reasoning for Smart Homes* by Gottfried, Guesgen, and Hübner, provides a survey of some relevant developments in the area of spatial and temporal reasoning and discusses their role for reasoning about the spaces and the times where activities develop within a house.

*Temporal Constraints with Multiple Granularities in Smart Homes*, by Combi and Rossato, describes how the problem of temporal granularities can affect the system in practical terms. The balance between reading and storing information from sensors as often as possible to keep good coverage of the main events occurring has to be weighted against the problems that storing and searching vast amounts of information pose for an efficient implementation of the system.

In *Causal Reasoning for Alert Generation in Smart Homes*, Galton considers a topic at the core of a reasoning system, namely, how to represent and use the causal laws governing the behavior of the system. This contribution illustrates how such a framework can be successfully used to implement an important module of the system where alerts are generated as a response to the recognition of meaningful events by the system.

*Plans and Planning in Smart Homes* by Simpson, Schreckenghost, LoPresti and Kirsch, focuses on the roles of plans and planning in the context of smart homes including their use in monitoring of activities to identify emergencies and on the provision of guidance to people with cognitive impairment.

*Temporal Data Mining for Smart Homes* by Galushka, Patterson and Rooney introduces temporal data mining and illustrates how the essential components of clustering, classification, and rule discovery and prediction can be used to develop a sophisticated smart home environment.

The next chapter, *Cases, Context, and Comfort: Opportunities for Case-Based Reasoning in Smart Homes* by Leake, Maguitman and Reichherzer, comments on three main areas where CBR can provide benefits for smart homes: supporting personalization, supporting interactive adjustment of the system by the user, and facilitating customization and knowledge acquisition by the developer.

Stankovski and Trnkoczy explain in *Applications of Decision Trees to Smart Homes* that decision trees can be used to evaluate how usual or unusual an activity or event in the smart home can be and in this way help the system to detect contexts where the inhabitant of the house may need assistance.

*Artificial Neural Networks in Smart Home* by Begg and Hassan explains how ANN can assist in the design of a smart home specially tailored to provide assistance during: entertainment, safety and security, caregiving and health monitoring.

Finally, *A Multi-Agent Approach to Controlling a Smart Environment* by Cook, Youngblood and Das discusses the application of multi-agent systems to control a smart environment and describes its implementation in the MavHome project.

This volume offers important contributions for the development of smart homes. It is expected that as the area reaches maturity a more scientific approach to the design of these systems will replace the less systematic approach currently employed. It is expected that the area will benefit from well-established domains of research like AI and we hope this volume offers a good range of examples of how AI can help those interested in the development of truly smart homes.

May 2006                                              JC Augusto and CD Nugent

# Acknowledgments

The editors would like to especially acknowledge Springer for the opportunity to create this contribution to the technical literature, and all the authors who contributed with their knowledge and shared their insights for other people to benefit. We also wish to give our sincere appreciation to the following reviewers, who patiently devoted their time to provide constructive feedback and helped to improve the quality of the volume:

Elena Camossi (Italian Research Council - Italy)
Carlo Combi (University of Verona - Italy)
Diane Cook (University of Texas at Arlington - USA)
John O'Donoghue (University College Cork - Ireland)
Dewar Finlay (University of Ulster - UK)
Antony Galton (University of Exeter - UK)
Bjoern Gottfried (Universitaet Bremen - Germany)
Hans Guesguen (University of Auckland - New Zealand)
Howard Hamilton (University of Regina - Canada)
Peter Hamilton (Queen's University Belfast - UK)
Weihong Huang (University of Hull - UK)
Sebastian Hübner (Universitaet Bremen - Germany)
Jos Lehman (Italian Research Council - Italy)
Ana Maguitman (Indiana University - USA)
Sylvia Miksch (Vienna University of Technology - Austria)
Debasis Mitra (Florida Institute of Technology - USA)
Constantinos Pattichis (University of Cyprus - Cyprus)
Niall Rooney (NIKEL - UK)
Rossalba Rossato (University of Verona - Italy)
Vlado Stankovski (University of Ljubljana - Slovenia)
John O'Sullivan (University College Cork - Ireland)
Elena Tamburini (Medea - Italy)
Alexey Tsymbal (Trinity College Dublin - Ireland)

# Alphabetic List of Contributors

**Juan Carlos Augusto**, School of Computing and Mathematics, University of Ulster at Jordanstown, UK (jc.augusto@ulster.ac.uk).

**Rezaul Begg**, Centre for Ageing, Rehabilitation, Exercise and Sport, Victoria University, Australia (Rezaul.Begg@vu.edu.au).

**Carlo Combi**, Department of Computer Science, University of Verona, Italy (combi@sci.univr.it).

**Diane Cook**, Computer Science and Engineering Department, University of Texas at Arlington, USA (cook@cse.uta.edu).

**Sajal Das**, Computer Science and Engineering Department, University of Texas at Arlington, USA (das@cse.uta.edu).

**Antony Galton**, School of Engineering, Computer Science and Mathematics, University of Exeter, UK (A.P.Galton@exeter.ac.uk).

**Mykola Galushka**, NIKEL, UK (mg.galushka@ulster.ac.uk).

**Björn Gottfried**, Intelligent Systems and Image Processing Department (TZI), Universitaet Bremen, Germany (bg@tzi.de).

**Hans W. Guesgen**, Computer Science Department, University of Auckland, New Zealand (hans@cs.auckland.ac.nz).

**Rafiul Hassan**, Department of Computer Science and Software Engineering, The University of Melbourne, Australia (mrhassan@cs.mu.oz.au).

**Sebastian Hübner**, Intelligent Systems Department (TZI), Universitaet Bremen, Germany (huebner@tzi.de).

**Ned Kirsch**, Department of Physical Medicine and Rehabilitation, University of Michigan, USA (nlkirsch@med.umich.edu).

**David Leake**, Computer Science Department, Indiana University, USA (leake@cs.indiana.edu).

**Ed LoPresti**, AT Sciences, USA (edlopresti@earthlink.net).

**Ana Maguitman**, School of Informatics, Indiana University, USA (anmaguit@cs.indiana.edu).

**Christopher D. Nugent**, School of Computing and Mathematics, University of Ulster at Jordanstown, UK (cd.nugent@ulster.ac.uk).

**David Patterson**, NIKEL, UK (wd.patterson@ulster.ac.uk).

**Thomas Reichherzer**, Computer Science Department, Indiana University, USA (treichhe@cs.indiana.edu).

**Niall Rooney**, NIKEL, UK (nf.rooney@ulster.ac.uk).

**Rosalba Rossato**, Department of Computer Science, University of Verona, Italy (rossato@sci.univr.it).

**Richard Simpson**, School of Health and Rehabilitation Sciences, University of Pittsburgh, USA (ris20@pitt.edu).

**Debra Schreckenghost**, Metrica Inc., USA (ghost@ieee.org).

**Vlado Stankovski**, Deparment of Construction Informatics, University of Ljubljana, Slovenia (Vlado.Stankovski@fgg.uni-lj.si).

**Jernej Trnkoczy**, Deparment of Construction Informatics, University of Ljubljana, Slovenia (Jernej.Trnkoczy@fgg.uni-lj.si).

**Michael Youngblood**, Computer Science and Engineering Department, University of Texas at Arlington, USA (youngbld@cse.uta.edu).

# Table of Contents

# Smart Homes Can Be Smarter

Juan C. Augusto and Chris D. Nugent

School of Computing and Mathematics,
University of Ulster at Jordanstown, UK
{jc.augusto, cd.nugent}@ulster.ac.uk

**Abstract.** Smart Homes have become firmly established as an active research area with potential for huge social and economic benefits. The concept of a Smart Home refers to the enrichment of a living environment with technology in order to offer improved habitual support to its inhabitants and therefore an improved quality of life for them.

In this article we purport how advances from the device and technological side have not necessarily been matched with a similar level of development in processing of the information recorded within the living environment from an algorithmic or 'intelligent' perspective. We surmise how traditional areas in Artificial Intelligence can bridge this gap and improve the experience for the user within a Smart Home.

## 1 Introduction

The term *Smart Homes* creates expectations of an environment which is capable to react 'intelligently' by anticipating, predicting and taking decisions with signs of autonomy. From a computational perspective there is a natural association between this expectation and the use of techniques from Artificial Intelligence (AI). However, research addressing Smart Homes ([1, 2, 3, 4]) has in the past largely focused on network and hardware oriented solutions. AI-based techniques which promote intelligent behaviour have not been examined to the same extent, although notable exceptions can be found (see for example the MavHome project [5]).

In this article we begin the discusion that well-established techniques in the AI field can be successfully applied to the area of Smart Home technology. Furthermore, we suggest that due to the characteristics of Smart Homes they (a) offer a context of application which can soon be deployed into society (b) can have a significant impact in our society and can offer fundamental services (e.g., in health-related applications) (c) they are much more amenable to the creation of feasible algorithms (as opposed to complex-AI problems where computational complexity makes system's construction prohibitively expensive or impossible).

Some of the functionalities offered by Smart Homes are related to economic and comfort-related aspects for example lights and heater systems automatically turning on/off according to the inhabitant's location/presence within the home. Nevertheless, one of the most beneficial elements witnessed from Smart Homes is the improvement in Independent Living such an environment can offer. An example of a cohort who could benefit from such an environment are those suffering from cognitive impairments. The introduction of technology and

J.C. Augusto and C.D. Nugent (Eds.): Designing Smart Homes, LNAI 4008, pp. 1–15, 2006.

technological support into the lives of such patients offers the potential for them to undertake daily activities which they previously would have relied upon from external support. With such a radical change in living environment and lifestyle it is possible to witness an improved quality of life, an improved level of independence and finally an extended amount of time where the person can remain within their own home without the need of institutionalisation.

We illustrate our hypothesis above by describing throughout this article an application of the Smart Home concept for the support of people with cognitive impairments in order to provide a protective environment but with more independence and privacy than in a traditional caring institution.

A scenario of common reference throughout this article will be introduced. Different limitations of state-of-the-art systems to consider such scenarios will subsequently be unravelled in relation to the described scenario and subsequently each will be related to areas of AI which have the potential to remove those limitations.

The remainder of this Chapter is organized as follows. Section 2 will describe the general concept of a Smart Home, then in Section 3 we introduce a typical specification, including typical sensors and problems which can be considered once the system is in operation. Section 4 presents a conceptualization by referring to concepts from an AI perspective (a system transitioning through states as the events occur in the house by, for example, sensors being triggered). Section 5 describes a possible context of interest where a hazardous situation develops and there is an expectation that the Smart Home will be able to react in a range of possible ways to address the problem. Finally in Section 6 we discuss how different well established areas within AI (spatio-temporal reasoning, temporal granularity, causal reasoning, planning, learning, case-based reasoning (CBR), decision trees, neural networks, and multi-agent systems (MAS)) can be considered to provide the kind of intelligent behaviour expected from a truly Smart Home.

## 2   Background on Smart Homes

To effectively address the needs within the realms of the 'Smart Home' environment requires a multidisciplinary collaboration. Such developments will usually involve specialists from Architecture, Computer Science, Electrical and Electronic Engineering and some applications related to the health sector may also require participation of professionals from Social Sciences, Medicine and Occupational Therapy. Within this text we endeavour to address one small component within the scope of Smart Homes namely the improvements in life style and safety that can be offered based upon the intelligent use of the characteristics of such homes and the intelligent processing of information which can be acquired.

The use of Smart Homes to support independent living refers here to the possibility of designing an intelligent monitoring system that can detect when an undesirable situation may be developing (e.g., hazard, security threat, etc). Although all people can be involved in such undesirable situations, elderly people and people with health problems require more exhaustive monitoring when they are not accompanied by a healthcare professional. It is possible for someone exhibiting early stages of cognitive impairments to, for example, begin to cook a meal, forgot they have started this activity and subsequently proceed to leave the house or take a bath/shower.

Smart Homes are usually equipped with embedded devices that can enhance the functionality of conventional domotic appliances. Within our work we have focused on improving the level of support offered by devices which are readily available from a commercial perspective and can be deployed with a simple user interface. 'Sensor' is a keyword in this area. By this we understand a coupling of hardware and software that is installed in one or more locations of the house and can provide information about what it is happening inside the house or in its vicinity. Examples of these can be a movement sensor, a smoke alarm and a timer fitted in a microwave. There are also enriched devices which besides providing information can also accept it, e.g., a tap can provide information detailing how long it has been turned on for and conversely the water flow to the tap can be remotely stopped.

Most of the work focused in the literature is devoted to individual sensors/devices that can bring new services. Our position is that for this technology to reach a second, and more evolved stage it has to introduce more AI-related problem solving strategies so that all the sensors available can be used to form : (a) a more cohesive diagnostic system combining different sources of information in order to provide a more global insight into the activities of a patient and (b) a more flexible diagnostic tool as the circumstances in which the semi-autonomous devices have to act can be better identified having a global view of the activities inside the home.

The essential point here is that, according to our experience, Smart Homes can be much more intelligent than they currently are. However, despite being thematically close, research in Smart Homes has remained quite disconnected from the software oriented AI community. On the AI side, researchers have not yet realized the potential of Smart Homes as a realistic and feasible scenario where their general problem solving discoveries can be applied to benefit society in the short term. Smart Homes can provide the AI community with a very interesting benchmark were different techniques can be compared against or integrated whilst research in AI can help make diagnostic systems more flexible and holistic regarding the state of the art in Smart Homes. This text attempts to build a bridge between the two areas.

## 3   Smart Home Scenario

We consider a model for a Smart Home based on a residential care institution in the United Kingdom. The environment is one of shared community care where approximately 30 individual one-person apartments are contained within the same building each offering high technology solutions to promote independent living for the elderly. At the core of the environment is a central monitoring facility (CMF) which has the ability to detect all sensor and alarm events

**KEY**

Motion Sensor

Emergency Switch

Door Bell Sensor

On/Off Switch/ Sensor

Pressure Pad

Smoke Alarm

Temperature Sensor

Medical Device

Motion Sensor

Radiator

Alarmed Window

**Fig. 1.** Layout of apartment indicating embedded technology to support independent living

concurrently from each apartment. However, to convey the concepts of this Chapter it will be sufficient to focus on just one such apartment. Figure 1 depicts the typical layout of a person's apartment.

## 3.1   Sensors

In this Section we provide a brief description of the sensors in the aforementioned scenario. Not all of them have to be present in a Smart Home and on the other hand new sensors can be incorporated. We focus here on a subset of sensors which are commercially available, affordable and combined can offer an autonomous living environment while maintaining the privacy of the inhabitant.

**Location Sensors:** The environment has motion sensors in the following locations which have the ability to identify the whereabouts of the person (kitchen, livingroom, toilet, reception, bedroom, outside (right below front door)).

In addition, it is assumed the person wears an electronic tag. Such a tag communicates with sensors on the doors to each room and has the ability to complement the aforementioned location sensors.

**Smokealarms.** The environment will have smoke alarms in all rooms.

**Sensors / Appliances.** The Smart Home will have control or monitoring abilities over the following common domestic appliances:

1. cooker
2. tv
3. fridge
4. kitchen tap
5. bathroom sink tap
6. bath tap
7. air conditioning
8. doorbell
9. phone
10. emergency pull cord switch
11. temperature sensor
12. radiators
13. bed

All the above will operate in a toggle fashion i.e. can only be active/non active. There is also a difference between items 1-7 and 8-13. The first group are also equipped with switches so that they can be remotely deactivated if needed.

The house will be fitted with a generic medical device which will have in built diagnostic capabilities and warning functionalities which can then be incorporated into the overall system. After the person has made a measurement, for example of blood pressure or glucose levels, the information is automatically sent to the CMF. The system can make an evaluation of the data received to check if a given threshold has been exceeded (e.g. high blood pressure or low blood sugar level).

## 3.2  Sensors at Work

An example of a possible sequence of primitive events for our case study would be: at_kitchen_on, cooker_on, cooker_off, alarm_kitchen_on, alarm_kitchen_off, at_living_on, tv_on, tv_off, doorbell_on, inbed_on, at_outside_on.

From the initial state, a possible sequence of primitive events (preceded by their instant of occurrence) arriving at the system would be:

| | |
|---|---|
| 0  at_kitchen_on | 1  cooker_on |
| 2  at_reception_on | 3  no_event |
| 4  at_toilet_on | 5  tapSinkBathroom_on |
| 6  no_event | 7  tapSinkBathroom_off |
| 8  no_event | 9  at_reception_on |
| 11  at_bedroom_on | 11  inbed_on |
| 12  no_event | 13  no_event |
| . . . | . . . |

Events with suffixes '_on' and '_off' represent sensors changing values from 'off' to 'on' and viceversa, respectively. One special event we considered is the absence of an event at a given point in time, we denote this as no_event. These represent that at a particular time no sensor changed its value. The fact that no sensor changed its value does not mean nothing happened inside the house but instead nothing that can be captured by the sensors occurred.

In order to develop the necessary approaches to process all of the information from these sensory elements and provide a means of support it is necessary to consider the possible activities that a person may undertake during normal and abnormal conditions. The key parameter is primarily to assess the current location of the person in the living environment. Once this has been realized, it is then possible to determine if the sequence of actions the person becomes involved in are 'normal' or 'abnormal'.

The diversity of the types of information generated by the sensors provides a number of dimensions to the information which can be generated for a person. These can be considered to be (a) their whereabouts (b) their interaction with appliances and (c) the duration of these events. Hence, with such information, rules may be modeled and used to discriminate between normal conditions and potentially hazardous situations when an alarm condition should be raised.

## 4  Smart Homes as Dynamic Systems

We can make an abstraction of a Smart Home and look at it as a system that starting in an initial state can then evolve through different states as events occur inside. Each state is defined by the place the person is in, which devices and alarms are activated, e.g. the temperature of the room. Each of these parameters are discrete values, either boolean 'on'-'off' or within ranges like those used for temperatures.

It is important to mention here from a computational point of view that all the constituent parts of the theory (houses, sensors, possible events, possible states and time spanning since the initial state until the current time of use) can be defined as finite sets. The sequence of events can potentially develop ad infinitum but from a practical perspective it would not make much sense to take the complete history and the possible 'sequence to be'. In reality what happens is that we look at a specific window in time to assess the history and another limited window to assess the possible future sequence in order to infer what may be the case in the next minutes. We do not consider if the cooker was left on by mistake one year ago and we do not try to infer if it will be left on by mistake in one year's time.

Once the initial state has been defined on the basis of the layout of the house, the sensors available and their initial values, subsequent states will be produced as events are triggered and their effects are recorded. Hence, from a perspective of knowledge representation, the evolution of the system will go through a cycle of sequence of states $S_i$ provoked by the event occurrences $E_i$ registered: $S_0, E_1, S_1, E_2, S_2, \ldots$. Lets suppose MDR represents the Movement Detector in the Reception area, TDRK the Tag Detector fitted around the door between the Reception area and the Kitchen and MDK the Movement Detector sensor in the Kitchen and events $n + 1 \ldots n + 3$ denotes the three events when the person is going through the door, walking into the kitchen and turning on the cooker. The evolution of the system in terms of what can be detected and perceived through the sensors is depicted in figure 2.

Lets suppose a patient/tenant is allocated one such house. The event of the door being opened triggers the anti-burglar sensor attached to the door. This will update the system to the next state where the front door is open. The movement sensor in the reception area will also detect movement and that event will trigger an update to a new state where movement in that room is explicitly included. While the patient is walking through the front door the movement sensor in the reception area will stay on. Eventually, if for example the patient enters the living room area then the movement sensor in the reception area will go off and the sensor in the living room will go on detecting movement of the person entering the room.

Movement sensors have to be strategically located; this posses the first practical challenge relating to the interaction between sensors and the reasoning

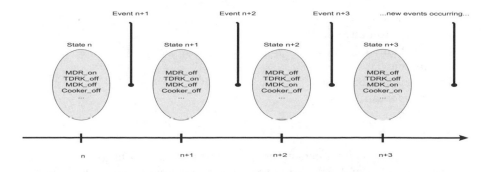

**Fig. 2.** Example of the smart house epistemic dynamics

system. Lets imagine two contiguous rooms like the living room and the reception area. Each one will have a movement sensor, lets call them $S_l$ and $S_r$ respectively. If $S_l$ and $S_r$ have an overlapping area of detection then when a person is moving in that particular area the system will believe they are in both areas simultaneously and automated analysis may become very difficult or at least it may decrease substantially the options the system can consider. On the contrary if there is a transition area such that it does not belong to any of the two regions then there may be important events/states that can pass unnoticed to the system, like the person staying in that area for a long time, e.g., alzheimer patients can stay in the same place for a prolonged duration during a time of crisis.

Occasionally the system can enter into loops. This is neither good nor bad and can be more or less frequent depending on how many moving objects there are inside the house, how many sensors there are and how sensitive they are. For example, imagine a state where the patient is sitting quietly in the living room on one side of the sofa watching TV, the movement sensor in the living room is off. Lets call this state $S_1$. Then the patient/tenant moves to the other side of the sofa activating the movement sensor. After a short period where the patient remains reasonably inactive in the new location the sensor will go off again. Lets call this state $S_2$. If no other sensors are triggered then the state of the house from the system's perspective, i.e., from outside and based on sensor values, will be exactly the same as in $S_1$.

Based on these notions further analysis of possible evolutions of the environment under consideration can be made. These analysis can be made before the system is built as an initial approximation during the modelling stage [6]. Alternatively they can also be used once the system is in operation to reason about the way the system itself is evolving, or may evolve, during real-time monitoring of activities in order to understand the context and decide how to react appropriately [7].

## 5   A Possible Scenario

Imagine the following sequences of events developing one after the other in sequence:

```
at_living_on,
at_reception_on,
at_kitchen_on,
cooker_on,
at_reception_on,
at_bedroom_on,
inbed_on,
...
```

These roughly depict a person moving from the living room to the kitchen to turn the cooker on and then going to bed. It is a common and normal sequence of activities. There are, however, potentially interesting issues in this sequence which depends on other aspects of the activities considered. For example, staying in bed for 'too long'.

To address those issues we need to consider explicitly the time when the events occurred, lets suppose we have:

```
0 at_living_on,
3 at_reception_on,
5 at_kitchen_on,
8 cooker_on,
10 at_reception_on,
13 at_bedroom_on,
15 inbed_on,
...
```

The reader can assume that at times when no meaningful event has been detected, for example at time 2, a default event no_event is recorded by the system to keep track of the activities developed in the house.

Also we omitted repetitions of events in the list above but a more realistic depiction of the scenario will have more information as movement sensors will be stimulated several times in sequence when a person is walking and also multiple sensors can be activated simultaneously. Hence a closer depiction of the information recorded in our scenario will be as follows:

```
0     at_living_on,
1     at_living_on,
2     at_door_reception-living_on,
3     at_reception_on,
4     at_door_reception-kitchen_on,
5     at_kitchen_on,
6     at_kitchen_on,
7     at_kitchen_on,                         cooker_on,
8     at_kitchen_on,                         cooker_on,
9     at_door_reception-kitchen_on,          cooker_on,
10    at_reception_on,                       cooker_on,
11    at_reception_on,                       cooker_on,
12    at_door_reception-bedroom_on,          cooker_on,
13    at_bedroom_on,                         cooker_on,
14    at_bedroom_on,                         cooker_on,
15    at_bedroom_on,                         cooker_on,     inbed_on,
...
```

Notice that in the list above at_door_reception-kitchen_on and at_reception_on correspond to what we generically described as $MDR$ and $TDRK$, respectively, in figure 2. Some sensors can be assumed to persist in an 'on' status once they have been activated, e.g. the cooker being on unless it is turned off, whilst other sensors tend to persist in an 'off' status, e.g. a movement sensor will be 'on' only while movement is detected.

Also it is worth mentioning that although we considered a way to attach temporal references to events in this section and to states in figure 2 which resemble instants we do not intend to suggest that this is a mandatory way to associate time with events and states.

# 6    Areas for Possible AI applications

AI techniques can be used to contribute in many ways to the development of Smart Homes like the one described in the previous sections. The Sections below exemplify this further, however, this should not be considered as an exhaustive set of possibilities but more an opportunity to offer some concepts of how the various levels of applications waiting to be explored may be deployed.

## 6.1    Spatio-temporal Reasoning

Analysis of the activities developed in the Smart Home described in Section 5 are not made based on visual aids due to privacy issues. Instead it is conducted based on the information obtained from the sensors. It is vital in this process for the system to be aware of the places visited by the patient and the order of events generated as well as their duration.

For example, in the list of events listed in the previous section it is fundamental to the understanding of a situation to be able to consider in which order the places where visited and realizing that by being in bed last the patient is now in a passive position and hence is more likely to forget about taking care of what has been left on the cooker. Detection of position can be achieved via the movement sensors in each room; to disambiguate some situations tag detectors on each door are needed.

Here it is important also to distinguish the patient from a visitor, pets, or other moving objects like a curtain moved by the wind. Keeping a history of the last movements of the patient can help to diagnose where the patient may be, sometimes tag detectors are essential for this task but then different questions arise, for example what does it mean if the patient stays for a long period of time under the door, has the patient fallen or are they talking to someone else in the house or perhaps they are having a rest?

Spatio-temporal reasoning is fundamental here to reason about where the patient can be and according to the time elapsed to diagnose if action is required on behalf of the caring personnel. The whole situation of leaving the cooker on followed by a period of time where the patient goes outside the kitchen leaving the cooker unattended is a complex event, depending on the condition that it takes more time than it is considered safe, this may or may not constitute a situation of interest for the monitoring system. Here *qualitative* as well as *quantitative* temporal reasoning is required to differentiate between these situations.

## 6.2    Temporal Granularity

Activities can be monitored at many different levels in terms of information granularity. Choosing the right level of information granularity is not trivial and can have important consequences in terms of what the system can achieve and how well it can perform in terms of efficiency.

In the list of activities presented in Section 5 sensors give information at a particular level of granularity which we also related to a particular level of temporal granularity. Let us say that data from the sensors are recorded each second.

There are reasoning activities that may demand to analyze only one, two or three successive activities and for that a few seconds are enough but to infer a trend a much more global view spanning for several minutes or days may be needed. For some diagnostic tasks low levels of time granularity are needed to allow the system to infer that the patient is in regular movement because of the speed at which they are moving through the successive rooms. But for other diagnostic tasks a way of abstracting different views of the system in terms of the different granularity levels of temporal information is very important, for example to identify a pattern indicating loss of memory or disorientation in the patient according to the frequency of episodes in which the patient left the cooker unattended or the apparently random process of wandering through rooms.

## 6.3   Causal Reasoning

Certainly the relation between the actions performed by the patient and the resulting states is a fundamental part of an automated diagnosis system however this issue has not yet been considered from the perspective of information analysis in Smart Homes and is not clear, for example, what system will be most effective in predicting possible outcomes given a trend of behaviour of a patient.

Suppose the cooker has no timer, it will stay on and if it persists in that state for a sufficiently long time the food may be burnt with the consequent frustration for the patient and the possibility of causing a fire and subsequently generating a call to the fire brigade. Persistency coupled with causal reasoning is fundamental here to predict possible outcomes and help the system to react in order to avoid possible problems.

Also of relevance here is the detection of complex events. Although there are some suggestions addressing this in the literature there is still no rigorous study for the case of Smart Homes on what complex events turn out to be more important, what characteristics the language to describe them should have and what the associated algorithms for their detections should be.

## 6.4   Planning

Planning can also be applied to the use of Smart Homes for healthcare. For example, according to the patient's demands for medicines, a plan can be constructed regulating medication intake hence its application or realization by the patient can be monitored by the system reporting instances of non-compliance or significant deviations from the prescribed medication regimen.

A variation of the scenario presented in Section 5 can be conceived where instead of the patient turning-on the cooker s/he takes some medicine. The system should monitor the medicine is taken within an appropriate time window, the frequency of its intakes, and if say, it has some side effects related to sleep disorders then the time the patient stays in bed can also be carefully observed.

## 6.5  Learning

Learning about the behaviour of the patient is essential in order to self-tune the system to further support the personalized independence the Smart Home can offer. Even when a system is prescribed for a Smart Home environment, different patients will have different conditions and habits which have to be taken into account for the system to be useful. For example, the normal time for a patient to be in bed may be from 11PM to 7AM and s/he may be expected every day to be up and active at 7:30 AM. Detecting this is not the case will be a cause for concern, while for other patients 9AM will be the normal time and being contacted at 7:30 AM by the nurse to check if they are well would be inappropriate.

Data Mining is useful here in order to learn new information from the statistics of the system, which can then be focused on a single patient, group of patients sharing a specific condition, or in a more heterogeneous group of people using a group of Smart Homes.

These learning capabilities are essential, for example, to assist a diagnostic system using CBR or any other diagnosis technique where, for instance, repetition of activities like the one leaving the cooker unattended or a persisting shift in habits will lead to a case being identified and suggested by the system.

## 6.6  Case-Based Reasoning

CBR can be used to identify patterns of patient behaviour. This can be used for diagnosis of situations which need urgent reaction on behalf of the system.

As shifts in habits are detected and learned by the system CBR-based techniques can be applied, for example, to diagnose when these shifts are similar or dissimilar to patterns of behaviour which constitutes a reason for concern.

Sometimes deviations from the expected time for taking meals or going to bed can be expected as daily activities can be changed by visits or exceptional events which are not related to any health problem affecting the patient. Differentiating these issues on the basis of contextual and historical information poses a real challenge for a diagnostic system to give useful advice whilst minimizing the chances of raising false alarms.

## 6.7  Decision Trees

Decision Trees may be used to monitor the sequence of events within the home and allow the monitoring system to react accordingly, especially in instances of concern where the person requires a form of intervention. Within the home environment it is common that sequences of events will be repeated, some of which will lead to hazardous situations requiring intervention and others can be considered as normal behaviour. These events, although occurring at different instances in time, should result in similar resulting supporting actions by the system. Although finite, it is possible to identify a large set of repeating actions with moderately varying degrees of support required.

For example, when considering the scenario described in Section 5 by simply turning the cooker on and going to bed requires a form of automated inter vention which could be considered as the terminating node of a branch of the tree. Here utility-related weights can be used to tune the decision support system about the risks involved when decisions to attend a possible emergency are made. For example, there is a cost on attending false alarms on behalf of the assisting personnel that has to be weighted against the risks involved if the call is ignored. There will be different costs associated with attending different alerts. For example, the system suggesting a possibility that the TV has been left on has different risks involved than when it is suggesting the possibility that the cooker has been left on.

Although the aforementioned are at the most simplistic levels they may be supported by such an approach. More intricate sequences and outcomes can be detected by longer term monitoring and profiling of activities which can be used as the basis to form the decision model and where appropriate introduce the notion of time.

## 6.8   Neural Networks

Neural Networks have long been established as powerful tools for classification and prediction. The vast array of topologies and supervised and un-supervised methods of learning offer the potential for a number of solutions to the management and processing of information within the Smart Home. For example, from a monitoring perspective Time Delay Neural Networks can be used to represent temporal relationships and hence within the given context of Smart Homes be used to predict likely activities of the person based on a preceding set of actions over time. Considering the scenario described in Section 5, the activities of the person and their time dependencies can be used as continuous inputs to the network and the output of the network can be trained to either automatically 'turn off the cooker' as in the scenario described in Section 5 or for a more generic sequence of time related events, automatically raise an alarm to the CMF.

## 6.9   Multi-agent Systems

MAS can be used as a development paradigm where a house is monitored for a group of agents with different skills and duties. The application of agent-oriented technology to healthcare is an area which is receiving increasing attention in the research community.

The scenario depicted in Section 5 can be assisted at a design level by including MAS-related developing methodologies where different parts of the system are seen as interacting agents with specific skills and monitoring duties. For example, an agent can be designed to monitor activities in the kitchen and another in the living and another in the bedroom or there can be agents specialized in different types of sensors. Hence, while one is dealing with devices another is in charge of movement monitoring sensors. Conclusions in the system can be reached after deliberation of different agents and using different techniques related to the representation of consensus and disagreement.

## 7   Conclusions

We present our view in this article which relates to the fact that much more needs and can be performed in terms of equipping Smart Home systems with advanced reasoning capabilities. Increasing the functionality of the available hardware with computational intelligence techniques will have the resultant effect of increasing the complexity of contexts to be understood, increasing the capabilities of the system to identify interesting situations, for example hazards, and to offer the ability of the system to react in a more appropriate way in terms of the quality of judgment.

We describe problems where a system should be able to intelligently detect a particular situation of interest and react intelligently and identified how traditional areas in AI can provide answers from dfferent perspectives to these problems. We hope this analysis will inspire, motivate and guide the development of the next generation of truly Smart Homes.

## References

1. Mokhtari, M., ed.: *Proceedings of 1st International Conference on Smart Homes and Health Telematics (ICOST'2003)*. In Mokhtari, M., ed.: *Independent living for persons with disabilities and elderly people*. Volume 12 of Assistive Technology Research Series., IOS Press (2003) Paris, France.
2. Zhang, D., Moktari, M., eds.: *Proceedings of 2nd International Conference On Smart homes and health Telematic (ICOST2004)*. In Zhang, D., Moktari, M., eds.: *Toward a Human Friendly Assistive Environment*. Volume 14 of Assistive Technology Research Series., IOS Press (2004) Singapore.
3. Giroux, S., Pigot, H., eds.: *Proceedings of 3rd International Conference On Smart homes and health Telematic (ICOST2005)*. In Giroux, S., Pigot, H., eds.: *From Smart Homes to Smart Care*. Volume 15 of Assistive Technology Research Series., IOS Press (2005) Sherbrooke, Canada.
4. Nugent, C.D., Augusto, J.C., eds.: *Proceedings of 4th International Conference On Smart homes and health Telematic (ICOST2006)*. In Nugent, C.D., Augusto, J.C., eds.: *Smart Homes and Beyond*. Assistive Technology Research Series, IOS Press (2006) Belfast, UK (In print).
5. Youngblood, G.M., III, E.O.H., Holder, L.B., Cook, D.J.: Automation intelligence for the smart environment. In: Proceedings of IJCAI 2005. (2005) 1513–1514.

6. Augusto, J., Nugent, C.: A new architecture for smart homes based on adb and temporal reasoning. In Zhang, D., Mokhtari, M., eds.: Toward a Human Friendly Assistive Environment (Proceedings of 2nd International Conference On Smart homes and health Telematic), IOS Press (2004) 106–113 Assistive Technology Research Series, Volume 14. September 15-17.
7. Augusto, J., Nugent, C.: The use of temporal reasoning and management of complex events in smart homes. In de Mántaras, R.L., Saitta, L., eds.: Proceedings of European Conference on Artificial Intelligence (ECAI 2004), IOS Press (Amsterdam, The Netherlands) (2004) 778–782 August, 22-27.

# Spatiotemporal Reasoning for Smart Homes

Björn Gottfried[1], Hans W. Guesgen[2], and Sebastian Hübner[1]

[1] Artificial Intelligence Group
Centre for Computing Technologies (TZI)
Universität Bremen
{bg, huebner}@tzi.de
[2] Computer Science Department
University of Auckland
hans@cs.auckland.ac.nz

**Abstract.** An important aspect in smart homes is the ability to reason about space and time. Certain things have to be done at certain times or at certain places, or they have to be done in relation with other things. For example, it might be necessary to switch on the lights in a room during the night and while a person is present in that room, but not if the room is the bedroom and the person is asleep. In this chapter, we discuss several AI-techniques for dealing with temporal and spatial knowledge in smart homes, mainly focussing on qualitative approaches to spatiotemporal reasoning.

## 1   Introduction and Motivation

Reasoning about space and time plays an essential role in our everyday lives: when navigating around our cities through road networks, when working according to schedules at our work places, or when finding our way around at home. In the latter case, smart homes can support us in this reasoning process, as they can remind us to do certain things at certain times or to be at certain places at certain times. This is of particular benefit for the elderly or people with cognitive impairments.

In a recent article in the AI Magazine [1], Martha Pollack paints the picture of an aging world, which experiences a demographic shift from a population with mainly relatively young people to one with many old people. Some of these need assistance if they want to be able to continue living in the homes they are used to. As an example of such an assistance, Pollack describes the Autominder system, which uses temporal reasoning in its plan manager. Temporal reasoning in this system is based on temporal constraints, for example, the time interval reserved for eating breakfast cannot overlap the interval set aside for taking a bath. When constructing a plan for the day, the system has to produce a plan that is consistent with the constraints, i.e. it has to assign time intervals to various activities in such a way that the intervals satisfy the temporal constraints.

Pollack's Autominder system is just one example of how temporal, spatial, and spatiotemporal approaches impact smart homes. Another one is the SLAM (simultaneous localisation and mapping) problem [2], which' occurs in smart

J.C. Augusto and C.D. Nugent (Eds.): Designing Smart Homes, LNAI 4008, pp. 16–34, 2006.

home to some extent. When an elderly person moves around in the house, her position cannot be determined with 100% accuracy, as one can hardly make the person wear sensor gloves, or any other technical equipment which is probably difficult to manage, but which is necessary in order to determine her position. Therefore, one has to rely on external sensor information, which means that there is a localisation problem. Additionally, the environment is usually not known completely. The layout of the rooms in the house might not change, but chairs can be moved around, doors can be opened or shut, etc., which means that there is also a mapping problem.

In robotics, SLAM problems are usually tackled with probabilistic approaches, which often require complex computations. We argue that in the context of smart homes, more light-weight approaches can be used, which for some problems can be restricted to qualitative approaches. Some of these approaches are based on topology, while others use spatial arrangements. The following section will discuss in more detail why qualitative approaches are often preferred over quantitative ones.

## 2    Qualitative vs. Quantitative Approaches

Reasoning about time and space in AI is always related to the ways in which human beings deal with time and space in their everyday life. This is different, for example, in physics where we are normally interested in the precise spatiotemporal behaviour of systems. Instead of precise measurements, in AI qualitative knowledge is employed and there are a number of reasons for this:

1. Binary decisions are frequently to be made, requiring a concise spatiotemporal assessment of the state of affairs, instead of precise measurements about space and time.
2. Coarse preliminary decisions are useful in planning since the world changes all the time. It makes no sense that an AI-system commits itself too early to precise spatiotemporal conditions.
3. Coarse qualitative representations frequently suffice for solving some problems which do not require precise measurements at all (*before* the elderly lies down in bed she has to take her medicine).
4. The usage of a number of qualitative distinctions leads to more efficient reasoning techniques than when using precise quantities and variables with continuous domains.
5. Actions are to be performed in space and time; for this purpose, additional knowledge beyond space and time must be integrated with the present spatiotemporal conditions (the preparation of a meal includes a list of ingredients, the order of their treatment, and information about how to combine them correctly). This knowledge is normally available in the form of symbolic representations which can be reconciled particularly well with spatiotemporal knowledge which is given qualitatively.

As we shall learn in the following sections, this rationale in particular applies to smart homes in which means for helping people are to be provided. Both temporal knowledge and spatial knowledge are expressible in terms of definitions about qualitative concepts which meet in a number of qualitative calculi, all of which share fundamental structural similarities. These calculi, in the first place, improve the efficiency of AI-systems and their modelling. However, whenever precise, quantitative information matters for the purpose of solving specific spatial problems, we refer to the field of *computational geometry* (cf. [3], [4]).

# 3   Temporal Calculi

Although there is a spectrum of approaches to temporal reasoning, two approaches within this spectrum stick out from the rest and are frequently referred to in applications: Allen's temporal logic [5] and the point algebra [6]. In the following subsections, we review these approaches and apply them to problems occurring in smart homes.

## 3.1   Allen's Temporal Logic

Instead of dealing with time points, it is common practice to describe scenarios by intervals which last over a period of time, and which describe specific events. Allen [5] introduced a temporal logic based on a set of thirteen atomic temporal relations between time intervals (see Figure 1). These relations are used to describe how an event relates to another event. For example, the event of a sensor in a room being triggered occurs during the event of a person being in that room. Or the event of the door to the room being opened occurs before the event of the person entering the room. If $I_1$ denotes the time intervals in which the door-opening event occurs, $I_2$ the one for the person-in-room event, and $I_3$ the one for sensor-triggering event, then we would have the following relations:

$$I_1 < I_2 \quad \text{and} \quad I_2 \text{di} I_3$$

Together with the 13 relations depicted in Figure 1, Allen introduced an algorithm to reason about networks of such relations. The basis of Allen's algorithm is a composition table, which determines the possible relations between two intervals like $I_1$ and $I_3$ given the relations between $I_1$ and another interval $I_2$ as well as the relation between $I_2$ and $I_3$. The composition table is shown in Figure 2.

If, for example, the door to the room is opened ($I_1$) before the person is in the room ($I_2$) and the sensor is triggered ($I_3$) during the person's presence in the room, then the composition table tells us that the door is opened before the sensor is triggered:

$$I_1 < I_2 \quad \text{and} \quad I_2 \text{di} I_3 \quad \text{then} \quad I_1 < I_3$$

If we then learn that the event of the sensor being triggered overlaps with the event of an automatic phone call being made to a helpline (represented by $I_4$),

| Relation | Illustration | Interpretation |
|----------|-------------|----------------|
| $I_1 < I_2$ <br> $I_2 > I_1$ | 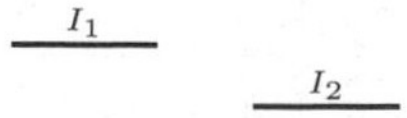 $I_1$ <br> $I_2$ | $I_1$ before $I_2$ <br> $I_2$ after $I_1$ |
| $I_1 m I_2$ <br> $I_2 mi I_1$ | 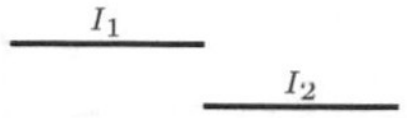 $I_1$ <br> $I_2$ | $I_1$ meets $I_2$ <br> $I_2$ met by $I_1$ |
| $I_1 o I_2$ <br> $I_2 oi I_1$ | 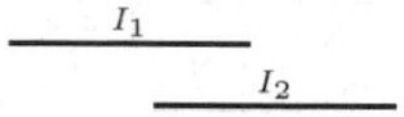 $I_1$ <br> $I_2$ | $I_1$ overlaps $I_2$ <br> $I_2$ overlapped by $I_1$ |
| $I_1 s I_2$ <br> $I_2 si I_1$ | 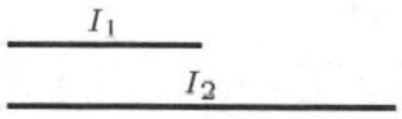 $I_1$ <br> $I_2$ | $I_1$ starts $I_2$ <br> $I_2$ started by $I_1$ |
| $I_1 d I_2$ <br> $I_2 di I_1$ | 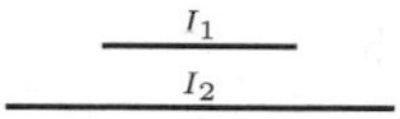 $I_1$ <br> $I_2$ | $I_1$ during $I_2$ <br> $I_2$ contains $I_1$ |
| $I_1 f I_2$ <br> $I_2 fi I_1$ | 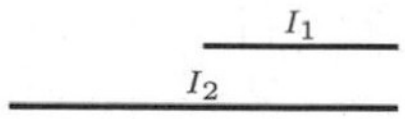 $I_1$ <br> $I_2$ | $I_1$ finishes $I_2$ <br> $I_2$ finished by $I_1$ |
| $I_1 = I_2$ | 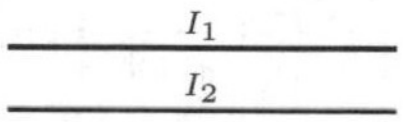 $I_1$ <br> $I_2$ | $I_1$ equals $I_2$ |

**Fig. 1.** Allen's thirteen atomic relations

we can conclude that the event of the person being in the room either overlaps the phone call, is finished by the phone call, or contains the phone call:

$$I_2 di I_3 \quad \text{and} \quad I_3 o I_3 \quad \text{then} \quad I_1 \{o, fi, di\} I_3$$

A set of possible relations such as $\{o, fi, di\}$ is also called a non-atomic Allen relation.

Non-atomic Allen relations provide a way to express uncertainty (which we discuss in detail in Section 5). Although in principle any subset of the 13 Allen relations is a non-atomic Allen relation, it is often the case that a non-atomic Allen relation is a set of relations that is connected under the neighbourhood relation. Whether or not a relation is a neighbour of another relation depends on the conceptual distance between the relations.

|   | < | m | o | fi | di | si | = | s | d | f | oi | mi | > |
|---|---|---|---|----|----|----|---|---|---|---|----|----|---|
| **<** | < | < | < | < | < | < | < | < | <, m, o, s, d | <, m, o, s, d | <, m, o, s, d | <, m, o, s, d | <, m, o, s, d, f, =, fi, di, si, oi, mi, > |
| **m** | < | < | < | < | < | m | m | m | o, s, d | o, s, d | o, s, d | f, =, fi | di, si, oi, mi, > |
| **o** | < | < | <, m, o | <, m, o | <, m, o, fi, di | o, fi, di | o | o | o, s, d | o, s, d | o, s, d, f, =, fi, di, si, oi | di, si, oi | di, si, oi, mi, > |
| **fi** | < | m | o | fi | di | di | fi | o | o, s, d | f, =, fi | di, si, oi | di, si, oi | di, si, oi, mi, > |
| **di** | <, m, o, fi, di | o, fi, di | o, fi, di | di | di | di | di | o, fi, di | o, s, d, f, =, fi, di, si, oi | di, si, oi | di, si, oi | di, si, oi | di, si, oi, mi, > |
| **si** | <, m, o, fi, di | o, fi, di | o, fi, di | di | di | si | si | s, =, si | d, f, oi | oi | oi | mi | > |
| **=** | < | m | o | fi | di | si | = | s | d | f | oi | mi | > |
| **s** | < | < | <, m, o | <, m, o | <, m, o, fi, di | s, =, si | s | s | d | d | d, f, oi | mi | > |
| **d** | < | < | <, m, o, s, d | <, m, o, s, d | <, m, o, s, d, f, =, fi, di, si, oi, mi, > | d, f, oi, mi, > | d | d | d | d | d, f, oi, mi, > | > | > |
| **f** | < | m | o, s, d | f, =, fi | di, si, oi, mi, > | oi, mi, > | f | d | d | f | oi, mi, > | > | > |
| **oi** | <, m, o, fi, di | o, fi, di | o, s, d, f, =, fi, di, si, oi | di, si, oi | di, si, oi, mi, > | oi, mi, > | oi | d, f, oi | d, f, oi | oi | oi, mi, > | > | > |
| **mi** | <, m, o, fi, di | s, =, si | d, f, oi | mi | > | > | mi | d, f, oi | d, f, oi | mi | > | > | > |
| **>** | <, m, o, s, d, f, =, fi, di, si, oi, mi, > | d, f, oi, mi, > | d, f, oi, mi, > | > | > | > | > | d, f, oi, mi, > | d, f, oi, mi, > | > | > | > | > |

**Fig. 2.** Allen's composition table including = as arranged in [7]. The entry at row $r_1$ and column $r_2$ in the table denotes the possible relations between $O_1$ and $O_3$, assuming that $O_1 r_1 O_2$ and $O_2 r_2 O_3$.

Given a particular interval relation, the other relations can be put in a partial order that indicates the conceptual distance between the given relation and each of the other relations [7]. For example, if two intervals are in relation m, then by moving or deforming the intervals slightly, we can change this relation to < or o. Therefore, < and o are conceptual neighbours of m. The relation f, for example, is not a conceptual neighbour of m, as f cannot be obtained from m by deforming or moving objects without passing through any third relation.

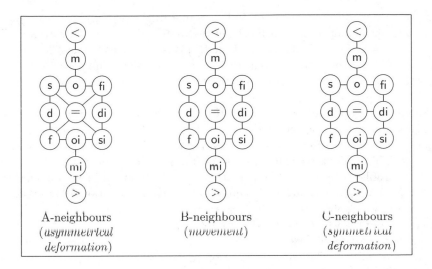

**Fig. 3.** The thirteen Allen relations arranged in conceptual neighbourhood structures

Freksa [7] distinguishes three different neighbourhood structures (A-, B-, and C-neighbours), depending on how intervals are allowed to be changed. If exactly one endpoint of one of the intervals is allowed to be moved whereas all other endpoints are fixed, we obtain the *A-neighbour* relation – this corresponds to an asymmetrical deformation. If the length of both intervals is fixed and we are allowed to move complete intervals, we obtain the *B-neighbour* relations. If we leave the location of intervals fixed at their midpoints and allow their length to vary, we obtain the *C-neighbour* relation – this corresponds to a symmetrical deformation. Figure 3 shows these neighbourhood graphs. For example, if the objects can be moved but not deformed, s is *not* a conceptual neighbour of =. However, if we allow for deformations, s and = are neighbours. Given a particular neighbourhood graph, the conceptual distance between two relations in that graph is defined as the length of the shortest path between the relations.

For example, if a person is supposed to take his or her medication (represented by $I_1$) before dinner (represented by $I_2$), then we would introduce a temporal constraint in our smart home scheduling system of the form $I_1 < I_2$. This constraint, however, might sometimes be too strict, which means that we might want to include a neighbouring relation in the constraint:

$$I_1\{<, \mathsf{m}\}I_2$$

Given a set of intervals and a set of interval relations (non-atomic relations or Allen relations) between these intervals, the purpose of Allen's algorithm is to remove inconsistent relations. It does this by repeatedly selecting three intervals from the set of all intervals and examining the interval relations between the selected intervals. The examination is performed by checking for each Allen relation in the third interval relation whether that relation can be obtained by concatenating an Allen relation from the first interval relation with an Allen relation from the second interval relation. If this is not the case, the Allen relation is removed from the third interval relation. Allen's algorithm terminates when no three intervals can be found anymore for which the examination of their relations leads to a change.

The result of applying Allen's algorithm to a network of interval relations is a locally consistent network of relations, which means that every triplet of relations is consistent with respect to the composition table, i.e. this is a path-consistent network. This does *not* mean that the network is globally consistent: it might not be possible to select an Allen relation from each interval relation such that the selected Allen relations form a consistent network of relations. This task is in general more complex and requires an algorithm whose runtime performance is exponential in the worst case (and not cubic, as in the case of Allen's algorithm). Researchers have recognised this problem and have suggested an alternative approach to solve it. The next subsection introduces this alternative approach, and [8] identify a number of tractable subalgebras and discuss complexity issues on the satisfiability on these algebras.

## 3.2   The Point Algebra

Not long after the publication of Allen's interval logic, Vilain and Kautz published a paper on constraint propagation algorithms for temporal reasoning [6], in which they proved the intractability of the interval logic and introduced the point algebra as a tractable alternative. The point algebra uses time points rather than time intervals for comparison. Given two points in time, $P_1$ and $P_2$, either of three relations can hold between the points. These relations are depicted in Figure 4.

| Relation | Illustration | Interpretation |
|----------|--------------|----------------|
| $P_1 < P_2$ | $P_1$      $P_2$   •      • | $P_1$ precedes $P_2$ |
| $P_1 = P_2$ | $P_1$ •   $P_2$ • | $P_1$ same as $P_2$ |
| $P_1 > P_2$ | $P_2$      $P_1$   •      • | $P_1$ follows $P_2$ |

**Fig. 4.** The three different point relations from the point algebra

Point relations can be used in a similar way as interval relations. For example, the time point at which we start to open the door precedes the time point at which we commence entering the room. In fact, Vilain and Kautz pointed out that many interval relations can be expressed as point relations by using the starting and finishing endpoints of the intervals:

| Interval relation | Corresponding point relations |
|---|---|
| $I_1 d I_2$ | $\underline{I}_1 > \underline{I}_2 \ \wedge \ \overline{I}_1 < \overline{I}_2 \ \wedge \ \underline{I}_1 < \overline{I}_1 \ \wedge \ \underline{I}_2 < \overline{I}_2$ |
| $I_1\{<, \mathsf{m}, \mathsf{o}\}I_2$ | $\underline{I}_1 < \underline{I}_2 \ \wedge \ \overline{I}_1 < \overline{I}_2 \ \wedge \ \underline{I}_1 < \overline{I}_1 \ \wedge \ \underline{I}_2 < \overline{I}_2$ |

In the table above, $\underline{I}_j$ and $\overline{I}_j$ represent the starting endpoint, respectively finishing endpoint, of the interval $I_j$.

The interval relations that can be expressed in terms of point relations are usually referred to as pointisable interval relations. Of course, not every interval relation is pointisable, or else the interval logic would be tractable. The relation $I_1\{<, >\}I_2$, for example, cannot be expressed as a set of point relations on the interval endpoints.

In the following section, it will become apparent that fundamental ideas which we have been discussed in the context of temporal reasoning are the same in spatial reasoning.

## 4 Spatial Calculi

There exist a number of calculi for reasoning about space. These calculi can be classified regarding their degree of precision, with topology at one extreme and Euclidean geometry at the other. As we shall learn in the current section, topological approaches and those which are based on ordering information are particularly useful in the context of smart homes, or more generally, in the context of *room space*; [9] surveys other kinds of spatial scales.

### 4.1 Topology

Topological relations, which describe the most abstract geometric concepts, are already sufficient for the purpose of representing which rooms link to other rooms by passages. While rooms are represented by the nodes of a topological net, edges correspond to the passages. As soon as specific regions and their relationships are to be described, more sophisticated representations are required. The same

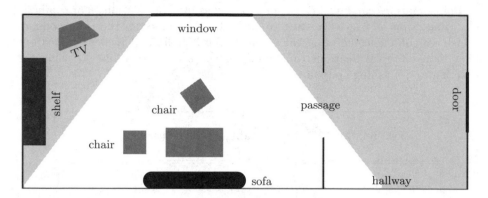

**Fig. 5.** A number of regions determining the spatial context in a living room and hallway - black regions are fixed, dark grey regions correspond to objects which can be removed, and bright regions (white and bright grey) can be occupied by people

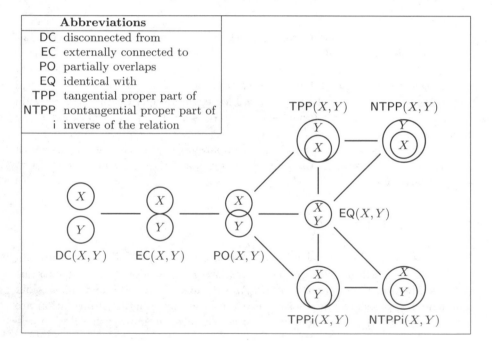

**Fig. 6.** The RCC8 relations arranged in a graph showing the conceptual neighbours

net allows the whereabouts of people to be represented. Regions in the present application context correspond to rooms, passages between rooms, or specific sub-regions dividing up a room into a number of (not necessarily disjoint) areas and places. Places correspond to specific regions which are connected to a land-mark (a specific identifier, such as the TV or window); areas on the other hand are less specific and refer to regions without landmarks. For instance, places correspond to the whereabouts of furniture, and the less specific areas correspond to those regions which can be occupied by objects and which can especially be passed by people. Each path through areas of the flat can then be described in terms of a number of landmarks which mark that path.

Topological relations for the purpose of spatial reasoning have been proposed by Randell, Cui, and Cohn [10] and by Egenhofer and Franzosa [11]. Randell, Cui, and Cohn define different dyadic relations between extended regions. In their *Region Connection Calculus* (RCC for short), they have chosen an axiomatic formalisation based on the binary predicate $C(x, y)$, which indicates whether two regions $x$ and $y$ are connected or not. Egenhofer and Franzosa derived their formalisation by considering the intersections of boundaries and interiors for two regions. This approach is therefore called the 4-intersection calculus. Considering the interior, boundary, and complement the relationship between two regions can be characterised by a 3x3-matrix called the 9-intersection. Both RCC and the 9-intersection calculus define topological relations between two regions, such as those depicted in Figure 6. These relations allow the spatial context of the flat in Figure 5 to be characterised. Some of these relations are:

{EC(living room, hallway), PO(passage, living room), PO(passage, hallway), TPP(window, living room), TPP(shelf, living room), TPP(sofa, living room), TPP(light-cone, living room), PO(light-cone, passage), TPP(sofa, light-cone), NTPP(chair1, light-cone), NTPP(chair2, light-cone), NTPP(table, light-cone)}

The same constraint satisfaction algorithm which has been proposed by Allen can be applied to these relations, since Allen's algorithm works for all those systems which define a number of *jointly exhaustive* and *pairwise disjoint* relations regarding some dimension, such as relations between events in time or between regions in two-dimensional space. That a set of relations are jointly exhaustive means that there exists no undefined relation between two objects regarding the considered dimension; that they are pairwise disjoint refers to the fact that there exists at most one relation for any given pair of objects, in this way, guaranteeing that every determined relation can be unambiguously described. In qualitative reasoning we attach great value to sets of *jepd*-relations, as they are referred to in short form.

By means of the topological relations of the RCC calculus alone (1.) or together with knowledge about time and further background knowledge (2.-3.) a number of inferences can be made:

1. NTPP(chair1, light-cone) ∧ TPP(light-cone, living room) → NTPP(chair1, living room)
2. If a sensor detects a person in the area of the light-cone, and if, after a short period of time, another sensor detects a person in the hallway, whereas the passage sensor did not detect anything in the meantime, it can be concluded that there are either two persons in the flat (one in the living room, the other one in the hallway), or that the sensor in the passage is out of order. The latter holds if the system knows there is only one person in the flat.

3. From the knowledge that a wheelchair enters the light-cone, it can be inferred that the chairs, the table, and the sofa are potential obstacles, whereas the shelf and the television are outside of the wheelchair's scope.

If more precise knowledge matters, for instance, in order to take into account the arrangement of obstacles, ordering information about objects becomes important.

## 4.2 Spatial Arrangements

Cardinal directions are frequently employed in spatial reasoning (mainly in geography), but they are inconvenient in room space. Instead, the layout of the apartment and the arrangements of furniture and other objects define the current spatial context relative to which spatial problems should be defined in room space.

Spatial arrangements between objects can be described by generalising Allen's relations (see section 3.1). In [12] an external reference frame is used relative to which positions are described. It is proposed to project orthogonally the endpoints of objects on both the axis of abscissae and the axis of ordinates. Allen's relations and his reasoning methods can then be used for describing the order of objects regarding both dimensions. It is then, for instance, possible to determine that there is one chair between the table and the window (regardless of what there else is between that chair and the window), and that there is another chair between the shelf and the table (compare Figure 5). This allows an ordering of obstacles to be determined which a wheelchair has to pass when being programmed to drive from the kitchen to the television. Precise measurements are only required as soon as local decisions are to be made, for example, to test whether the wheelchair fits through the gap between window and chair — a local decision which can generally entail a lot of changes, though not in this case, since the chair is not attached to the floor, so it can be pushed aside. The idea of suspending local decisions is in accordance with [13] in which is shown the effectiveness of hierarchical planning with detailed decisions being delayed as long as possible until a high level plan has been achieved.

[12] is limited to adequately representing those objects which are aligned with the axes of the underlying reference frame. In order to capture all possible two-dimensional relationships between disconnected objects in room space, another generalisation of Allen has been introduced in [14]. This approach defines relations which are depicted in Figure 7, and which allow arrangements between arbitrarily aligned objects to be described at the same granularity level as Allen. Rather than using external frames of references, approaches like this one make use of intrinsic reference systems, that is, objects themselves define a spatial context relative to which other objects can be described. As a consequence, the ordering between arbitrarily aligned furniture and other objects can be adequately considered. For instance, the spatial relation *in front of the TV* can then correctly be represented, and so can alignments between the oblique light-cone and other objects (compare Figure 5).

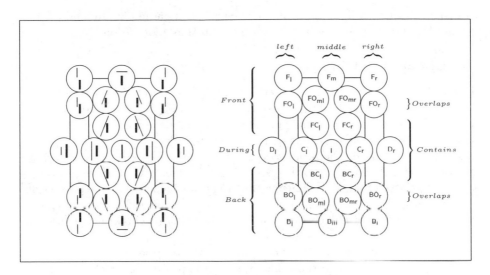

**Fig. 7.** Interval relations embedded in two dimensions, arranged in their neighbourhood graph; the vertical reference interval is displayed bold; a mnemonic code on the right

As with the RCC calculus a number of inferences can be made with these relations:

1. $D_l$(chair1, table) $\wedge$ $C_r$(sofa, table) $\rightarrow$ $D_l$(chair1, sofa)
2. As the TV is slanted with respect to the room, and as its orientation can be defined in a way that its front points to the window, it can be inferred that daylight comes from the right when sitting on the sofa or on one of the chairs and looking to the TV. If this arrangement is unfavourable another arrangement can be found, by formulating appropriate constraints which determine appropriate conditions, for instance, that daylight must not shine onto the TV: not $D_l$(TV, window).
3. From the knowledge that a wheelchair enters the living room, it can be inferred that one of the chairs poses a threat within the given arrangement of furniture, if the wheelchair is programmed to drive to the shelf; compare the less accurate conclusion at the topological level in the previous section. For the position of this chair, and if both the shelf and the passage is defined to be oriented upwards regarding the image plane, it holds that $D_r$(chair, schelf) and $D_l$(chair, passage). As a consequence, it is probable that the chair lies on the path between the passage and the shelf.

Like in this example, arrangement information is particularly useful for robot navigation, as has been shown in [15]. Navigating through a furnished environment amounts to crossing virtual lines connecting specific furniture or other landmarks found in the house. The wheelchair can be programmed in terms of those landmarks and in terms of virtual lines it has to pass in order to find its way from the kitchen to the television. Further approaches which relate to arrangement information applicable in room space are found in [16] and [17], as well as [18] and [19] which relate more to orientation information.

### 4.3   Distances and Sizes

So far we have considered a number of spatial relations between regions and objects. In doing so we neglected distances between objects and also their size. It shows that often precise distances and sizes are unnecessary for the purpose of making abstract spatial decisions. For instance, in order to provide the elderly a seating-accommodation the *nearest* object must be found — this can be a chair, the sofa, or the bed. The smart system has to decide which of these objects is nearest to the fatigued person for providing her help to get to the seating. A simple distance metric such as the one from [20] suffices for these purposes. Here, directions are combined with simple distance information, such as *far* and *close*.

Spatial representations of distances can be divided up into those which measure on absolute scales, and those like in the former example which use relative measurements. Absolute scales are mainly necessary when precise local manoeuvre are executed. A combination of these kinds of approaches is the delta calculus [21] which introduces a triadic relation: $x(>, d)y$ indicating that $x$ is larger than $y$ by an amount $d$. For instance, *living room*$(>, 1.2)$*light-cone* indicates that daylight pervades most of the living room. This is of importance for the system's knowledge base which has to adapt the sensitivity of the motion sensors accordingly when the sun is shining. That is, the delta calculus allows qualitative statements about sizes of regions and objects to be described.

### 4.4   Activity Patterns

There are also issues which relate to both space and time. Whenever people move around, for example, they perform specific patterns of movement-activity which we refer to as *activity patterns*. Whereas the consideration of patterns and shapes is generally an important issue in spatial reasoning, it is frequently sufficient to

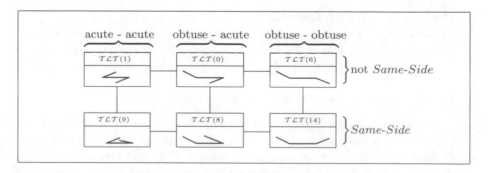

**Fig. 8.** Six primitives distinguished by $\mathcal{TLT}$ arranged in a neighbourhood graph

 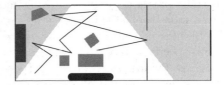

**Fig. 9.** Two different activity patterns: the left hand side shows a goal-oriented behaviour; by contrast, the right hand side shows a seeking-like pattern

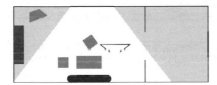 

**Fig. 10.** Depending on its size the same $\mathcal{TLT}$ relation refers to two different meanings. On the left hand side, it shows a running to and fro in the passage, on the right hand side it shows a large arc around the lounge (extending even the large light cone).

abstract away precise shapes, confining oneself to points and describing their relative positions [19], using bounding boxes [22], or convex hulls ([23], [24]). Since for privacy issues no cameras are used in the current application setting, object recognition (which would involve shape) is not employed and we can confine the discussion about shapes to activity patterns.

When atypical behaviours are to be distinguished from normal behaviours activity patterns come into play. For this purpose it does not matter to precisely record each movement. It is rather necessary to provide means for obtaining the overall activity of a person, and to qualitatively distinguish a number of clearly different patterns. Such patterns are then used to recognise, for example, goal-oriented, seeking, and chaotic activities, and they thus trigger appropriate support, or provide assurance that the elder is performing normally, or assess the elder's cognitive status. Figure 8 from [25] shows a number of jointly exhaustive and pairwise disjoint pattern-primitives using which it is possible to characterise trajectories. Whereas trajectories which are made up of $\mathcal{TLT}(6)$ and $\mathcal{TLT}(14)$ relations show rather goal-oriented patterns, chaotic activities of confused elderly are related to $\mathcal{TLT}(1)$ and $\mathcal{TLT}(9)$ which show more compact movements as when running to and fro. Combinations of these primitives allow arbitrarily long activity patterns to be characterised. Figure 9 shows two examples.

The characterisation of activity patterns can be improved by topological relations between regions and pattern primitives, in that there is a difference whether a $\mathcal{TLT}(9)$-relation *is contained* in a region or *extends outside* that same region (compare Figure 10). In the former case such a relation could indicate a hectic running to and fro, whereas in the latter case a $\mathcal{TLT}(9)$-relation could refer to a circle-like path indicating, for example, a systematic search. Describing primitive activity patterns by spatial arrangements and using information about distances, even more sophisticated patterns can be distinguished.

Besides movement patterns, there are also *hand gestures* conceivable which form specific activity patterns and which can be employed for easily instructing devices, for instance, for the purpose of easily opening doors and windows, or for switching on and off devices such as coffee machine and dish washer. Hand gestures are comparable to graphical gestures as employed for easily instructing a personal digital assistant. They are carried out in front of the device without the need for touching it, thus not requiring to reach the respective device which is probably not easily accessible.

### 4.5 Combining Space and Time

Although activity patterns already bring together spatial and temporal aspects, in this context we have still treated them individually. Clearly, this will suffice most of the smart home utilities conceivable. But for the sake of completeness let us also refer to some work in which space and time is combined more closely. Instead of considering space and time separately, [26] combine the two by bringing in the consideration of the continuity of motion. They formalise the intuitive notion of spatiotemporal continuity and provide a qualitative theory of motion. [27] and [28] address similar issues about continuity, namely what it implies for a commonsense theory of motion. [27] characterises continuity as a set of logical constraints on transitions in a temporal framework, while [28] proposes a mereotopological theory of space-time.

## 5   Handling Spatiotemporal Uncertainty

Though defining different sets of relations, the approaches introduced in the previous sections have in common that they provide structures for dealing with imprecise and incomplete data in a specific way. Both the temporal and the spatial calculi define finite sets of qualitative relations (such as $<$, m, and o). Each of these relations subsumes infinitely many metrically distinguishable situations. By this means they are robust against small changes, generally not changing the qualitative concept at hand. On the other hand, if the situation is close to two different relations ($<$ and m) we are always concerned with conceptually neighbouring relations which are also semantically close to each other. As a consequence imprecision is dealt with by conceptual neighbourhood graphs such as those depicted in Figs. 3, 6, 7, and 8. Either the relation given is true, or one of the relations in its neighbourhood.

Incompleteness is treated as follows. If nothing can be said about the spatial or temporal relation between two objects, all relations are to be taken into account (this is the universal relation). If a subset of all relations is known the description is not completely undetermined but still incomplete. In this case, however, known relations can be used for deriving possible relations for the unknown dependencies. For this purpose, one has to proceed as described in Section 3.1. At first, the universal relation is taken as the domain of unknown relations (between two objects); after that, triples of objects are considered in order to find pairs of relations which are consistent between three objects. Inconsistent relations are deleted from the domains, allowing the domains of unknown dependencies to be restricted by propagating knowledge about known relations.

Another way to handle uncertainty is to use different granularities: the more uncertain the spatiotemporal information, the coarser the granularity of the description. One way to express granularities in the time domain is discussed in the next chapter [29]. Yet another way of dealing with uncertain temporal and spatial knowledge, namely with fuzzy knowledge, is shown in [30]. There, conceptual neighbourhood graphs are employed for determining membership values for the purpose of fuzzy qualitative reasoning. This becomes of interest when regions are to be used which gradually diminish towards their surrounding environments. Among other things, this concerns light, draught, odours, and the scope of sensors. Essentially, the algorithms for fuzzy reasoning are the same as those described in Section 3.1. There are only some modifications necessary which are outlined in [31] and [32]. The idea behind the fuzzy algorithms is to replace the standard set operations, which build the basis for Allen's algorithm, with their fuzzy counterparts. Rather than removing inconsistent atomic relations from the set of interval relations, the fuzzy algorithms change the membership grades associated with the atomic relations.

Eventually, another author who deals with fuzzy representations is [33]. He compares fuzzy and qualitative approaches with a specific emphasis on the representation of distance information. He also discusses their relation to linguistic and cognitive issues, and how well each of them models human perception and expression of distance information, which may be of particular interest for the purpose of modelling how humans deal with distance information in their smart home. For a general and thorough discussion on Fuzzy techniques and AI we refer to [34].

# 6   Conclusion

In this chapter we presented AI-techniques for dealing with temporal and spatial knowledge in smart homes. Having their seeds in Allen's approach [5], in the last fifteen years a number of calculi have been proposed from which many still rely on the same reasoning mechanisms as Allen's algorithm (see section 3.1). In the meantime, improvements have been made, among other things, concerning the efficiency with the aid of neighbourhood based reasoning [7], and concerning soft computing by incorporating fuzziness into qualitative approaches [30]. Further on, many different qualitative reasoning approaches have been devised, focusing on different application areas, scales, or spatial dimensions, such as shape [23], size [21], discussing ontological issues [35], or considering even spatiotemporal combinations [28]. A domain-independent overview of qualitative spatial and temporal approaches is provided by [36].

While most approaches in spatial reasoning are motivated by problems arising in geography and navigation, we have shown here how such approaches can be employed in smart homes. This is a challenging issue insofar as smart homes are defined at quite a different spatial scale than geographical objects, demanding the distinction between *room space* and *geographic space*. In room space, besides topological approaches, spatial arrangements become important, whereas topology sometimes suffices in geographical information systems. By contrast, there is no difference in applying temporal reasoning to room space or to other spatial scales — temporal reasoning is more abstract than spatial reasoning, though spatial reasoning is more complex. In the future, advances in the context of smart homes and also the conquest of other areas might put further challenges to the field of spatiotemporal reasoning in AI, not later than when smart homes become inhabited by smart service robots.

# References

1. Pollack, M.E.: Intelligent Technology for an Aging Population: The Use of AI to Assist Elders with Cognitive Impairment. AI Magazine **26** (2005) 9–24
2. Thrun, S.: Robotic mapping: A survey. In Lakemeyer, G., Nebel, B., eds.: Exploring Artificial Intelligence in the New Millenium. Morgan Kaufmann, San Mateo, California (2002) 1–35
3. Preparata, F.P., Shamos, M.I.: Computational Geometry: An Introduction. Springer, New York (1985)
4. de Berg, M., van Kreveld, M., Overmars, M., Schwarzkopf, O.: Computational Geometry. Springer (1997)
5. Allen, J.: Maintaining knowledge about temporal intervals. Communications of the ACM **26** (1983) 832–843
6. Vilain, M., Kautz, H.: Constraint propagation algorithms for temporal reasoning. In: Proc. AAAI-86, Philadelphia, Pennsylvania (1986) 377–382
7. Freksa, C.: Temporal reasoning based on semi-intervals. Artificial Intelligence **54** (1992) 199–227
8. Krokhin, A., Jeavons, P., Jonsson, P.: Reasoning about temporal relations: The tractable subalgebras of allen's interval algebra. J. ACM **50** (2003) 591–640
9. Freundschuh, S., Egenhofer, M.: Human Conceptions of Spaces: Implications for GIS. Transactions in GIS **4** (1997) 361–375
10. Randell, D., Cui, Z., Cohn, A.: A spatial logic based on regions and connection. In: Proc. KR-92, Cambridge, Massachusetts (1992) 165–176
11. Egenhofer, M., Franzosa, R.: Point-set topological spatial relations. International Journal of Geographical Information Systems **5** (1991) 161–174
12. Guesgen, H.: Spatial reasoning based on Allen's temporal logic. Technical Report TR-89-049, ICSI, Berkeley, California (1989)
13. Tate, A., Hendler, J., Drummond, M.: A review of AI planning techniques. In Allen, J., Hendler, J., Tate, A., eds.: Readings in Planning. Morgan Kaufman, San Mateo, CA (1990)
14. Gottfried, B.: Reasoning about intervals in two dimensions. In Thissen, W., Wieringa, P., Pantic, M., Ludema, M., eds.: IEEE Int. Conference on Systems, Man and Cybernetics, The Hague, The Netherlands, Omnipress (2004) 5324–5332

15. Kuipers, B.J., Levitt, T.: Navigation and mapping in large-scale space. AI Magazine **9** (1988) 25–43
16. Murkerjee, A., Joe, G.: A qualitative model for space. In: 8th-AAAI. (1990) 721–727
17. Hernandez, D.: Qualitative Representation of Spatial Knowledge. LNAI 804. Springer (1994)
18. Renz, J., Mitra, D.: Qualitative direction calculi with arbitrary granularity. In Zhang, C., Guesgen, H.W., Yeap, W.K., eds.: PRICAI. Volume 3157 of Lecture Notes in Computer Science., Springer (2004) 65–74
19. Zimmermann, K., Freksa, C.: Qualitative Spatial Reasoning Using Orientation, Distance, and Path Knowledge. Applied Intelligence **6** (1996) 49–58
20. Frank, A.: Qualitative Spatial Reasoning about Distance and Directions in Geographic Space. Journal of Visual Languages and Computing **3** (1992) 343–373
21. Zimmermann1995, K.: Measuring without Distances: the delta calculus. In Frank, A.M., Kuhn, W., eds.: COSIT 1995, Spatial Information Theory. LNCS 988, Springer-Verlag (1995) 59–68
22. Clementini, E., Di Felice, P.: Approximate Topological Relations. International Journal of Approximate Reasoning **16 (2)** (1997) 173–204
23. Cohn, A.G.: A hierarchical representation of qualitative shape based on connection and convexity. In Frank, A.M., Kuhn, W., eds.: COSIT 1995, Spatial Information Theory. Lecture Notes in Computer Science, Springer-Verlag (1995) 311–326
24. Davis, E., Gotts, N.M., Cohn, A.G.: Constraint networks of topological relations and convexity. Constraints **4(3)** (1999) 241–280
25. Gottfried, B.: Tripartite Line Tracks, Qualitative Curvature Information. In Kuhn, W., Worboys, M., Timpf, S., eds.: Spatial Information Theory: Foundations of Geographic Information Science, Int. Conference COSIT 2003. LNCS. Springer-Verlag, Ittingen, Switzerland (2003) 101–117
26. Hazarika, S.M., Cohn, A.G.: Qualitative spatio-temporal continuity. In Montello, D.R., ed.: Spatial Information Theory: Foundations of Geographic Information Science, International Conference, COSIT 2001, Morro Bay, CA, USA, September 19-23, 2001, Proceedings. Volume 2205 of LNCS., Springer (2001) 92–107
27. Galton, A.: Qualitative Spatial Change. Oxford University Press, Oxford, New York (2000)
28. Muller, P.: A qualitative theory of motion based on spatio-temporal primitives. In Cohn, A., Schubert, L., Shapiro, S., eds.: Proceedings of the 6th International Conference on Principles of Knowledge Representation and Reasoning, Morgan Kaufmann (1998) 131–141
29. Combi, C., Rossato, R.: Temporal constraints with multiple granularities in Smart Homes. In Augusto, J.C., Nugent, C.D., eds.: Smart Homes and AI. Chapter 3 (this volume). (Springer, forthc.)
30. Guesgen, H.: Fuzzifying spatial relations. In Matsakis, P., Sztandera, L., eds.: Applying Soft Computing in Defining Spatial Relations. Physica, Heidelberg, Germany (2002) 1–16
31. Guesgen, H., Hertzberg, J., Philpott, A.: Towards implementing fuzzy Allen relations. In: Proc. ECAI-94 Workshop on Spatial and Temporal Reasoning, Amsterdam, The Netherlands (1994) 49–55
32. Guesgen, H.: When regions start to move. In: Proc. FLAIRS-03, St. Augustine, Florida (2003) 465–469
33. Hernández, D.: Qualitative vs. fuzzy represenations of spatial distance. In Freksa, C., Jantzen, M., Valk, R., eds.: Foundations of Computer Science: Potential - Theory - Cognition. Volume 1337 of Lecture Notes in Computer Science., Springer (1997) 389–398

34. Freksa, C.: Fuzzy Systems in AI. In Kruse, R., Gebhardt, J., Palm, R., eds.: Fuzzy systems in computer science. Vieweg, Braunschweig (1994)
35. Bittner, T., Smith, B.: Granular Spatio-Temporal Ontologies. In Guesgen, H.W., Mitra, D., Renz, J., eds.: AAAI Symposium: Foundations and Applications of Spatio-Temporal Reasoning (FASTR), AAAI Press (2003) 12–17
36. Cohn, A.G., Hazarika, S.M.: Qualitative spatial representation and reasoning: An overview. Fundamenta Informaticae **43** (2001) 2–32

# Temporal Constraints with Multiple Granularities in Smart Homes

Carlo Combi and Rosalba Rossato

Dipartimento di Informatica
Università di Verona
{combi, rossato}@sci.univr.it

**Abstract.** In this chapter, we propose a logic-based approach to describe temporal constraints with multiple time granularities related to events occurring in Smart Homes. We identify a time granularity as a (possibly) infinite sequence of time points properly labeled with propositional symbols marking the starting and the ending points of each granule. In particular, *sensor granularities* describe time intervals during which Smart Home sensors are in the state "ON". Both time and sensor granularities and temporal constraints are expressed by means of PPLTL formulae. Temporal constraints for Smart Home are satisfied when the specific relationships between time/sensor granularities, involved in the described constraints, hold.

## 1 Introduction

Every day, we show the ability to represent temporal knowledge of actions and events (more generally, facts) in the world in order to model causation, construct complex plans, anticipate possible outcomes of actions. Usually facts can be temporally characterized by means of the *valid time* dimension [26], which allows one to represent the time when the fact is true in the reality. For example, if a person turns on the cooker on July 17, 2005 at 12:00 and she turns off it at 12:45 of the same day, then the valid time of the fact "the cooker is ON" is represented by means of the time interval [2005July17 12:00, 2005July17 12:45].

The temporal units, used to specify the temporal validity of facts, are *time granularities*; any time granularity can be viewed as a partition of a time domain in groups of indivisible elements (*granules*). For example, by considering the time interval [12:00, 12:45] regarding to the fact "the cooker is ON", we can note that it is defined with respect to the bottom granularity of *minute*; bottom granularity represents the minimal granularity for a particular application.

The ability of providing and relating the temporal representation of facts at different levels of granularity is an important research theme in computer science and, in particular, in the database area [4, 14, 18, 41].

In this area, one of the earliest formalization of the concept of time granularities is described in [14]. The possibility of describing temporal constraints on data stored in a database and possibly related to user defined calendars (*i.e.,* sets of granularities), is a very interesting topic which has been studied in several papers [8, 17, 18, 35, 38, 43, 44, 45].

J.C. Augusto and C.D. Nugent (Eds.): Designing Smart Homes, LNAI 4008, pp. 35–56, 2006.

Other relevant works on time granularities has been done in the context of classical and temporal logics [11, 31, 32, 33] and some of these works have been applied to the verification of real-time system specifications and to temporal reasoning in the artificial intelligence area. In this context, several problems of scheduling, planning, diagnosis, and natural language understanding often involve different time granularities [21, 24, 27, 29, 30, 39, 41].

The representation and reasoning about temporal constraints related to several granularities is very important also for *Smart Home* applications, which are applications related to environments which are capable to react "in an intelligent way" to some occurring situations [2, 3, 23, 42]. Smart Home is a term commonly used to denote a residence that uses a home controller to integrate various automation systems. A Smart Home is usually equipped with a set of sensors, such as movement sensors, smoke alarm, and device sensors; a central monitoring facility is able to detect all sensors and alarm events. Several projects deal with the design of Smart Home architectures [1, 23], and some works focus on formal specifications for Smart Home applications [2, 3].

In this context, the goal is to define an intelligent system which is able to anticipate, predict, and take decisions with autonomy. In particular, the modeling of temporal events occurring in a Smart Home and related to the people with some disabilities (for example, cognitive disabilities) and elderly people is an important question [42]. Temporal constraints possibly related to different time granularities could model "normal" activities; if a temporal constraint is not satisfied, then a potential "abnormal" or "critical" situation may occur inside the house.

In this chapter we focus our attention on the description of temporal constraints for Smart Homes. We adopt a logic-based approach to describe temporal constraints with multiple time granularities related to events occurring in Smart Homes. We identify a time granularity as an infinite sequence of time points properly labeled with propositional symbols marking the starting and the ending points of each granule. Moreover, we identify *sensor granularities* which allow one to describe time intervals during which sensors are in the state "ON"; granules of a sensor granularity describe the time intervals related to the validity of the considered sensor. Both time and sensor granularities, and temporal constraints are expressed by means of logical PPLTL formulae.

For example, a temporal constraint we can model by means of our framework allows one to describe that "the cooker cannot be turned on if the person is not at the kitchen". During a "normal" behavior with respect to the considered constraint, the person goes into the kitchen and then he turn on the cooker; in an "abnormal" situation, the cooker changes its state from OFF to ON even if nobody is in the kitchen. As we will show in the following, temporal properties related to sensor granularities require specific relationships between the granularities involved in the constraint.

*Structure of the Chapter.* Section 2 introduces the basic notions about time granularities with particular emphasis on relationships between granularities.

In Section 3, we consider the context of Smart Homes and highlight why it is important to describe temporal constraints related to multiple granularities in order to detect undesirable situations which may occur in the house.

Section 4 introduces a logical framework for the description of time granularities and, in Section 5, we extend the framework to the description of *sensor granularities*, which can be considered as time granularities associated to the state "ON" of Smart Home sensors. In this way, temporal constraints related to events occurring in a Smart Home can be described by means of specific constraints between sensors granularities.

In Section 6, we discuss the problem of checking temporal constraints on our logical framework and we propose an evaluation of the computational complexity of the constraint checking phase related to the well-known results of model checking problems for PPLTL.

In Section 7, we consider the advantages and limitations of our proposal with respect to other approaches for the specification and verification of temporal constraints. Section 8 reports the conclusions.

## 2  Background: Time Granularities

A time granularity can be perceived as a partition of a temporal domain in groups of indivisible units called *granules*. Granularities are, for example, Day, Month, and WorkingDay, which correspond to the usual partition on the timeline. By using these granules it is possible to describe a fact providing a temporal qualification.

The standard definition [16] of time granularity is the following.

**Definition 1.** *A granularity is a mapping $G : \mathbb{N} \to 2^{\mathbb{N}}$ such that:*

1. *for all $i < j$, for any $n \in G(i)$ and $m \in G(j)$, $n < m$;*
2. *for all $i < j$, if $G(j) \neq \emptyset$, then $G(i) \neq \emptyset$.*

The domain of a granularity $G$ is called *index set* and an element of the codomain of $G$ is called a *granule*. The first condition of the definition states that granules in a granularity do not overlaps and that their order is the same as their time domain order. The second condition states that the subset of the index set that maps to nonempty granules forms an initial segment.

The reported definition of time granularity specializes the definition given in [4], assuming that both the index set and the time domain are the linear discrete domain $(\mathbb{N}, <)$.

Most approaches proposed in the literature for representing and reasoning about time granularities can be classified into *algebraic* approaches and *logical* ones [16]. In the algebraic framework, a bottom granularity is assumed, and a finite set of operators are introduced in order to create new granularities by manipulating other granularities [5, 21, 35, 36]. In the logical framework for time granularities, the different granularities and their relationships are described by means of suitable mathematical structures (layered structures); these structures allow one to represent a possibly infinite set of related differently-grained temporal domains. Suitable operators make it possible to move within a given temporal domain and across temporal domains. Temporal properties involving different time granularities are expressed by means of logical formulae by mixing such operators [22, 31, 33, 34].

## 2.1 Properties of Time Granularities

By considering the features of the partition that a time granularity induces over the timeline, we can define the following properties.

**Definition 2.** *A granularity G is said [4]:*

- *externally continuous, if there are no gaps between its nonempty granules;*
- *internally continuous, if there are no gaps inside its granules;*
- *continuous, if it is both internally and externally continuous;*
- *total, if the granules of G cover all the time domain;*
- *uniform, if all the nonempty granules of G have the same cardinality.*

For example, with reference to the time granularities of the Gregorian calendar, the granularity Day is continuous, uniform and total; granularities Month and Year are not uniform, YearSince2002 is not total, BusinessWeek is not externally continuous, and BusinessMonth is not internally continuous.

The organization of human activities often deals with a temporal context, which is expressed in terms of an appropriate *time granularity*. New kinds of time granularities can be defined in order to characterize the time intervals devoted to working activities. For example, WorkingDay represents a time interval during which some kind of working activity is performed and specifically it describes a set of hours within a day. Different from the granularity Day, we can observe that there is a gap between two consecutive working days and this means that the granularity WorkingDay is not externally continuous.

## 2.2 Relationships Between Time Granularities

In a granularity system (*i.e.,* a set of granularities), it is important to identify the relationships between granularities defined on the same domain. For example, by observing the granularities Day and WorkingDay, we can observe that each working day is contained in a day.

A number of meaningful relationships [36] can be established between pairs of time granularities $G_1$ and $G_2$, as reported in the following definitions [4].

**Definition 3.** *A granularity $G_1$ is finer than a granularity $G_2$ if each granule of $G_1$ is contained into a granule of $G_2$.*
*In particular,* FinerThan$(G_1, G_2)$ *holds if and only if:*

$$\forall i \; \exists j \; s.t. \; G_1(i) \subseteq G_2(j)$$

Figure 1 depicts a *finer than* relationship between two granularities $G_1$ and $G_2$. For example, the granularity Day is finer than Month, but the granularity Week is not finer than Month because a week can spread over two consecutive months.

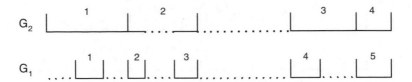

**Fig. 1.** The *finer than* relationship between the granularities $G_1$ and $G_2$

**Fig. 2.** The *subgranularity* relationship between the granularities $G_1$ and $G_2$

**Fig. 3.** The *granule refinement* relationship between the granularities $G_1$ and $G_2$

**Definition 4.** *A granularity* $G_1$ *is a subgranularity of* $G_2$ *if each granule of* $G_1$ *is equal to a granule of* $G_2$.

*In particular,* SubGranularity($G_1, G_2$) *holds if and only if:*

$$\forall i \; \exists j \; s.t. \; G_1(i) = G_2(j)$$

Figure 2 depicts a *subgranularity* relationship between two granularities $G_1$ and $G_2$. For example, the granularity Monday is a subgranularity of Day.

**Definition 5.** *A granularity* $G_1$ *is a granule refinement of* $G_2$ *if each granule of* $G_1$ *is contained into the corresponding granule of* $G_2$.

*In particular,* GranuleRefinement($G_1, G_2$) *holds if and only if:*

$$\forall i \; G_1(i) \subseteq G_2(i)$$

For example, Weekend is a granule refinement of Week. The graphical representation of a relationship *granule refinement* is reported in Figure 3.

**Definition 6.** *A granularity* $G_1$ *is a group of* $G_2$ *if each granule of* $G_2$ *is obtained by grouping an arbitrary number of consecutive granules of* $G_1$.

*In particular,* Group($G_1, G_2$) *holds if and only if:*

$$\forall i \; \exists S = \{j, j+1, \ldots, j+k\} \; s.t. \; G_2(i) = \bigcup_{l \in S} G_1(l)$$

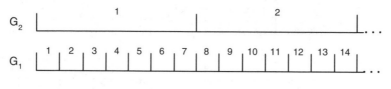

**Fig. 4.** The *group* relationship between the granularities $G_1$ and $G_2$

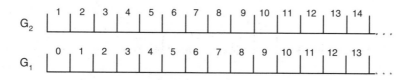

**Fig. 5.** The *shift* relationship between the granularities $G_1$ and $G_2$

For example, we have that Group(Day, Week) holds. In particular, Group$_7$(Day, Week) holds, where Group$_p$($G_1$, $G_2$) holds if each granule of $G_2$ is obtained by grouping p consecutive granules of $G_1$.

**Definition 7.** *A granularity* $G_1$ *is a shifting of* $G_2$ *with size* p, *with* $p \geq 0$, *if the granules of* $G_2$ *are obtained by backward shifting of* p *positions the granules of* $G_1$.
*In particular,* Shift$_p$($G_1$, $G_2$) *holds when:*

$$\forall i \quad G_2(i) = G_1(i + p)$$

For example, suppose London-Hour stands for the hours in London. Since the hours in Rome are 1 hour later that those in London, the granularities Rome-Hour and London-Hour satisfy the relation: Shift$_1$(Rome-Hour, London-Hour).

## 3   Motivation: Smart Home Applications

The possibility of designing an intelligent monitoring system that can detect when an undesirable situation may arise, makes Smart Homes a protective environment more independent and private than traditional caring institution. During the time, a Smart Home can be represented by means of a system composed by *states*; the evolution between states is characterized by *events*, such as the change of the state of some sensor. The initial state of the system is defined on the basis of the layout of the house. The evolution of the system is represented by means of a sequence of states $S_i$; the system changes its state from $S_i$ to $S_{i+1}$ when an event $E_{i+1}$ occurs.

*Example 1.* Let us suppose *Rec* represents the movement detector in the reception area, TDRK the tag detector fitted around the door between the reception area and the kitchen and *Kit* the movement detector sensor in the kitchen. Figure 6 shows an evolution on time of events occurring in a Smart Home. At time $n$, the sensor *Rec* is on state "ON", while the others sensors are "OFF";

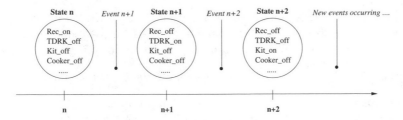

**Fig. 6.** Evolution of the state of some sensors in time

it means that the hosted person is in the reception area. The evolution between the state $n$ and the state $n+1$ occurs when the person is going through the door between the reception area and the kitchen; at the state $n+1$ the sensor TDRK is "ON", while $Rec$ is "OFF", while at the state $n+2$ the sensor TDRK is "OFF" while $Kit$ is "ON". The evolution between states $n+1$ and $n+2$ describes the fact that the person is going through the door, walking into the kitchen.

## 4    A Logical Approach to Represent and Reason About Granularities

In [15, 16] the authors have proposed a labeled linear time structure in order to define possibly infinite sets of granularities by means of suitable linear time formulae described in the context of the propositional temporal linear logic (PPLTL). The idea is to identify the starting point of an arbitrary granule of the granularity $G$ in the structure with the propositional symbol $P_G$ and the ending point of an arbitrary granule of G in the structure with the symbol $Q_G$.

Let $\mathcal{G} = \{G_1, G_2, \ldots, G_n\}$ be a finite set of granularities (*i.e.*, a *calendar*) and let $\mathcal{P}_\mathcal{G} = \{P_{G_i}, Q_{G_i} | 1 \leq i \leq n\}$ be a set of propositional symbols associated with the calendar $\mathcal{G}$. Given an alphabet of propositional symbols $\mathcal{P} \supseteq \mathcal{P}_\mathcal{G}$, the $\mathcal{P}$-*labeled (discrete) linear time structure* has the form $(\mathbb{N}, <, V)$, where $(\mathbb{N}, <)$ is the set of natural numbers with the usual ordering modeling the time domain, and $V : \mathbb{N} \to 2^\mathcal{P}$ is a labeling function mapping the natural number set to sets of propositional symbols.

The notion of *consistency* of a labeled structure with respect to a temporal granularity $G$, is described as follows [16]:

**Definition 8.** *A labeled linear time structure* $\mathcal{M} = (\mathbb{N}, <, V)$ *is G-consistent when:*

1. *if* $P_G \in V(i)$ *for some* $i \in \mathbb{N}$, *then either* $Q_G \in V(i)$ *or* $Q_G \in V(j)$ *for some* $j > i$ *such that* $P_G \notin V(k)$ *for each* $i < k \leq j$ *and* $Q_G \notin V(k)$ *for each* $i \leq k < j$;
2. *if* $Q_G \in V(i)$ *for some* $i \in \mathbb{N}$, *then either* $P_G \in V(i)$ *or* $P_G \in V(j)$ *for some* $j < i$ *such that* $Q_G \notin V(k)$ *for each* $j \leq k < i$ *and* $P_G \notin V(k)$ *for each* $j < k \leq j$.

A set of granularities is defined in an intensional declarative way by means of a formula of a propositional linear time logic (PPLTL), extended with future temporal operators [19]. The syntax of the considered logic is the following:

**Definition 9.** *Formulae of PPLTL are inductively defined as follows:*

- *any propositional symbol $p \in \mathcal{P}$ is a PPLTL formula;*
- *if $\phi$ and $\psi$ are PPLTL formulae, then $\phi \wedge \psi$ and $\neg\phi$ are PPLTL formulae;*
- *if $\phi$ and $\psi$ are PPLTL formulae, then $\mathbf{X}\phi$, $\phi \, \mathbf{U} \, \psi$, $\mathbf{X}^{-1}\phi$ and $\phi \, \mathbf{S} \, \psi$ are PPLTL formulae.*

It is possible to define the logical operators $\vee$, $\rightarrow$, and $\Leftrightarrow$ by means of the operators $\neg$ and $\wedge$ as follows:

$$\phi \vee \psi \stackrel{\text{def}}{=} \neg(\neg\phi \wedge \neg\psi)$$
$$\phi \rightarrow \psi \stackrel{\text{def}}{=} \neg\phi \vee \psi$$
$$\phi \Leftrightarrow \psi \stackrel{\text{def}}{=} (\phi \rightarrow \psi) \wedge (\psi \rightarrow \phi)$$

Moreover, $\mathbf{F}\alpha$ ($\alpha$ will hold in the future), $\mathbf{G}\alpha$ ($\alpha$ will always hold in the future), $\mathbf{P}\alpha$ ($\alpha$ held in the past), and $\mathbf{H}\alpha$ ($\alpha$ always held in the past) are shorthand for

$$\mathbf{F}\alpha \stackrel{\text{def}}{=} true\mathbf{U}\alpha$$
$$\mathbf{G}\alpha \stackrel{\text{def}}{=} \neg\mathbf{F}\neg\alpha$$
$$\mathbf{P}\alpha \stackrel{\text{def}}{=} true\mathbf{S}\alpha$$
$$\mathbf{H}\alpha \stackrel{\text{def}}{=} \neg\mathbf{P}\neg\alpha$$

where $true \stackrel{\text{def}}{=} p \vee \neg p$, for some $p \in \mathcal{P}$.

Temporal operators in the set $\{\mathbf{X}, \mathbf{U}, \mathbf{X}^{-1}, \mathbf{S}\}$ have priority over Boolean operators $\{\wedge, \vee\}$. Moreover, $\neg$ has priority over $\wedge$ and over $\vee$, and $\wedge$ has priority over $\vee$. For example, the formula $\neg\alpha \wedge \neg\beta\mathbf{U}\gamma \vee \delta$ requires the priorities $((\neg\alpha) \wedge ((\neg\beta)\mathbf{U}\gamma)) \vee \delta$.

The PPLTL formulae are interpreted over the $\mathcal{P}$-labeled linear time structures; the semantics of PPLTL is as follows.

**Definition 10.** *Let $\mathcal{M} = (\mathbb{N}, <, V)$ be a $\mathcal{P}$-labeled linear time structure and $i \in \mathbb{N}$. The truth of a PPLTL-formula $\psi$ in $\mathcal{M}$ with respect to the time point $i$, denoted as $\mathcal{M}, i \models \psi$, is defined as follows:*

| | | |
|---|---|---|
| $\mathcal{M}, i \models p$ | *iff* | $p \in V(i)$ *for $p \in \mathcal{P}$;* |
| $\mathcal{M}, i \models \phi \wedge \psi$ | *iff* | $\mathcal{M}, i \models \phi$ *and* $\mathcal{M}, i \models \psi$; |
| $\mathcal{M}, i \models \neg\phi$ | *iff* | *it is not the case that* $\mathcal{M}, i \models \phi$; |
| $\mathcal{M}, i \models \phi\mathbf{U}\psi$ | *iff* | $\mathcal{M}, j \models \psi$ *for some $j \geq i$ and* |
| | | $\mathcal{M}, k \models \phi$ *for each $k$ such that $i \leq k < j$;* |
| $\mathcal{M}, i \models \mathbf{X}\psi$ | *iff* | $\mathcal{M}, i+1 \models \psi$; |
| $\mathcal{M}, i \models \phi\mathbf{S}\psi$ | *iff* | $\mathcal{M}, j \models \psi$ *for some $j \leq i$ and* |
| | | $\mathcal{M}, k \models \phi$ *for each $k$ such that $j < k \leq i$;* |
| $\mathcal{M}, i \models \mathbf{X}^{-1}\psi$ | *iff* | $i > 0$ *and* $\mathcal{M}, i-1 \models \psi$. |

$\mathcal{M}$ is a model for $\psi$ if $\mathcal{M}, 0 \models \psi$. A formula $\psi$ is satisfiable if and only if there exists a labeled linear time structure with propositional symbols $\mathcal{P}$ that is a model of $\psi$; the formula $\psi$ is valid if and only if every $\mathcal{P}$-labeled linear time structure is a model of $\psi$. $\psi$ is valid if and only if $\neg\psi$ is not satisfiable.

*Example 2.* Figure 7 shows the labeled linear time structure representing the time granularity $G$ such that $G(0) = \{1, 2, 3\}$, $G(1) = \{4, 5, 6\}$, and $G(2) = \{7, 8, 9\}$.

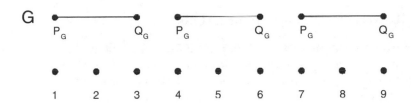

**Fig. 7.** A labeled linear time structure inducing the granularity G

### 4.1 Extending Granularities with Gaps

The above proposal does not consider granularities with gaps inside the granules (only internally continuous granularities are treated): thus, it is not possible to represent, for example, business months, which have gaps inside, corresponding to weekends. This kind of time granularities can be described by extending the set of propositional symbols, representing the time granularities composing a calendar, with suitable symbols denoting the start and the end of a gap inside a specific granularity [16]. Let $\mathcal{G}$ be a calendar and $\mathcal{P}_{\mathcal{G}} = \{ P_G, Q_G, P_{H_G}, Q_{H_G} \mid G \in \mathcal{G} \}$ be set of propositional symbols associated to the calendar $\mathcal{G}$: symbols $P_G$ and $Q_G$ to delimit the granules of $G$ as mentioned before while symbols $P_{H_G}$ and $Q_{H_G}$ bound the gaps inside the granules of $G$. The description of the gaps of $G$ is itself a granularity $H_G$ and, in particular, $H_G$ is finer than $G$. The notion of $G$-consistency for granularities non internally continuous is extended as follows.

**Definition 11.** *A labeled linear time structure $\mathcal{M} = (\mathbb{N}, <, V)$ is G-gap-consistent whether:*

- *$\mathcal{M}$ is G-consistent with respect to both the granularities $G$ and $H_G$;*
- *every granule of $\mathcal{M}$ with respect to $H_G$ is a subset of some granule of $\mathcal{M}$ with respect to $G$;*
- *no granule of $\mathcal{M}$ with respect to $G$ is the union of some granules of $\mathcal{M}$ with respect to $H_G$.*

## 5    Temporal Constraints in Smart Home Applications

Smart Homes are equipped with a set of sensors such as movement sensors, smoke alarm and sensing devices. The core of a Smart Home is the *central monitoring facility* (CMF) which has the ability to detect all sensor and alarm events concurrently from each apartment of the residential care institution.

In this section, we explain how it is possible to represent events occurring in a Smart Home by means of a logical structure which allows one to describe temporal properties related to multiple granularities. We describe some kinds of temporal constraints related to time granularities and denote some sequences of "normal" actions; if a temporal constraint is not satisfied, then a possible undesirable situation may be occurring.

## 5.1  Representing Smart Home Events

The sensors present in a Smart Home give information about what is happening inside the home. Every second, the CMF of the Smart Home receives the state of the sensors; according to this assumption, the bottom granularity of our structure is the second one, *i.e.*, each point in the temporal axis represents a second.

Let $S = \{ Coo, Tv, Fri, \dots \}$ be the symbols denoting sensors related to appliances or to locations: the description of the meaning of these sensors is reported in Tables 1 and 2, respectively. For example, *Kit* represents the sensor associated to the kitchen room, *Coo* is the sensor associated to the cooker and *Tv* represents the Tv-sensor.

In order to represent the events occurring in a Smart Home, the idea is to describe the temporal validity of the state "ON" of some sensor $s \in S$ by means of a temporal granularity s; each granule of s describes a time interval during which the sensor $s$ is in the state "ON".

In particular, when at time $i$ the state of a sensor $s$ changes its value from "OFF" to "ON", then we associate the symbols $s_{on}$ to the time point $i$ of our structure; in this way we can denote the fact that $i$ is the starting point of a time interval during which the sensor $s$ is "ON". Moreover, if at time $j$ $(j > i)$ the

**Table 1.** Symbols related to appliance sensors

| Sensor Name | Appliance |
|:---:|:---:|
| *Coo* | Cooker |
| *Tv* | TV |
| *Fri* | Fridge |
| *K-Tap* | Kitchen tap |
| *BatSinkTap* | Bathroom sink tap |
| *BatTap* | Bath tap |
| *Bed* | Bed |
| *Doo* | Doorbell |
| *Pho* | Phone |
| *Eme* | Emergency pull cord switch |
| *Tem* | Temperature |
| *Rad* | Radiators |
| *Air* | Air conditioning |

**Table 2.** Symbols related to location sensors

| Sensor Name | Location |
|:---:|:---:|
| *Kit* | Kitchen |
| *Liv* | Livingroom |
| *Toi* | Toilet |
| *Rec* | Reception |
| *BedR* | Bedroom |
| *Out* | Outside |

sensor $s$ changes its value from "ON" to "OFF", then we associate the symbols $s_{off}$ to the time point $j-1$ in order to describe the fact that during the time interval $[i, j-1]$ the sensor $s$ is "ON".

The labeling function $L$ associates to each time point in the structure the set of symbols denoting the granularities related to sensors as follows:

$$\begin{cases} s\_off \rightsquigarrow^i s\_on & then & s_{on} \in L(i) \\ s\_on \rightsquigarrow^i s\_off & then & s_{off} \in L(i-1) \end{cases}$$

According to the nature of these sensors, the following properties have to be satisfied:

*Property 1.* It is not possible that a sensor changes its state from "ON" to "ON".

*Property 2.* It is not possible that a sensor changes its state from "OFF" to "OFF".

*Property 3.* At the same time, a sensor cannot be both in the states "ON" and "OFF".

According to the properties reported above and related to the specific application we are considering, in the following we require that each sensor granularity must be internally continuous. Moreover, we denote with "no_event" the fact that the state of a sensor is not changed between time $i-1$ and $i$:

$$\begin{cases} s\_off \rightsquigarrow^i s\_off & then & no\_event \\ s\_on \rightsquigarrow^i s\_on & then & no\_event \end{cases}$$

*Example 3.* Let us now consider the possible sequence of primitive events arriving at the system starting from the initial state, reported in Table 3.

By observing the sequence of events, we can note that the sensor *Kit* assumes value "ON" at time 1 and its state is changed to "OFF" only at time 8. For this reason, we can say that the time interval describing the validity of the sensor *Kit* is the interval [1,7]. The time interval related to the validity of the sensor *Coo* is [2,6] while, in the portion of sequence we are observing, the time interval related to the validity of the sensor *Tv* is still valid, *i.e.*, it is in the form [3, $\perp$] because we assume that in some future time instant, there will be a change from its state "ON" to "OFF". The portion of the labeled linear time structure that maps this set of events with respect to the time is reported in Figure 8.

**Table 3.** A possible sequence of primitive events

| Time | Event | State of Sensors |
|------|-------|------------------|
| 1 | at_kitchen_on | $\{\,Kit\_on\,\}$ |
| 2 | cooker_on | $\{\,Kit\_on, Coo\_on\,\}$ |
| 3 | tv_on | $\{\,Kit\_on, Coo\_on, Tv\_on\,\}$ |
| 4 | no_event | $\{\,Kit\_on, Coo\_on, Tv\_on\,\}$ |
| 5 | no_event | $\{\,Kit\_on, Coo\_on, Tv\_on\,\}$ |
| 6 | no_event | $\{\,Kit\_on, Coo\_on, Tv\_on\,\}$ |
| 7 | cooker_off | $\{\,Kit\_on, Coo\_off, Tv\_on\,\}$ |
| 8 | at_kitchen_off | $\{\,Kit\_off, Coo\_off, Tv\_on\,\}$ |

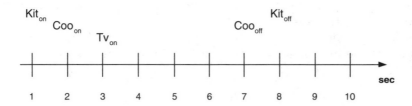

**Fig. 8.** The portion of labeled linear time structure mapping the validity of some sensors

Let $\mathcal{P}_\mathcal{S} = \{\,s_{on}, s_{off} \mid s \in \mathcal{S}\,\}$ be the set of propositional symbols describing the granularities denoting the validity of each sensor $s \in \mathcal{S}$ in the structure $\mathcal{M}$. Let us also assume to have a set $G = \{\,\mathsf{lunch, dinner}, \dots\,\}$ of time granularities describing the granularities of lunch time (*i.e.*, the temporal interval [12:00, 2:00] of each day), the granularity of dinner time (*i.e.*, temporal interval [18:30, 20:30] of each day) and other granularities related to particular time intervals (of a day) during which it is important to observe the events occurring into the house. The set $\mathcal{P}_G = \{\,P_g, Q_g \mid g \in G\,\}$ contains the propositional symbols associated to these granularities. Let $L : \mathbb{N} \to 2^{\mathcal{P}_\mathcal{S} \cup \mathcal{P}_G}$ be the labeling function mapping the natural number set to the set of symbols denoting sensor granularities and symbols related to time granularities.

According to the definition of consistency of a labeled structure with respect to a granularity, the sensor-granularities of $\mathsf{Kit}$, and $\mathsf{Coo}$, shown in Figure 8, are consistent, while the presence of the symbol $Tv_{on}$ at time 2 is not enough to define a granule of the sensor granularity $\mathsf{Tv}$. For these reasons, the granularity $\mathsf{Tv}$ is not consistent in the portion of timeline reported in Figure 8.

The syntax and semantics of the formulae for the description of Smart Home events are simple extensions of syntax and semantics proposed in Definitions 9 and 10. In particular, each propositional symbol $p \in \mathcal{P}$, where $\mathcal{P} = \mathcal{P}_\mathcal{S} \cup \mathcal{P}_G$, is a PPLTL formula. A structure $\mathcal{M}$ satisfies the formula $p$ at time $i$, denotes as $\mathcal{M}, i \models p$, if and only if $p \in L(i)$ for $p \in \mathcal{P}_\mathcal{S}$ or $p \in \mathcal{P}_G$.

The proposed framework allows one to represent possibly infinite time/sensor granularities. A single sequence may represent a calendar, by using different pair of marking proposition symbols for any granularities. In particular, it is possible to model non-periodical finite granularities, such as the sensor granularities related to the activation of sensors during a day, and periodical granularities. An example of a periodical granularity may be a sensor granularity describing the fact that a sensor may be activated with a periodic temporal pattern; for example, if a sensor is auto-activated during the first three minutes of each hour, than the corresponding granularity is a periodical one.

## 5.2 Description of Temporal Constraints

In this section we describe some temporal constraints related to events which can occur in a Smart Home.

*Example 4.* Let us now consider the constraint requiring that:

> "*the cooker cannot be on if the person is not at the kitchen*".

The logical formula describing this constraint is the following:

$$\mathbf{G}(Coo_{on} \rightarrow (\neg Kit_{off} \mathbf{S} Kit_{on}))$$

The formula states that, for each time point $i$ (*i.e.*, it must be always ($\mathbf{G}$) true), if the symbol $Coo_{on} \in L(i)$, then there exists a time point $j \leq i$ such that $Kit_{on} \in L(j)$ and, for each $j < k \leq i$, $\{ Kit_{on}, Kit_{off} \} \notin L(k)$.

The formula is satisfied when $Kit_{on}$, denoting the event "the person is at kitchen", precedes the symbol $Coo_{on}$, denoting the starting point of a time interval associated to the event "the cooker is turn on".

*Example 5.* Let us now describe the constraint requiring that:

> "*during the lunch time, the person has to go into the kitchen*".

The logical formula describing this constraint is the following:

$$\mathbf{G}(P_{Lunch} \rightarrow (\neg Q_{Lunch} \mathbf{U}(Kit_{on} \wedge \neg Q_{Lunch})))$$

The formula states that, it must be always true that if the symbol $P_{Lunch} \in L(i)$, then there exists a time point $j \geq i$ such that $Kit_{on} \in L(j), Q_{Lunch} \notin L(j)$ and, for each $i < k < j$, $Q_{Lunch} \notin L(k)$. Note that we have forced the fact that $Q_{Lunch} \notin L(j)$ to describe that during the lunch-time, the person stays in the kitchen for at least 1 second.

If we want to describe that:

> "*during the lunch time, the person goes into the kitchen and he remains there for at least 10 minutes*"

then we can use the following formula:

$$\mathbf{G}(P_{Lunch} \rightarrow (\neg Q_{Lunch} \mathbf{U}(Kit_{on} \wedge \bigwedge_{i=0}^{600} \mathbf{X}^i \neg Kit_{off})))$$

The formula states that the size of the overlapping between a granule of Lunch and one of Kit is at least equal to 10 minutes (*i.e.*, 600 seconds); in particular $\mathbf{X}^0 \alpha$ stands for $\alpha$ and, for every $n > 0$, $\mathbf{X}^n \alpha$ stands for $\mathbf{X} \mathbf{X}^{n-1} \alpha$.

*Example 6.* Let us now suppose to model the situation *"cooker unattended"* in a strong way, *i.e.,* this situation occurs when the person leaves the kitchen but the cooker is still on. This situation cannot happen when each granule of the sensor granularity Coo is included in some granule of Kit; it means that the granularities Coo and Kit have to satisfy the *finer than* relationship. Figure 9 shows an example of *finer than* relationship between the granularities Coo and Kit; we can note that three granules of Coo is included in the first granule of Kit.

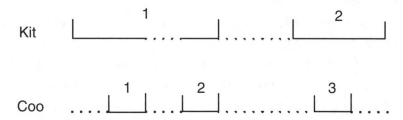

**Fig. 9.** The *finer than* relationship between the granularities Coo and Kit

The relationship FinerThan(Coo, Kit) is described by means of the following formula; in particular, it allows that more than one granule of Coo is included in the same granule of Kit.

IntContGran(Coo) $\wedge$ IntContGran(Kit) $\wedge$

$\mathbf{G}(Coo_{on} \rightarrow ((\neg Kit_{on} \wedge \neg Kit_{off})\mathbf{S}Kit_{on} \wedge (\neg Kit_{on} \wedge \neg Kit_{off})\mathbf{U}Coo_{off}))$

The formula IntContGran(Coo), reported in the following, describes that the granularities Coo is *internally continuous*; as just said before, these constraints are related to the specific application we are considering. In a similar way it is possible to define the formula IntContGran(Kit).

$$\text{IntContGran(Coo)} = \mathbf{G}((Coo_{on} \rightarrow \alpha) \wedge (Coo_{off} \rightarrow \beta))$$

where

$\alpha$ is $Coo_{off} \vee \mathbf{X}(\neg(Coo_{on} \vee Coo_{off})\mathbf{U}(\neg Coo_{on} \wedge Coo_{off}))$
$\beta$ is $Coo_{on} \vee \mathbf{X}^{-1}(\neg(Coo_{on} \vee Coo_{off})\mathbf{S}(Coo_{on} \wedge \neg Coo_{off}))$

A (too) stronger constraint could be imposed by the formula

GranuleRefinement(Coo, Kit)

which requires that each granule of Kit contains a granule of Coo: each time a people enter the kitchen, he must use the cooker and only one time.

*Example 7.* Let us now suppose to model a more complex situation, we name *"cooker unattended and fridge energy conservation"*: we want to exclude both that a person leaves the kitchen but the cooker is still on or the fridge is open. Moreover, we want to exclude that the person turns on or off the cooker when the fridge is open. This situation cannot happen when each granule of the sensor granularity Coo is included in some granule of Kit and each granule of Fri is included in some granule of Kit and each granule of Fri does not contain any event related to the cooker, *i.e.*, $Coo_{on}$ and $Coo_{off}$. The following formula represents the described constraint.

$$\mathsf{FinerThan}(\mathsf{Coo}, \mathsf{Kit}) \wedge \mathsf{FinerThan}(\mathsf{Fri}, \mathsf{Kit}) \wedge$$
$$\mathbf{G}(Fri_{on} \rightarrow \neg(Coo_{on} \vee Coo_{off})\mathbf{U}Fri_{off})$$

## 6 Checking Temporal Constraints

Given a labeled structure $\mathcal{M}$, representing the events occurring in a Smart Home, it is interesting to check whether some temporal constraints are satisfied: for example, it could be useful to check whether the situation *"cooker unattended"*, described in the *Example 6*, never happens.

This corresponds to apply the model checking problem [13] to our framework. In the proposed example, the *model checking problem* allows one to check whether the labeled structure $\mathcal{M}$ defined a model for the following relationship:

$$\mathsf{FinerThan}(\mathsf{Coo}, \mathsf{Kit})$$

Model checking has emerged as a promising and powerful approach to automatic verification of systems. A *model checker* is a procedure that decides whether a given structure $\mathcal{M}$ is a model for a logical formula $\phi$ (*i.e.*, $\mathcal{M} \models \phi$). $\mathcal{M}$ is usually modeled as a finite automata and $\phi$ is a temporal logical formula describing the property to check. Generally, model-checking depends on a discrete model of a system and the system's behavior is represented by means of a graph structure where the nodes represent the states of the system while the arcs represent the transitions between the states.

The common discrete representation of a system is based on the a *Kripke structure*.

**Definition 12.** *Let AP a set of atomic propositions. A Kripke structure (KS) M over AP is a four tuple*
$$M = \langle S, s_0, R, L \rangle$$
*where $S$ is a finite set of states, $s_0 \subseteq S$ is the set of initial states, $R \subseteq S \times S$ is a total transition relation (i.e. for every state $s \in S$ there is a state $s' \in S$ such that $(s, s') \in R$), and $l : S \rightarrow 2^{AP}$ is a function that labels each state with the set of atomic propositions true in that state.*

A *path* in the structure $M$ from the state $s$ is a finite sequence of states $\pi = s_0 s_1 s_2 \ldots$ such that $s_0 = s$ and $R(s_i, s_{i+1})$ holds for all $i \geq 0$. An *execution* is an infinite sequence of states $\sigma = s_0 s_1 s_2 \ldots$ such that $s_0$ is the initial state and $(s_i, s_{i+1}) \in R$, for all $i \geq 0$.

The KS represents the discrete state transition behavior as a direct labeled graph. Temporal logic [20] is used to specify the allowed computation of the system. There are two main kinds of temporal logics, *linear time* logics and *branching time* logics. Linear-time logics (LTLs) are related to properties of paths while the branching time logics describe properties that depend on the branching structure of the model; LTL can be extended with past temporal modalities, *i.e.*, temporal operators that refer to the truth of subformulae in the past and it is usually denoted as PLTL. The *Computational Tree Logic* (CTL) was the first temporal logic for which it was proposed an efficient model-checking procedure [12].

Let us now focus our attention on a finite portion of the labeled structure $\mathcal{M}$ associated to the time interval $[0, n]$, with $n \in \mathbb{N}$. We describe how it is possible to derive a KS describing a finite portion of the labeled linear time structure we are considering. We assume that the set $AP = \{ s_{on}, s_{off}, In_s \mid s \in \mathcal{S} \}$ contains the atomic propositions denoting that the sensor $s$ is turn on, is turn off or is just on (by means of $s_{on}, s_{off}$ and $In_s$, respectively). Each state $s_i \in S$, with $i \in [0, n]$, is used to represent the state of the Smart Home sensors at the specific time $i$. In particular, $s_0$ is the initial state. The total transition relation $R$ is composed by the transitions $(s_j, s_{j+1})$, with $j \in [0, n-1]$. The label function $l : S \to 2^{AP}$ is defined, with respect to the structure $\mathcal{M}$, as follows:

$$s_{on} \in L(j), 0 < j \leq n \Rightarrow s_{on} \in l(s_j)$$
$$s_{off} \in L(k), 0 < k \leq n \Rightarrow s_{off} \in l(s_k)$$

Moreover,

$$s_{on} \in L(j), s_{off} \in L(k), \forall j < h < k \ s_{on}, s_{off} \notin L(h) \Rightarrow \forall j < h < k \ In_s \in l(s_h)$$

According to the above condition, when a sensor is on during the time interval $[j, k]$, then each state of the KS $s_h$, with $j < h < k$, will be label with the atomic proposition $In_s$.

*Example 8.* The portion of the Kripke Structure derived from labeled linear time structure $\mathcal{M}$ reported in Figure 8, is shown in Figure 10.

As just said before, the situation *"cooker unattended"* cannot happen when the granularities Coo and Kit satisfy the *finer than* relationship. We can say that the structure $\mathcal{M}$ satisfies the logical formula associated to the relation

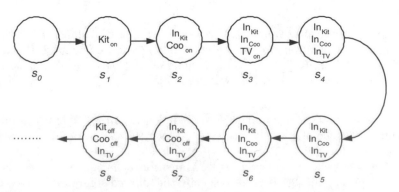

**Fig. 10.** The KS representing a portion of the labeled linear time structure

if and only if, in each state of the associated Kripke Structure, the following
formula holds:

$$(Coo_{on} \rightarrow In_{Kit}) \vee (In_{Coo} \rightarrow In_{Kit}) \vee (Coo_{off} \rightarrow In_{Kit})$$

Sometimes graphs alone are too weak to provide an interesting description of a
system, so they are annotated with more specific information. A very common
approach to the system's representation is the *Kripke Transition System (KTS)*,
where nodes are annotated with *atomic propositions* and arcs are annotated with
*actions*. Paths in KTS model computations of the system.

**Definition 13.** *A Kripke Transition System over a set $\Pi$ of atomic propositions
is a structure $\mathcal{K} = \langle \Sigma, Act, \mathcal{R}, I \rangle$, where $\Sigma$ is a set of states, Act is a set of actions
$(\Pi \cap \Sigma = \emptyset)$, $\mathcal{R} \subseteq \Sigma \times Act \times \Sigma$ is a total relation, and $I : \Sigma \rightarrow \wp(\Pi)$ is an
interpretation.*

In a KTS, the interpretation $I$ defines local properties of states. Sometimes it is
important to describe global properties connected to the transitional behavior,
such as the fact that from the initial state it is possible to reach a state where
the property $P$ holds. There are two ways in which the model-checking problem
can be specified:

**Definition 14.** *The local model checking: given a KST $\mathcal{K}$, a formula $\phi$, and a
state $s$ of $\mathcal{K}$, verifying whether $s \models \phi$. The global model checking: given a KST
$\mathcal{K}$, and a formula $\phi$, finding all states $s$ of $\mathcal{K}$ such that $s \models \phi$.*

Both the local and global model-checking problems are usually formulated for
$\Sigma$ finite. In [12] it has been proved that the global model-checking problem for
a CTL formula $\phi$ can be solved in linear running time on $|\phi| \cdot (|\Sigma| + |\mathcal{R}|)$. The
model checking problem for PLTL and LTL is PSPACE-complete [40].

Let us now focus our attention on a finite portion of the labeled structure $\mathcal{M}$
associated to the time interval $[0, n]$, with $n \in \mathbb{N}$. We describe how it is possible
to derive a KTS representing a finite portion of the labeled linear time structure
we are considering.

Starting from the fact that, at each time point we can have more than one
symbol to denote granularity sensors, we assume that the label of each transition
may be composed by a set of actions. The set of actions $Act$ of the Kripke
Transition System contains the symbols $p \in \mathcal{P}_S$ (*i.e.*, the symbols $s_{on}$ and $s_{off}$,
for each sensor $s$) and the special action $Time$ denoting that there is a (time)
clock which determines the transition from a state to the next one (*i.e.*, the label
of each transition always contains the action $Time$). The KTS will be composed
by $n + 1$ states (a state for each time point in the interval $[0, n]$). The total
transition relation $\mathcal{R} \subseteq \Sigma \times Act \times \Sigma$ is defined as follows:

$$p \in L(i), p \in \mathcal{P}_S \Rightarrow (s_{i-1}, \mathcal{A}, s_i) \in \mathcal{R} \wedge p \in \mathcal{A}$$
$$\forall i \in [0, n-1] \Rightarrow (s_{i-1}, \mathcal{A}, s_i) \in \mathcal{R} \wedge Time \in \mathcal{A}$$

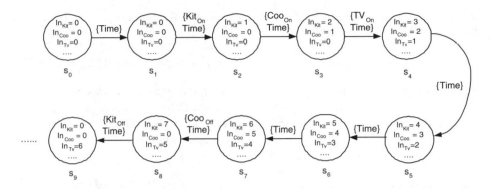

**Fig. 11.** The Kripke Transition System representing a portion of the labeled linear time structure

The initial state $s_0$ contains atomic propositions $In_s = 0$, for each $s \in \mathcal{S}$; this means that at the beginning, each sensor is in the state "OFF".

The idea is that each state of the transition system will be labeled with atomic proposition in the form $In_s = k$, where $k$ is a natural number denoting the duration of the state "ON" of the sensor $s$. By considering the label of the transition from a state to another one[1], the set of atomic propositions associated to each state $s_i \in \Sigma$ ($i > 0$) can be derived as follows:

$$(s_{i-1}, \mathcal{A}, s_i) \in \mathcal{R} \wedge \exists p \equiv s_{on} \in \mathcal{A} \wedge (In_s = 0) \in I(s_{i-1})$$
$$\Rightarrow (In_s = 1) \in I(s_i)$$

$$(s_{i-1}, \mathcal{A}, s_i) \in \mathcal{R} \wedge \exists p \equiv s_{off} \in \mathcal{A} \wedge (In_s = k) \in I(s_{i-1}), \ k > 0$$
$$\Rightarrow (In_s = 0) \in I(s_i)$$

$$(s_{i-1}, \mathcal{A}, s_i) \in \mathcal{R} \wedge \not\exists p \equiv s_{off} \in \mathcal{A} \wedge (In_s = k) \in I(s_{i-1}), \ k > 0$$
$$\Rightarrow (In_s = k+1) \in I(s_i)$$

*Example 9.* The Kripke Transition System derived from the portion of the labeled linear time structure reported in Figure 8, is shown in Figure 11.

In this case, we can say that the structure $\mathcal{M}$ satisfies the logical formula associated to the relation

$$\mathsf{FinerThan(Coo, Kit)}$$

if and only if, in each state of the KTS, the following property holds:

$$In_{Kit} > In_{Coo}$$

The complexity of checking the proposed property on the KTS has linear cost with respect to the number of state.

---

[1] Remark: we are considering a linear time system.

# 7   Comparison with Related Work

In the Artificial Intelligence, the Event Calculus (EC) [28] is a frequently used approach to representing and reasoning about events and their effects. Several variants of EC have been proposed by different authors, but, unlike the original version, based on time periods, most of them are based on time points [37]. From a description of events which occur in the real world and properties they initiate or terminate, EC is used to derive the maximal validity intervals over which properties hold. The notions of event, property, time point and time interval are the primitives of the formalism: *events* happen at *time points* and initiate and/or terminate *time intervals* over which some *property* holds, provided than some other property already holds (*precondition*). Properties are assumed to persist until an event occurs that terminates them (*default persistence*). In the application domain of Smart Homes, events model the change of a sensor value (ON/OFF or OFF/ON) and basic properties represent the state of sensors being ON or OFF; further properties can be defined to explicitly represent some anomalous situations, e.g. leaving the kitchen while the cooker is on. Indeed, these properties can be defined as initiating when the corresponding sensor event happens and some other properties hold: in the previous example, a property *anomalousS* can be defined as initiated by the event $Coo_{on}$ provided than the precondition *outsideKit* holds. The efficient implementation of a PRO-LOG based language supporting EC is not trivial and the related computational complexity is discussed in [10]. Cervesato et al. [7] discuss different extensions of EC to deal with partially ordered events. Chittaro and Combi [9] propose TGIC (Temporal Granularity and Indeterminacy event Calculus), an approach based on the EC to represent and reason on events given either with temporal indeterminacy or with different temporal granularities.

With respect to the above mentioned EC-based contributions, our proposal has some limitations, as it is not possible to represent events given at multiple granularities: indeed, we assume to have a single bottom time line, over which sensor events are precisely located. On the other hand, temporal constraints related to events which can occur in a Smart Home are modeled in a simple way in our proposal, while EC-based formalisms would require the definition of ad-hoc properties (as, in the previous example, being outside a given room). Moreover, our approach, which is closely related to the model checking problem, could benefit from the adoption of some general model checkers, as SPIN or KRONOS [6, 25], to implement a real world system prototype.

# 8   Conclusions

In this chapter, we proposed a logic-based approach to describe temporal constraints with multiple time granularities related to events occurring in Smart Homes. We identified time and sensor granularities as infinite sequences of time points properly labeled with propositional symbols marking the starting and the ending points of each granule. In particular, a *sensor granularity* describes time intervals during which a sensor is in the state "ON", *i.e.,* the time interval related to the validity of the considered sensor. Both time and sensors granularities and temporal constraints are expressed by means of logical PPLTL formulae. Temporal constraints we modeled describe temporal relationships related to sensors providing the right control of the environment of a Smart Home.

# References

1. P. G. Argyroudis and D. O'Mahony. Securing communications in the smart home. In L.T. Yang, M. Guo, G.R. Gao, and N.K. Jha, editors, *International Conference on Embedded and Ubiquitous Computing*, volume 3207 of *LNCS*, pages 891–902. Springer, 2004.
2. J. C. Augusto. Temporal reasoning for decision support in medicine. *Artificial Intelligence in Medicine*, 33(1):1–24, 2005.
3. J. C. Augusto and C. D. Nugent. The use of temporal reasoning and management of complex events in smart homes. In Ramon López de Mántaras and Lorenza Saitta, editors, *16th Eureopean Conference on Artificial Intelligence (ECAI'2004)*, pages 778–782. IOS Press, 2004.
4. C. Bettini, S. Jajodia, and X. S. Wang. *Time granularities in Databases, Data Mining, and Temporal Reasoning*. Springer, 2000.
5. C. Bettini and R. De Sibi. Symbolic representation of user-defined time granularities. *Annals of Mathematics and Atificial Intelligence*, 30(1–4):53–92, 2000.
6. M. Bozga, C. Daws, O. Maler, A. Olivero, S. Tripakis, and S. Yovine. KRONOS: A Model-Checking Tool for Real-Time Systems. In *10th International Conference on Computer Aided Verification (CAV '98)*, volume 1427 of *LNCS*, pages 546–550. Springer, 1998.
7. I. Cervesato, M. Franceschet, and A. Montanari. A guided tour through some extensions of the event calculus. *Computational Intelligence*, 16(2):307–347, 2000.
8. R. Chandra, A. Sergev, and M. Stonebraker. Implementing calendars and temporal rules in next generation databases. In A.K. Elmagarmid and E. Neuhold, editors, *International Conference on Data Engineering*, pages 264–273. IEEE Computer Society Press, 1994.
9. L. Chittaro and C. Combi. Temporal granularity and indeterminacy in reasoning about actions and change: An approach based on the event calculus. *Annals of Mathematics and Artificial Intelligence*, 36(1-2):81–119, 2002.
10. Luca Chittaro and Angelo Montanari. Efficient temporal reasoning in the cached event calculus. *Computational Intelligence*, 12:359–382, 1996.
11. E. Ciapessoni, E. Corsetti, A. Montanari, and P.S. Pietro. Embedding time grnaularity in a logical specification language for synchronous real-time systems. *Science of Computer Programming*, 20:141–171, 1993.
12. E. M. Clarke, E. A. Emerson, and A. P. Sistla. Automatic verification of finite-state concurrent systems using temporal logic specifications. *ACM Transaction on Programming Languages Systems*, 8(2):244–263, 1986.
13. E. M. Clarke, O. Grumberg, and D. A. Peled. *Model Checking*. MIT Press, 2000.
14. J. Clifford and A. Rao. A simple, general structure for temporal domains. In *Temporal Aspects in Information Systems*, pages 17–28. North-Holland/Elsevier, 1987.
15. C. Combi, M. Franceschet, and A. Peron. A logical approach to represent and reason about calendars. In *9th International Symposium on Temporal Representation and Reasoning, (TIME-2002)*, pages 134–140. IEEE Computer Society, 2002.

16. C. Combi, M. Franceschet, and A. Peron. Representing and reasoning about temporal granularities. *Journal of Logic and Computation*, 14(1):51–77, 2004.
17. C. Combi, A. Montanari, and R. Rossato. A uniform algebraic characterization of temporal functional dependencies. In *12th International Symposium on Temporal Representation and Reasoning (TIME-2005)*, pages 91–99. IEEE Computer Society Press, 2005.
18. C. Combi and R. Rossato. Temporal functional dependencies with multiple granularities: A logic based approach. In F. Galindo, M. Takizawa, and R. Traunmüller, editors, *15th International Conference on Database and Expert Systems Applications (DEXA 2004)*, volume 3180 of *LNCS*, pages 864–873. Springer, 2004.
19. E. A. Emerson. Temporal and modal logic. In J. van Leeuwen, editor, *Handbook of Theoretical Computer Science*, volume B, chapter 16, pages 995–1072. MIT Press, 1990.
20. E. A. Emerson. Temporal and modal logic. In *Handbook of Theoretical Computer Science, Volume B: Formal Models and Sematics (B)*, pages 995–1072. 1990.
21. D. Foster, B. Leban, and D. McDonald. A representation for collections of temporal intervals. In *Proceedings of the American National Conference on Artificial Intelligence (AAAI)*, pages 367–371. Morgan Kaufmann, 1986.
22. M. Franceschet and A. Montanari. Branching within time: an expressively complete and elementarily decidable temporal logic for time granularity. *Journal of Language and Computation*, 1(3-4):229–263, 2003.
23. M. Ghorbel, M.T. Segarra, J. Kerdreux, A. Thepaut, and M. Mokhtari. Networking and communication in smart home for people with disabilities. In *9th International Conference on Computers Helping People with Special Needs (ICCHP 2004)*, volume 3118 of *LNCS*, pages 937–944. Springer, 2004.
24. J. R. Hobbs. Granularity. In *Proc. of International Joint Conference on Artificial Intelligence*, pages 432–435. Morgan Kaufmann, 1985.
25. Gerard J. Holzmann. *The SPIN Model Checker: Primer and Reference Manual*. Addison Wesley Professional, 2004.
26. C. S. Jensen, R. T. Snodgrass, J. Clifford, S. K. Gadia, and A. Sergev. A glossary of temporal databases concepts. *SIGMOD Record*, 21(3):35–43, 1992.
27. E. T. Keravnou. A multidimensional and multigranular model of time for medical knowledge-based systems. *Journal of Intelligent Information Systems (JIIS)*, 13(1-2):73–120, 1999.
28. R. A. Kowalski and M. J. Sergot. A logic-based calculus of events. *New Generation Computing*, 4(1):67–95, 1986.
29. P. B. Ladkin. Time representation: A taxonomy of internal relations. In *Proceedings of the American National Conference on Artificial Intelligence (AAAI)*, pages 360–366. Morgan Kaufmann, 1986.
30. P. B. Ladkin. Models of axioms for time intervals. In *American National Conference on Artificial Intelligence (AAAI-1987)*, pages 234–239. Morgan Kaufmann, 1987.
31. A. Montanari. Metric and layered temporal logic for time granularity. ILLC Dissertation Series 1996-02, Institute for Logic, Language and Computation, University of Amsterdam, 1996.
32. A. Montanari, E. Maim, E. Ciapessoni, and E. Ratto. Dealing with time granularity in the event calculus. In *Proc. of International Conference on Fifth Generation Computer Systems*, pages 702–712. IOS Press, 1992.
33. A. Montanari, A. Peron, and A. Policriti. Decidable theories of $\omega$-layered metric temporal structures. *Logic Journal of the IGPL*, 7(1):79–102, 1999.
34. A. Montanari, A. Peron, and A. Policriti. Extending Kamp's theorem to model time granularity. *Journal of Logic and Computation*, 12:641–677, 2002.

35. M. Niezette and J. Stevenne. An efficient symbolic representation of periodic time. In *Proceedings of the International Conference on Information and Knowledge Management*, volume 752 of *LNCS*, pages 161–168, Baltimore, Maryland, November 1993.

36. P. Ning, S. Jajodia, and X. S. Wang. An algebraic representation of calendars. *Annals of Mathematics and Artificial Intelligence*, 36:5–38, 2002.

37. F. Sadri and R. A. Kowalski. Variants of the event calculus. In *Twelfth International Conference on Logic Programming*, pages 67–81. MIT Press, 1995.

38. A. Segev and R. Chandra. A data model for time-series analysis. In N.R. Adam and B.K. Bhargava, editors, *Advanced Database Systems*, volume 759 of *LNCS*, pages 191–212, 1993.

39. Y. Shahar. A framework for knowledge-based temporal abstraction. *Artificial Intelligence*, 90(1-2):79–133, 1997.

40. A. P. Sistla and E. M. Clarke. The complexity of propositional linear temporal logics. *Journal of the ACM*, 32(3):733–749, 1985.

41. P. Terenziani. Integrating calendar dates and qualitative temporal constraints in the treatment of periodic events. *IEEE Transaction on Knowledge and Data Engineering*, 9(5):763–783, 1997.

42. Ti-Shiang Wang. When smart home meets pervasive healthcare services using mobile devices and sensor networks - status and issues. In Soraya Kouadri Mostéfaoui and Zakaria Maamar, editors, *2nd International Workshop on Ubiquitous Computing (IWUC 2005)*, pages 67–74. INSTICC Press, 2005.

43. X. S. Wang, C. Bettini, A. Brodsky, and S. Jajodia. Logical design for temporal databases with multiple granularities. *ACM Transaction on Database Systems*, 22(2):115–170, 1997.

44. J. Wijsen. Reasoning about qualitative trends in databases. *Information Systems*, 23(7):469–493, 1998.

45. J. Wijsen. Temporal FDs on complex objects. *ACM Transactions on Database Systems*, 24(1):127–176, 1999.

# Causal Reasoning for Alert Generation in Smart Homes

Antony Galton

School of Engineering, Computer Science, and Mathematics,
University of Exeter, UK
A.P.Galton@ex.ac.uk

**Abstract.** In this chapter we discuss some of the features of causal reasoning, and present a simple formalism for handling a restricted form of such reasoning applicable to the Smart Homes domain. The formalism handles the manner in which certain conjunctions of *independent states* (i.e., readings from the sensors) can be used to trigger a variety of *dependent states*, notably those which give alert regarding potential emergency situations.

## 1 The Nature of Causality

Causality is a large topic, which has received extensive discussion in the philosophical literature [7]. It is not my intention here to paraphrase or summarise this discussion; instead, in this section I shall draw attention to a number of issues that are central to the modelling of causal reasoning and which will play an important role in what follows.

It is generally held that causation is a relation of some kind. For example, flipping the switch causes the light to come on: this is a relationship between two events, the flipping of the switch and the coming on of the light. This can be expressed in several different ways, e.g., the light came on because the switch was flipped, or, the result of flipping the switch was that the light came on. But causal relations need not only be between events: the water on the floor caused the floor to be slippery. This appears to be a causal relation between the water (an object) and the floor's being slippery (a state of affairs). Perhaps more carefully expressed, this should be: the presence of water on the floor caused the floor to be slippery; this now looks like a causal relation between two states of affairs. One might express it differently again and say that the spilling of the water onto the previously dry floor (an event) caused the floor to become slippery (another event). Even if we take the last of these as the correct expression of the causal relation in this case, we cannot reason correctly about the state of affairs in question if we do not include another principle to the effect that the slipperiness of the floor was *perpetuated* by the continuing presence of the water, which certainly seems to be a relationship between two states of affairs, a relationship, moreover, with a distinctly causal 'flavour'.

We must distinguish between general and particular causal relations. When the flipping of the switch on a particular occasion causes the light to come on, this is a particular causal relation: it is a relation between two individual occurrences (sometimes called *event tokens*), namely the flipping of a particular switch at a particular time and the coming on of a particular light almost immediately afterwards. On the other hand, there is also a general rule to the effect that flipping a light switch causes the associated light to come on. Of course, as stated, this rule is not strictly true: there are innumerable

J.C. Augusto and C.D. Nugent (Eds.): Designing Smart Homes, LNAI 4008, pp. 57–70, 2006.

'background conditions' that must be satisfied for any particular switch-flipping to result in a light's coming on. Some examples are: that the light is not already on, that the power-supply is on, that the light circuit is in good order, that the bulb has not blown, and so on. Thus the general causal statement has to be qualified by a disclaimer along the lines of 'assuming that everything is functioning normally'; this means that causal reasoning is very often non-monotonic [5].

It is not always easy to distinguish between true causality and mere regularity. We may infer the existence of a causal relation between events of type X and events of type Y on the grounds that (given suitable background conditions) events of type X are regularly followed by events of type Y. A child might observe that whenever the light switch is flipped, the light comes on, and infer from this observation that the switch-flipping *causes* the light to come on. Hume famously argued that the only empirical access we have to causal relations must be of this sort, that is, through observation of regularities in the pattern of events. Equally famously, there are clear cases where the inference of causation from regular succession is not justified: during the winter months, whenever the clock strikes six, the heating comes on, but the latter event is not caused by the former.

It is not always clear whether a particular relationship should count as causal, and indeed this may not matter. It is clearly an important piece of knowledge (one so fundamental that we generally take it for granted) that if a body is in a certain position P and moving in a certain direction D then a little later it will be in a position P' such that the line PP' is (at least approximately) in the direction D. Would it be true to say that the body's being in position P' is *caused* by its earlier having been in position P and moving in direction D? Possibly; but whether or not it is, we will need to be able to reason about this kind of relation as well as the ones which are more unequivocally causal. A similarly 'anaemic' form of causality shows up when we reason that if a state has obtained for 10 minutes then if it does not cease to obtain over the next minute, at the end of that minute it will have obtained for 11 minutes. We could say that the earlier fact that the state had obtained for 10 minutes was the cause of the later fact it has obtained for 11 minutes, but again, since the best that we can suggest for a causal mechanism is the mere passage of time, this is not same kind of full-blooded causality (involving transfer of energy) that relates the flipping of a light-switch to the illumination of the light.

In a practical setting, we are interested in causality because we want to be able to predict and control the future and to explain the past. Often, we want to explain the past in order to allow us to control the future better. For example, we flip the switch and the light does not come on, whereas causal reasoning suggests that it should have done. We infer that one of the background conditions was absent; if we know what the background conditions are, we may be able to determine which was at fault. By doing so, we can then rectify the situation so that the when the switch is flipped in future the light does indeed come on.

## 2   Causal Theories

Our knowledge of causal relations can, in principle, be enshrined in a *causal theory*, that is, a set of rules which, when applied to any given state of affairs, will enable us to deduce the causal consequences of that state of affairs. This should be distinguished from a purely logical theory, which will only give us the *logical* consequences. One should be a little careful about terminology here. Given the facts that a pot of water is placed on the gas-ring and the gas-ring is lit at full power, and that this state of affairs is maintained over a period of ten minutes, it is a causal consequence, but not a logical consequence, that at the end of the ten minutes the water is boiling. We can turn this into a logical consequence if we add to the original particular facts a general rule to the effect that whenever a pot of water is placed over a gas-ring on full power for ten minutes, the water will boil. This general rule is a causal rule because its presence enables the causal consequences of a situation to be established as logical consequences — not of the situation alone but of the situation together with the rule. It is rules of this kind that constitute a causal theory.

What form should the causal rules take? There are many possibilities, and the most appropriate choice may vary with the kinds of situations we are modelling. In the first place, causal theories may be classified into two broad categories, depending on whether they contain explicit reference to the notion of cause. By explicit reference we mean the presence of a predicate or function $Cause$ within the formalism. A simple 'caricature' of a system of this kind might be something like

$$Cause(X, Y) \rightarrow \forall t(Occurs(X, t) \rightarrow Occurs(Y, t + 1)).$$
$$Cause(DropGlass, BreakGlass).$$
$$Cause(ThrowBrick, BreakWindow).$$

Here the first formula provides a general rule characterising the $Cause$ predicate: for an event-type $X$ to cause an event-type $Y$, it must be (and here the over-simple nature of our particular formulation becomes apparent!) that whenever $X$ occurs at a time $t$, $Y$ will occur at the succeeding time $t + 1$. The other formulas provide specific instances of that predicate to which the general rule can apply. This kind of theory takes causation to be a primitive relation, which is characterised through the general axioms (such as the first formula above) in which it features. The advantage of choosing a theory of this kind is that it forces one to think explicitly about what causes what, and thus to attend to the true causal structure of the domain being modelled.

Note that a $Cause$ predicate can quite well appear under another name, and then the question arises as to whether it is 'really' causal in meaning. In the Event Calculus [3], for example, the predicate $Initiates$ is used: the formula $Initiates(e, s, t)$ says that state $s$ holds after the occurrence of event $e$ at time $t$. This is neutral as between what I earlier called 'full-blooded' and 'anaemic' notions of causality. To illustrate, the Event Calculus formulation of the notorious Yale Shooting Problem [6], makes use of both $Initiates(load, loaded, t)$ and $Initiates(shoot, dead, t)$. The former says that the action of loading a gun initiates the state of the gun's being loaded; this is 'anaemic' in that one might reasonably claim it to be true simply by virtue of the definition of loading as an action which results in the gun being loaded. On the other hand, shooting can be characterised as an action independently of the fact that, under certain circumstances, it results in someone's being dead. Thus $Initiates(shoot, dead, t)$ expresses a more weighty (or, if you will, less 'trivial') fact than does $Initiates(load, loaded, t)$.

The Event Calculus was inspired by the earlier Situation Calculus [4], in which causality may be expressed by means of a binary function $result$ such that $result(a, s)$

is the situation resulting from performing action $a$ in situation $s$.[1] In this formalism, we could write $Holds(loaded, result(load, s))$ and $Holds(dead, result(shoot, s))$, showing that here, too, the ostensibly causal function $result$ can be used for a range of causal-like relations.

The other kind of causal theory encodes the causal information not by way of an explicit predicate, but implicitly by means of causal rules. Our caricature example would come out as

$$\forall t(Occurs(DropGlass, t) \rightarrow Occurs(BreakGlass, t+1))$$
$$\forall t(Occurs(ThrowBrick, t) \rightarrow Occurs(BreakWindow, t+1))$$

Here we have no general characterisation of the notion of cause; instead we have a set of individual causal rules, one for each of the instances of the $Cause$ relation in the explicit theory. This type of theory has the advantage of parsimony, in the sense that it shows that it is strictly unnecessary to have an explicit cause predicate; its disadvantage is that it becomes less easy to separate out the causal component of the theory from whatever other rules and principles the theory embodies, and in particular one is no longer forced to think about causal relations as such, as opposed to more general temporal relations.[2]

To illustrate this, consider the theory of the gas heater presented by Cervesato and Montanari [1]. This is not presented as an explicitly causal theory, and indeed the word 'cause' is absent not only from the prolog clauses used to implement the theory, but also from the explanatory text. On the other hand, since the framework employed is broadly similar to the Event Calculus [3] the 'initiates' predicate `init` occurs frequently in clauses which have the look and feel of causal rules. But are they really?

The scenario described is that of a gas heater. Amongst the rules used to formalise the theory of the gas heater are the following:

```
init(coolDown, cold, [], []).
init(coolDown, thermoVOpen, [], []).
init(coolDown, burning, [], [pilotOn]).
```

These rules state that if a cooling down event occurs, this will bring about the following states: it is cold, the thermostatic valve is open, and, so long as the pilot light was on at the time of cooling down, the gas is burning. Indeed, this is precisely what happens when the gas heater is functioning as it should. Although these may be thought of as causal rules, they do not, in fact, capture the true causal sequence, which is that the event `coolDown` initiates the state `cold`;[3] this causes the state `thermoVOpen`, which in turn

---

[1] A situation represents the state of the world at one time.

[2] In addition, it does not allow one to express general truths about causation such as 'An effect cannot precede its cause'. Practical causal reasoning must make use of an extensive supply of specific instances of this general truth, and such instances may be expressed without the use of an explicit 'cause' predicate; whether we ever need to invoke the rule in its full generality, requiring explicit reference to causation, is less clear.

[3] This is an example of 'anaemic' causality: the state `cold` can be seen to follow from the event `coolDown` as a matter of logical necessity, given a definition of the latter as that event which results in the former. In the absence of such an explicit definition, of course, the connection must be enshrined in a rule, and whether or not we wish to call such a rule causal, it certainly has a similar form to more full-blooded causal rules.

causes burning. Thus while it is certainly true that coolDown causes burning, it does so only indirectly, by way of the sequence just described. As a consequence of the way Cervesato and Montanari have modelled the gas heater, the first two rules above play no part in inferring that burning is initiated as a result of coolDown, this inference being instead secured by the third rule alone. This means that their model does not correctly capture the causal structure of the gas heater's operation. Likewise, they have the composite event par(prLighter, prDisable) (i.e., simultaneous pressing of the lighter switch and the safety-valve disable button) initiating both the states burning and pilotOn, whereas the true causal sequence is that pressing the disable button causes the safety valve to open, allowing gas to flow to the pilot, while at the same time pressing the lighter switch causes sparking, the two conditions together ensuring that the pilot light comes on; it is *this* that initiates burning.

The init predicate illustrates one form of causal rule, which states that an event, under suitable conditions, will bring about a state. This is only one out of a number of possible types of causal relation. As remarked above, we sometimes speak of events causing other events, sometimes of an event causing a state, sometimes of a state causing an event, and sometimes of a state causing a state, and sometimes what is in reality a single instance of causation may be described in several different ways. Whatever causes the water to come to the boil (an event) is also causing the water to be boiling (a state). In this case the cause is the initial placing of the pot of water on the gas-ring (an event), combined with the fact that over a sufficiently long interval it is not removed or the gas turned off (a background condition); or alternatively, it is the state which consists of the fact that the pot has been on the gas-ring for ten minutes. The possibility of redescribing both causes and effects in this way means that we have a considerable amount of lee-way in choosing the form of our causal rules; it would be incorrect to suppose that there is a unique 'right' way of doing it. Rather, the choice should be informed by what is most convenient in relation to the particular scenario being modelled.

In the smart homes scenario, the information available is entirely in the form of sensor readings. If the sensors are all binary, i.e., they are each capable of reporting only two states — that the associated device is either 'on' or 'off' — then in effect the basis for our reasoning is purely state-based. However, even if we only explicitly refer to states, events are implicit whenever we have a *change* of state. For example, if a certain sensor reports 'off' at time $t$ and then 'on' at time $t + 1$, we can say that an event, namely the switching on of the device which is being monitored by the sensor, has taken place. We do not necessarily need to refer to this event explicitly, since any causal consequence it may have is also a causal consequence of the state of the device being on, given the background condition that it was off at the immediately previous moment.

For this reason, the formalism to be developed in the next section will not refer explicitly to events. The causal rules will only make use of states. These include both the states that are immediately reported by the sensors and also various logical constructs out of these, such as the state which consists of a particular device having been on for a certain period of time. We emphasise that no claims are made for the generality of this formalism; it is specifically designed to operate within a tightly circumscribed domain, and in this application is used to handle only a specific aspect of that domain—namely the triggering of alerts in response to certain conjunctions of sensor readings. Within that context we have aimed to produce a formalism that is as simple as possible. The larger problem of devising a flexible formalism for causal reasoning which might be applied universally lies outside the scope of the present treatment.

## 3   A Formalism for Causal Reasoning About States

We shall make use of a *stratified* system of states similar to that described in [2].[4] We assume we have a set of *atomic states*, which come in pairs, each positive atomic state $S$ being paired with its negation $-S$. We shall use $\overline{S}$ to refer to the state paired with $S$: if $S$ is positive, then $\overline{S} = -S$, while if $S = -S_1$ (a negative state) then $\overline{S} = S_1$. We write $S_1 \sqcap S_2$ to denote the (non-atomic) state that holds when $S_1$ and $S_2$ both hold, and at no other times.

Let $S$ be the set of all atomic states (both positive and negative); these states are partitioned into two classes, called *dependent* and *independent*. We use $S_D$ and $S_I$ for the sets of dependent and independent atomic states, respectively. The idea is that an independent state does not depend causally on other states holding at the same time, whereas a dependent state can do so. In the smart homes scenario, the independent states are those which are directly reported by the sensors, e.g., cooker_on. Note that because we have state-negation, we do not need a separate state cooker_off; instead we can write −cooker_on. Because of this, for brevity, we shall write Cooker instead of cooker_on, and likewise with all the other sensors. We shall call $S$ *co-independent* if $\overline{S}$ is independent.

The dependent states will include various states of emergency alert which are triggered by particular combinations of circumstances. These will be discussed in the context of the smart homes scenario in the next section. Another important class of dependent states called *duration states* will play an important causal role in relation to the aforementioned alert states; these are described below.

Time is represented as a discrete series of instants, labelled by the natural numbers. We assume that a constant time elapses between each pair of consecutive instants: for example, they might be one second apart. In the Smart Homes scenario, for example, these instants correspond to the times at which the readings from the sensors are sampled; for simplicity we assume this will take place at regular intervals. At each instant $t$, the state $S$ either holds or does not hold; in the latter case, its negation $-S$ holds. If both $S_1$ and $S_2$ hold at $t$, then we say that their conjunction $S_1 \sqcap S_2$ holds at $t$; this is an associative operator, so we can write multiple conjunctions of the form $S_1 \sqcap S_2 \sqcap \cdots \sqcap S_n$ without the need for pairwise bracketing.

There are two kinds of causal rule. *Same-time rules* take the form

$$S_1 \sqcap S_2 \sqcap \cdots \sqcap S_n \rightsquigarrow S,$$

---

[4] In [2] this formalism is applied to the gas-heater example of [1], and to an automatic handdrier with a time-out mechanism. In a longer, unpublished paper, we have also applied it to an electrical circuit, the Yale Shooting Problem, the falling of an arrangement of dominos, and the swinging of a pendulum.

where each $S_i$ is an atomic state and $S \in S_D$. *Next-time rules* have the form

$$S_1 \sqcap S_2 \sqcap \cdots \sqcap S_n \rightsquigarrow \bigcirc S;$$

here it is not required that $S \in S_D$.

Same-time rules are required to be *stratified*. This is explained as follows.

1. A state $S$ is called *0-dependent* if and only if it is independent, i.e., $S \in S_I$. (This means it cannot appear as the consequent of a same-time rule.)

2. For $k \geq 1$, a Stage $k$ rule is a same-time rule $S_1 \sqcap S_2 \sqcap \cdots \sqcap S_n \rightsquigarrow S$ where each of $S_1, \ldots, S_n$ is at most $(k-1)$-dependent, and at least one of them is $(k-1)$-dependent. Then $S$ is said to be *k-dependent*. In this case we also say that $\bar{S}$ is *co-k-dependent*.

3. A set of same-time rules is stratified so long as for every rule in the set there is a number $k$ such that the rule is a Stage $k$ rule.

A same-time rule $S_1 \sqcap S_2 \sqcap \cdots \sqcap S_n \rightsquigarrow S$ can be *applied* at time $t$ so long as $S_1, S_2, \ldots, S_n$ all hold at $t$. The result of applying it is that we may assert that $S$ holds at $t$. Under the same condition we can also apply a next-time rule $S_1 \sqcap S_2 \sqcap \cdots \sqcap S_n \rightsquigarrow \bigcirc S$, and the result of applying it is that we may assert that $S$ holds at $t + 1$. If a rule can be applied, it is said to be *live*.

The rules are applied in accordance with the following algorithm for $t = 0, 1, 2, 3, \ldots$ for as many steps as required:

1. First determine the current value of each independent state (e.g., from the sensor readings).

2. For $k = 1, 2, 3, \ldots,$

   (a) Apply any live same-time rules of Stage $k$ (note that some rules may become live as a result of applying others of a lower stage).

   (b) If $t = 0$, for any positive state $S$ whose value is not already determined, assume that $-S$ holds.

   (c) If $t > 0$, then for any co-$k$-dependent state $S$, if $S$ holds at $t - 1$, and $\bar{S}$ has not already been asserted to hold then $S$ may be asserted to hold at $t$. (This is applying the assumption that a state $S$ persists from one instant to the next unless there is reason to assert the contrary.)

3. Apply any live next-time rules.

To illustrate, we shall show how the Yale Shooting Problem can be formulated in this system.[5] The scenario may be described informally as follows: at time 0, the victim is alive, the gun is not loaded, the trigger is not being pressed, and the bullet is not being fired. The gun (assumed to be pointing at the victim) becomes loaded at time 1, and the trigger is pressed at time 3; no actions are specified between these times. The problem is to formulate this scenario in such as way that the desired conclusion, that the victim

---

[5] We do not, of course, claim that this simple formulation provides a complete solution to the YSP, but merely that, within the context of the type of scenario we can model, YSP does not present any problems for us. The non-monotonic persistence of the state Loaded is secured by step 2(c) of the algorithm.

is dead at time 4, follows. We use four positive states Alive, Trigger, Loaded, and Bullet. The only dependent state is Bullet, which is governed by the same-time rule

1. Loaded ⊓ Trigger ⤳ Bullet.

This says that if the gun is loaded and the trigger is pressed then the bullet fires. In addition we have three next-time rules[6]

2. Bullet ⊓ Alive ⤳ ○(−Alive)
3. Bullet ⤳ ○(−Loaded)
4. Bullet ⤳ ○(−Bullet)

The history can be computed as follows:

$t = 0$ We have Alive ⊓ −Loaded ⊓ −Trigger ⊓ −Bullet.

$t = 1$ From information given, we have Loaded. The co-independent states Alive and −Trigger and the co-1-dependent state −Bullet all persist, so we have Alive ⊓ Loaded ⊓ −Trigger ⊓ −Bullet.

$t = 2$ All states persist, giving Alive ⊓ Loaded ⊓ −Trigger ⊓ −Bullet again.

$t = 3$ We are given Trigger. The co-independent state Loaded persists, so Rule 1 becomes live, giving Bullet. The complete state is thus Alive ⊓ Loaded ⊓ Trigger ⊓ Bullet. The next-time rules 2–4 all become live, so we have

$t = 4$ −Alive from rule 2, −Loaded from rule 3, and −Bullet from rule 4. The co-independent state Trigger persists (the trigger remains depressed since the person holding the gun has not released it). The complete state is now

−Alive ⊓ −Loaded ⊓ Trigger ⊓ −Bullet.

This history is summarised in the following table:

|        | 0 | 1 | 2 | 3 | 4 |
|--------|---|---|---|---|---|
| Alive   | + | + | + | + | − |
| Loaded  | − | + | + | + | − |
| Trigger | − | − | − | + | + |
| Bullet  | − | − | − | + | − |

Within the system we have described we can define the duration states that were mentioned above. Given a state $S$, the duration state $\mathrm{dur}(S)=n$ is that state which holds when $S$ itself has held for the previous $n$ atomic intervals. Note that we have used a function notation $\mathrm{dur}(S)$ here rather than a relation $\mathrm{Dur}(S, n)$. This is because at any given time there is only one value of $n$ for which $\mathrm{Dur}(S, n)$ would hold; hence we can notate this value $\mathrm{dur}(S)$. Thus $\mathrm{dur}(S)$ is in effect a *fluent*, i.e., a function from times to values; ordinary states such as $S$ (and, indeed, $\mathrm{dur}(S) = n$ for any given $n$) may likewise be regarded as *Boolean fluents*, i.e., functions from times to values from the set {true,false}.

The causal rules governing duration states are as follows:

$$(\textbf{dur1})\quad \overline{S} \rightsquigarrow \mathrm{dur}(S)=0$$
$$(\textbf{dur2})\quad S \sqcap \mathrm{dur}(S)=n \rightsquigarrow \bigcirc(\mathrm{dur}(S)=n+1)$$

---

[6] Note that dependence, as defined for the purpose of the algorithm, is determined by same-time rules only, so these rules do not make −Alive, −Loaded and −Bullet dependent states.

In addition, we assume that if $\mathrm{dur}(S)$ cannot be determined by the rules, then its default value is 0.

To see how these rules work, we shall apply the algorithm to a system which contains a single independent state $S$. Assume that the sequence of sensor readings for $S$ is $-, -, +, +, +, -, +, +, -, -, -, \ldots$, where '$-$' represents 'off' and '$+$' represents 'on'. The reasoning, as determined by the algorithm, proceeds as follows:

$t = 0$   We have $-S$ from the sensor. Same-time rule **(dur1)** gives $\mathrm{dur}(S)=0$. By default, we also have $\mathrm{dur}(-S)=0$. Then, given $-S \sqcap \mathrm{dur}(-S)=0$, next-time rule **(dur2)** yields $\mathrm{dur}(-S)=1$ at $t = 1$.

$t = 1$   We have $-S$ from the sensor and $\mathrm{dur}(-S)=1$ from $t = 0$. Same-time rule **(dur1)** gives $\mathrm{dur}(S)=0$. Given $-S \sqcap \mathrm{dur}(-S)=1$, **(dur2)** yields $\mathrm{dur}(-S)=2$ at $t = 2$.

$t = 2$   We have $S$ from the sensor and $\mathrm{dur}(-S)=2$ from $t = 1$. However, given $S$, same-time rule **(dur1)** yields $\mathrm{dur}(-S)=0$. This *overrides* the previously determined value for $\mathrm{dur}(-S)$ at this time.[7] The value of $\mathrm{dur}(S)$ has not been determined, so it defaults to 0: $\mathrm{dur}(S)=0$. We now have $S \sqcap \mathrm{dur}(S)=0$ so by **(dur2)** we infer $\mathrm{dur}(S)=1$ at $t = 3$.

$t = 3$   We have $S$ from the sensor and $\mathrm{dur}(S)=1$ from $t = 2$. By **(dur1)** we infer $\mathrm{dur}(-S)=0$. From $S \sqcap \mathrm{dur}(S)=1$ and **(dur2)** we have $\mathrm{dur}(S)=2$ at $t = 4$.

Continuing in this way, we generate a history which may be summarised in the following table:

|             | 0 | 1 | 2 | 3 | 4 | 5 | 6 | 7 | 8 | 9 | 10 |
|-------------|---|---|---|---|---|---|---|---|---|---|----|
| $S$         | $-$ | $-$ | $+$ | $+$ | $+$ | $-$ | $+$ | $+$ | $-$ | $-$ | $-$ |
| $\mathrm{dur}(S)$   | 0 | 0 | 0 | 1 | 2 | 0 | 0 | 1 | 0 | 0 | 0 |
| $\mathrm{dur}(-S)$  | 0 | 1 | 0 | 0 | 0 | 0 | 0 | 0 | 0 | 1 | 2 |

From the table we can read off that, for example, at $t = 4$, $S$ has obtained for a duration of 2 time units (i.e., over the interval $[2, 4]$).

Note that although $-S$ comes to hold at $t = 5$, it does not persist to the next instant, and hence it does not register a positive duration on this occasion. However, the fact that $-S$ held at $t = 5$ shows up in the fact that $\mathrm{dur}(S)$ is 'reset to zero'. Thus the fact that $\mathrm{dur}(S)=1$ at $t = 7$ indicates that $-S$ must have held two time intervals ago, i.e., at $t = 5$. This means that we can use $\mathrm{dur}$ to describe complex states such as '$S_1$ has not held at any time since $S_2$ last held'. This can be represented as the state $\mathrm{dur}(-S_1) \geq \mathrm{dur}(-S_2)$, which holds just when the length of time for which $S_1$ has failed to hold exceeds the length of time since $S_2$ last held.

## 4  Application to the Smart Homes Scenario

The purpose of the sensors in the smart home is to monitor the patient's activities and to trigger an alert if something untoward happens. In order to handle alerts, we introduce a set of dependent states indicating the subject and degree of urgency of an alert. For

---

[7] Note that this shows why the '$\rightsquigarrow$' symbol in the causal rules cannot be replaced by '$\rightarrow$': if they were ordinary material implications, we would now have a contradiction.

example, the state `alert(bath)=1` indicates that a state of alertness exists in relation to the bath, but its urgency is currently low. We shall assume a scale of three degrees of urgency, namely 1 (low), 2 (medium), and 3 (high), with 0 to indicate the absence of an alert.

In this section we shall consider the following sequence of events:

> Initially, the patient is in the kitchen, where she switches the cooker on to a high setting. She then goes (via the reception area) into the bathroom and turns on the tap at the basin. Leaving it on, she returns to the kitchen, turns the cooker to a low setting, and then returns to the bathroom, where, after a short delay she turns off the tap. Finally she goes back once more to the kitchen.

It should be noted that while this *could* be an entirely innocuous piece of behaviour, it does have the makings of a potential emergency and hence we should expect some alerts to be triggered at various points during the course of it. We describe below the causal rules needed to make this happen.

Before beginning the formalisation, we should note that the set of sensors described in the introductory chapter will need to be expanded somewhat if we are to handle this sequence of events adequately. 'Switching on the cooker' is rather vague: a typical cooker will have a hob containing four gas or electric rings, an oven, and possibly a grill as well. It makes a difference which of these is switched on in the above scenario: switching on the oven and then leaving it for an extended period is normal and to be expected; with the hob, on the other hand, it is more of a matter for concern. Similarly, there is less to worry about if a gas-ring is on a low setting than if it is on a high setting. Thus instead of having a single state `Cooker` to indicate that the cooker is on, we will use structured states such as `setting(hob)=high` or `setting(oven)=off`. For simplicity we shall assume four settings, abbreviated as `O` (off), `L` (low), `M` (medium), `H` (high). It will be assumed that the sensors attached to the cooker are able to detect and report this information.

The sequence described in words above can be represented by the following table, in which it is assumed that the sensor readings take place at one-minute intervals.

|  | 0 | 1 | 2 | 3 | 4 | 5 | 6 | 7 | 8 | 9 | 10 | 11 | 12 |
|---|---|---|---|---|---|---|---|---|---|---|---|---|---|
| InKitchen | + | + | − | − | − | − | + | + | − | − | − | − | + |
| InReception | − | − | + | − | − | + | − | − | + | − | − | + | − |
| InBathroom | − | − | − | + | + | − | − | − | − | + | + | − | − |
| setting(hob) | O | H | H | H | H | H | H | L | L | L | L | L | L |
| BathroomBasinTap | − | − | − | − | + | + | + | + | + | − | − | − | − |

If the hob is switched on at a high setting, we would normally expect the patient to remain in attendance, at least for most of the time. Thus a state of alert should be generated if, while the hob is on a high setting, the patient is absent from the kitchen for more than, say, two minutes. The urgency level could begin at 1, and increase to 2 after a further two minutes, and then to 3 after two minutes more.[8] These results will be secured by the following same-time rules:[9]

$$\mathrm{dur}(\mathrm{setting}(\mathrm{hob}){=}\mathrm{H} \sqcap -\mathrm{InKitchen}) \leq 2 \rightsquigarrow \mathrm{alert}(\mathrm{hob}) = 0$$
$$2 < \mathrm{dur}(\mathrm{setting}(\mathrm{hob}){=}\mathrm{H} \sqcap -\mathrm{InKitchen}) \leq 4 \rightsquigarrow \mathrm{alert}(\mathrm{hob}) = 1$$
$$4 < \mathrm{dur}(\mathrm{setting}(\mathrm{hob}){=}\mathrm{H} \sqcap -\mathrm{InKitchen}) \leq 6 \rightsquigarrow \mathrm{alert}(\mathrm{hob}) = 2$$
$$\mathrm{dur}(\mathrm{setting}(\mathrm{hob}){=}\mathrm{H} \sqcap -\mathrm{InKitchen}) > 6 \rightsquigarrow \mathrm{alert}(\mathrm{hob}) = 3$$

Similarly, we would normally expect a tap to be switched off when the patient is out of the room (an exception being if she is running a bath). Thus the following rules are appropriate:

$$\mathrm{dur}(\mathrm{BathroomBasinTap} \sqcap -\mathrm{InBathroom}) \leq 2 \rightsquigarrow \mathrm{alert}(\mathrm{bathroomBasin}){=}0$$
$$2 < \mathrm{dur}(\mathrm{BathroomBasinTap} \sqcap -\mathrm{InBathroom}) \leq 4 \rightsquigarrow \mathrm{alert}(\mathrm{bathroomBasin}){=}1$$
$$4 < \mathrm{dur}(\mathrm{BathroomBasinTap} \sqcap -\mathrm{InBathroom}) \leq 6 \rightsquigarrow \mathrm{alert}(\mathrm{bathroomBasin}){=}2$$
$$\mathrm{dur}(\mathrm{BathroomBasinTap} \sqcap -\mathrm{InBathroom}) > 6 \rightsquigarrow \mathrm{alert}(\mathrm{bathroomBasin}){=}3$$

Note that $2 < \mathrm{dur}(\mathrm{BathroomBasinTap} \sqcap -\mathrm{InBathroom}) \leq 4$ is 'syntactic sugar' for the state conjunction

$$\mathrm{dur}(\mathrm{BathroomBasinTap}) > 2$$
$$\sqcap \, \mathrm{dur}(-\mathrm{InBathroom}) > 2$$
$$\sqcap \, \mathrm{dur}(\mathrm{BathroomBasinTap}) \leq 4$$
$$\sqcap \, \mathrm{dur}(-\mathrm{InBathroom}) \leq 4,$$

and likewise with the other composite states used here.

We can now use the algorithm presented in §3, together with the rules there given for dur and the rules just given for alert to infer the times at which alerts occur in the scenario under consideration. To this end, we repeat the above tabulation, with extra rows for the dependent states inferred using these rules.

|  | 0 | 1 | 2 | 3 | 4 | 5 | 6 | 7 | 8 | 9 | 10 | 11 | 12 |
|---|---|---|---|---|---|---|---|---|---|---|---|---|---|
| InKitchen | + | + | − | − | − | − | + | + | − | − | − | − | + |
| InReception | − | − | + | − | − | + | − | − | + | − | − | + | − |
| InBathroom | − | − | − | + | + | − | − | − | − | + | + | − | − |
| setting(hob) | O | H | H | H | H | H | H | L | L | L | L | L | L |
| BathroomBasinTap | − | − | − | − | + | + | + | + | + | + | − | − | − |
| dur(setting(hob)=H $\sqcap$ −InKitchen) | 0 | 0 | 0 | 1 | 2 | 3 | 0 | 0 | 0 | 0 | 0 | 0 | 0 |
| dur(BathroomBasinTap $\sqcap$ −InBathroom) | 0 | 0 | 0 | 0 | 0 | 0 | 1 | 2 | 3 | 0 | 0 | 0 | 0 |
| alert(hob) | 0 | 0 | 0 | 0 | 0 | 1 | 0 | 0 | 0 | 0 | 0 | 0 | 0 |
| alert(bathroomBasin) | 0 | 0 | 0 | 0 | 0 | 1 | 0 | 0 | 1 | 0 | 0 | 0 | 0 |

We see that two low-level alerts occur, but they each persist for no more than a minute. This is in keeping with our earlier suggestion that the sequence of events being

---

[8] These specific figures are, of course, purely speculative and suggested for the sake of having some definite figures to work with; in reality, it would be necessary to conduct detailed research to determine what the most appropriate figures should be.

[9] Note that although we do not explicitly use the next-time operator here, it is none the less present implicitly, since the function dur is goverened by the next-time rule **dur2**.

described is not in itself cause for major alarm, but at certain points displayed the potential for developing into something more serious. Of course, the fact that *two* alerts occur in quick succession may be indicative of something wrong, e.g., that the patient is in a state of mild mental confusion which if it persists might lead her to do something with more serious consequences. We could introduce a further layer of 'meta-alerts', by which the system monitors the pattern of alerts and draws attention to cases which we wish to regard as cause for possible intervention.

While this initial illustration is inevitably rather crude and over-simplified, it does indicate that the kind of formalism proposed here might be usefully deployed as a way of handling the generation of alert conditions from those patterns of sensor readings which require it. There are a number of further observations that can be made here.

First, for each appliance, there are typical patterns of application, and there are typical relationships between appliance activation and the movements of the patient. For example, if the doorbell or telephone rings, then this would normally be followed by movement towards the door or telephone, an exception being if the patient is asleep in bed, as evidenced by a sufficiently long period of inactivity following a most recent movement detected in the bathroom. These normal or typical sequences of events are for the most part not causal in the truest sense of the word, and we do not need to treat them as such. However, it is important to be able to recognise when departures from such sequences occur, as these will be precisely the conditions under which we might wish to trigger an alert state. The rules for the hob given above in effect encapsulate the observation that normally, if the patient switches on the hob at a high setting, it is expected that they will remain in the vicinity of the hob until such time as it is switched to a lower setting. Other rules will correspond to other regularities in expected behaviour. For example, the absence of detected movement over a long period during the day would normally be cause for alarm.

It should be noted, however, that behavioural patterns are likely to differ from patient to patient. One patient might typically go to the kitchen to prepare a nightcap just before going to bed, and different patients may have different patterns of bathroom use in relation to breakfast and other mealtimes. Normally, if the patient is in bed and gets up in the middle of the night to go to the bathroom, they should return to bed after a few minutes. But some individual patients might quite usually get up for fairly long periods during the night. Deviations from the normal pattern for the patient being monitored can be used to trigger alarms, but in order for this to happen, the system will have to learn what the normal patterns are for that patient, so there is an important pattern detection element here. The learning process might make use of feedback from false alarms: if a particular conjunction of circumstances several times leads the system into generating an alert state that proves to be unfounded, the rule should be modified so that that conjunction of circumstances is no longer treated as cause for an alert.

In addition to normal or typical patterns of behaviour, there will also be some universals: for example, a person cannot be in two rooms at once, and a person cannot move directly between two non-adjacent rooms (continuity of movement). If either of these conditions is detected, it suggests the possibility of an intruder in the flat.[10] Of course, it is possible that the patient has a visitor, but if this is the case, the system should know

---

[10] Of course, it could also be an indication of a faulty sensor!

about it since at some stage the doorbell will have rung, followed by movement in the vicinity of the front door. Thus we could have a state `Visitor`, whose default value is false, and which becomes true only after a sequence of sensor readings characteristic of the patient's admitting a visitor into the flat. The first 'possible intruder' alarm can then be readily handled by rules of the form

$$-\texttt{Visitor} \sqcap \texttt{InKitchen} \sqcap \texttt{InBathroom} \rightsquigarrow \texttt{alert(possibleIntruder)} = 2,$$

by which a medium-level 'possible intruder' alert is triggered by the simultaneous detection of movement in two different rooms when the patient is supposedly alone. To handle the second case, we need to enforce conditions to the effect that if, say, `InBathroom` holds at $t-1$ and `InKitchen` holds at $t$ then `alert(possibleIntruder)` should be set to the value 2. However, the same-time and next-time rules as we have them do not readily lend themselves to this. One (perhaps rather inelegant) possibility would be to introduce a new state-forming operator $\texttt{prec}$ such that $\texttt{prec}(S)$ holds at time $t$ if and only if $S$ holds at time $t-1$. The rules governing $\texttt{prec}$ are

$$S \rightsquigarrow \bigcirc\texttt{prec}(S)$$
$$\texttt{prec}(S) \rightsquigarrow -\texttt{prec}(\overline{S})$$

(where these need only be implemented for independent states $S$). We then have the rule

$$\texttt{InKitchen} \sqcap \texttt{prec(InBathroom)} \rightsquigarrow \texttt{alert(possibleIntruder)} = 2.$$

## 5  Concluding Remarks

The Smart Home, as perceived by the array of sensors it contains, is a rather well-defined, constrained environment in which much of what happens is likely to conform to certain invariable, or almost invariable, patterns that can be specified in a simply-formulated language of limited expressive power. As such, it is an excellent test bed for various formalisms that have been developed in AI for reasoning about closed domains. It seems reasonable to hope that many problems, which prove to be intractable when they arise in the context of a wider world in which it is impossible to specify in advance even the *kinds* of things that can happen, may be much more benign when they arise in this more restricted arena. In this chapter we have examined the case of causal reasoning; specifically, the detection of emergencies or potential emergencies from the monitoring of activity taking place within the Smart Home. We have suggested that for this purpose a comparatively simple formalism, devised originally for modelling deterministic devices and protocols, might be an appropriate tool to use.

Of course, there is more scope for causal reasoning in the Smart Home environment than what has been described here. In the introductory chapter, the example is given of food being left too long on the cooker, causing a fire. Behind this we can discern a causal law to the effect that, given suitable background conditions, if the cooker is left on for too long (however 'too long' may be defined), then a fire will ensue. Does the central computer system that is monitoring the Home need to 'know' this? Here we would argue not: what is needed is that the system can detect that a condition has arisen that is cause for alarm. By generating an alert state, it draws this condition to the attention of humans who are, we may assume, watching out for such things. At that point, human commonsense reasoning takes over; depending on the details of the case, it may or may not be judged necessary to call the fire brigade.

One of the goals of AI is, of course, to emulate human commonsense reasoning, so it is natural to ask at which point we should expect humans to have to intervene in the monitoring process. Can we, for example, build into the computer system sufficient 'common sense' for us to allow it to make decisions such as whether to call the fire brigade when it detects a condition that appears to warrant it? Here it would seem prudent to proceed with caution: the computer emulation of human common sense does not at present appear to have advanced sufficiently to allow us to deploy such computers outside the comparatively constrained environments in which 'reasoning' is reducible to a kind of mechanical calculation. This is not common sense but perhaps provides a foundation on which something more like true common sense can be built. Here I must reveal my own prejudices and express a guarded scepticism as to whether any such thing will ever be achievable. Even if it is not, the kind of system described in this chapter can function as a useful tool, providing essential support for the decisions we humans have to make, even if not making any such decisions itself. A parallel can be drawn with decision-support systems in medicine. In the early days of AI there was much optimism that expert systems could be used for completely automated diagnosis; although this proved not to be the case, the ensuing research effort has led to a widespread acceptance that computer-based systems can usefully support the human physician in the decision-making process.

# References

1. Iliano Cervesato and Angelo Montanari. A calculus of macro-events: Progress report. In A. Trudel and S. Goodwin, editors, *Proceedings of the Seventh International Workshop on Temporal Representation and Reasoning*, pages 47–58. IEEE Computer Society Press, 2000.
2. Antony Galton and Juan Carlos Augusto. Stratified causal theories for reasoning about deterministic devices and protocols. In Michael Fisher and Alessandro Artale, editors, *Proceedings of the Ninth International Symposium on Temporal Representation and Reasoning (TIME-02)*, pages 52–54. IEEE Computer Society, 2002.
3. R. A. Kowalski and M. J. Sergot. A logic-based calculus of events. *New Generation Computing*, 4:67–95, 1986.
4. John McCarthy and Patrick J. Hayes. Some philosophical problems from the standpoint of artificial intelligence. In B. Melzer and D. Michie, editors, *Machine Intelligence 4*. Edinburgh University Press, Edinburgh, 1969.
5. Erik Sandewall and Yoav Shoham. Non-monotonic temporal reasoning. In Dov M. Gabbay, C. J. Hogger, and J. A. Robinson, editors, *Handbook of Logic in Artificial Intelligence and Logic Programming*, volume 4, pages 439–498. Oxford University Press, 1995.
6. Murray P. Shanahan. The event calculus explained. In M.J.Wooldridge and M.Veloso, editors, *Artificial Intelligence Today*, number 1600 in Lecture Notes in Artificial Intelligence, pages 409–430. Springer, 1999.
7. Ernest Sosa and Michael Tooley, editors. *Causation*. Oxford Readings in Philosophy. Oxford University Press, 1993.

# Plans and Planning in Smart Homes

Richard Simpson[1], Debra Schreckenghost[2], Edmund F. LoPresti[3],
and Ned Kirsch[4]

[1] University of Pittsburgh, Pittsburgh, PA 15260
ris20@pitt.edu
[2] TRACLabs, Houston, TX 77058
schreck@traclabs.com
[3] AT Sciences, Pittsburgh, PA 15213
edlopresti@at-sciences.com
[4] University of Michigan, Ann Arbor, MI 48108
nlkirsch@med.umich.edu

**Abstract.** In this chapter, we review the use (and uses) of plans and planning in Smart Homes. Plans have several applications within Smart Homes, including: sharing task execution with the home's inhabitants, providing task guidance to inhabitants, and to identifying emergencies. These plans are not necessarily generated automatically, nor are they always represented in a human-readable form. The chapter ends with a discussion of the research issues surrounding the integration of plans and planning into Smart Homes.

## 1 Introduction

In this chapter, we discuss the use of plans and planning by smart homes. *Plans* are a series of *steps* or *actions* by which an *activity* or *task* (e.g., bake cookies, do the laundry) is completed or a *goal* (e.g., remain hydrated throughout the day) is achieved. *Planning* refers to the act of creating a plan. While all of the systems described in this chapter *make use of* plans, not all of these systems can *generate plans* on their own.

### 1.1 Planning

Planning software solves the problem of how to achieve desired goal states given an initial state of the world. The classical approach to planning is to model states in the world with deterministic actions that define transitions between states. Plans are built by searching the space of state sequences derived from this model to find a sequence that starts at the initial state(s) and ends with the desired goal state(s). Scheduling addresses a different problem than planning. Given a set of tasks with resource and temporal ordering constraints, scheduling determines when to perform these tasks. It applies optimization criteria to determine which of these tasks to schedule first and constraint satisfaction techniques to place tasks on a timeline.

Deliberative techniques for solving the planning problem can be partitioned into three areas [1]. Classical planning encompasses a variety of techniques, including

J.C. Augusto and C.D. Nugent (Eds.): Designing Smart Homes, LNAI 4008, pp. 71–84, 2006.
© Springer-Verlag Berlin Heidelberg 2006

forward and backward search and graph-based analysis like Graphplan [2]. Decision theoretic techniques like Markov Decision Processes [3] define functions for identifying actions from states. Hierarchical planning techniques (e.g., SIPE-2, [4]; O-Plan, [5]) pre-define hierarchical groupings of goals and associate them with constraints that are matched during search (i.e., goal decomposition).

The challenges of planning for complex, real-world domains, like human activity planning, have been addressed by developing a variety of specialized techniques [6]. *Planning with uncertainty* is addressed by modeling beliefs with non-deterministic or probabilistic actions that define the belief transitions. *Anytime planning* provides algorithms that don't have to complete to determine a useful partial plan. *Temporal planning* models actions that include duration and temporal constraints, which permits solving problems with concurrent and covering goals. *Knowledge-based planning* models domain specific information to speed up search (e.g., action models with domain-specific constraints such as action performer or *agent*). Problem-based heuristics can be used to improve search. Examples of *heuristic planning* include progressive planning (using forward search) and regressive planning (using backward search).

*Reactive planning* (e.g., RAPS, [7]; PRS, [8]) handles uncertainty by sensing states in the environment and using them to adjust the plan during execution. Reactive planning uses such sensed information to guide goal decomposition during execution and to determine if the execution of a task has the intended effect on the environment. Reactive plans can be adjusted during execution in response to changing conditions in the environment or failure to achieve desired states.

*Mixed initiative planning* [9] supports either humans or the planner in taking the initiative to guide the planning process. It provides a means for incorporating human knowledge during plan building to revise goals and guide search, and during plan execution to indicate the success of activities in achieving their goals. Mixed initiative planning is particularly useful when automatically building plans that humans must understand or follow. Because humans participate in building the plan, human satisfaction with the plan can be improved significantly.

## 1.2  Planning and Scheduling in Smart Homes

There are three ways in which smart homes use plans:

1. Provide guidance or reminders to a resident during a task;
2. Perform actions to help the resident complete a task;
3. Identify emergencies, because the resident isn't doing what they're supposed to be doing, or is doing something the wrong way.

Systems that provide guidance need an explicit representation of the steps within each task, but this representation may be generated by a person rather than planning software. For example, the COACH [10-12] has an internal representation of the steps involved in washing one's hands, but this information was provided by the system developers rather than derived by COACH. The advantage of this approach is that COACH has a much more detailed and complete representation of hand washing than could be generated by planning software. However, the trade-off is that COACH has limited ability to re-plan in response to unforeseen events.

Systems that perform actions instead of the resident or monitor the resident's actions to identify emergencies, on the other hand, may operate from a "plan" that was learned through observation of previous events rather than forward-looking reasoning. For example, The Adaptive Control of Home Environments (ACHE) project at the University of Colorado [13, 14] uses neural networks to monitor the relationship between the date, the time of day, and operation of light switches and temperature controls. In this case there is no step-by-step representation of a plan that would be recognizable to a person, but a sequence of actions is nonetheless encoded within the neural network.

Similarly, systems that focus on identifying emergencies don't need an explicit representation of plans or schedules. In fact, these systems don't even need to know when tasks have begun or ended. Instead, these systems often use machine learning techniques to identify expected patterns of sensor readings, which are then compared against subsequent readings for deviation. For example, the MavHome [15] uses Hidden Markov Models (HMMs) to cluster sequences of sensor readings to allow the system to predict the next action based on observations of a series of previous actions.

Smart homes are an attractive environment for planning research because they offer significant advantages over assistive agents that are "embodied" in devices like hand-held computers [16] or mobile robots [17]. Not even a sophisticated mobile robot platform like the Nursebot [17] can support the number and variety of sensors that can be integrated within an entire home, and a smart home can use multiple modalities, devices and interfaces to exchange information with the user. On a more practical level, a smart home can extend through all rooms of the house, including places a mobile robot cannot reach or fit into, and a smart home has access to much greater power and bandwidth.

## 2  Providing Task Guidance

There is a long history of research [18] in using technology to compensate for impairments in *executive reasoning tasks*. Executive reasoning refers to cognitive activities related to planning, initiating and carrying out activities, interleaving the execution of multiple tasks, re-planning the steps of a task, or rescheduling tasks in response to external events. These skills can be compromised by a variety of disabilities, and even people without such disabilities may desire assistance with such planning tasks. Early technological interventions consisted of alarm clocks, paper "day planners" and picture books, while more recent systems (e.g., Neuropage [19]) have made use of pagers, cell phones and personal digital assistants (PDAs).

A pioneering use of planning technology for cognitive assistance is the Plan Execution Assistant and Trainer (PEAT) [16]. PEAT uses planning software to present step-by-step guidance to the user, and is capable of re-scheduling activities in response to unanticipated events. PEAT is, however, entirely "disembodied" and receives no information from the outside world other than what is provided by the user. This significantly limits the amount of information at PEAT's disposal for making planning and scheduling decisions and makes it impossible for PEAT to perform actions on the user's behalf.

While PEAT functions quite well without sensor input, there are clear benefits to integrating sensors into a cognitive assistant. First, knowledge of context can allow a device to be more specific and relevant in its prompts and cues. If the device was aware of the user's location, for example, it could give reminders relevant to that location. Information about the user's environment might also provide cues to the device on what reminders might be important (e.g., hand washing if the person is in the washroom) or unnecessary (a reminder to go to the cafeteria if the person is already there). Social cues might allow the device to know when a reminder would be inappropriate; such as when the user is talking with another person and might not want to be interrupted.

Secondly, traditional memory aides are limited to reminding the user about items on their daily schedule. However, users might wish to initiate tasks on their own, and still receive assistance to complete those tasks. A context-sensitive reminding system could potentially infer a person's desired task based on observed activities, and be prepared to provide appropriate reminders for the user-selected task [20, 21]. This would help satisfy the desire expressed by some users for a memory aid "being responsive to you but not controlling you [22]."

Third, a context-sensitive reminder could support the method of vanishing cues. This training technique provides as much cue information as patients need to make a correct response and then gradually withdraws it across learning trials [23]. A context-sensitive memory aid could apply this technique automatically, only providing those cues which are truly needed and otherwise allowing the user to independently perform their daily tasks. A therapist could monitor the user's progress and adjust the maximum or minimum support provided by the device, or the speed of response of the device, in order to promote greater independence on the part of the

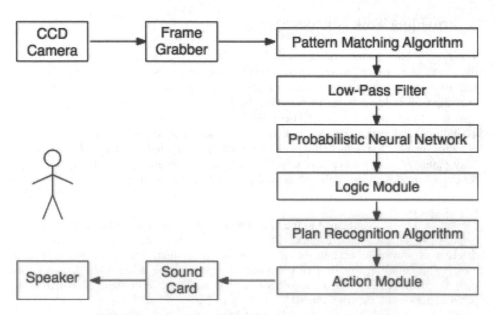

**Fig. 1.** Overview of the COACH System (adapted from [12])

user. Unfortunately, a person's abilities may decrease instead of increase. In this instance as well, a context-sensitive system can detect difficulties a person is having and adapt as the user's abilities change over time.

The Cognitive Orthosis for Assisting aCtivities at Home (COACH) is an example of a system that uses input from sensors to provide activity guidance, in this case for washing one's hands [10-12]. As shown in Fig. 1, a video camera is used to locate the user's hands, which serve as input to the COACH agent software. The agent software identifies which step within the activity corresponds to the input, and then determines which plan from a pre-existing plan library matches the observed steps. If the user makes a mistake (e.g., skipping a step or performing a step out of sequence), a prerecorded verbal cue is provided to the user. If the user continues to ignore the cues, a caregiver can be notified.

COACH uses of a probabilistic neural network (PNN) to determine which step corresponds with the observed hand location. The PNN comprises an input level, a pattern level, a summation level and an output level. PNNs use the Bayes optimal decision rule to categorize an input pattern $(X)$ as belonging to the population $(i)$ which maximizes the value of:

$$h_i c_i f_i(X),$$

where $h_i$ is the prior probability of an unknown sample being drawn from population $l$, $c_i$ is the cost of misclassifying an input pattern as belonging to population $i$, and $f_i(X)$ is the probability density function (PDF) for population $i$. PNNs require less training time than other types of neural networks, but the training data must be highly representative of the actual task data.

COACH uses a simple plan recognition algorithm. The sequence of steps is first compared to a library of plans, to see if the observed actions match an existing plan. If an exact match cannot be found, the agent finds the "closest" plan by eliminating observed steps (beginning with the most recent) until a match is identified. A situated planning agent is then used to guide the user through the remaining steps of the plan.

## 3   Perform Actions for the Resident

Instead of providing guidance, some systems take over parts or all of an activity for the user. There are a number of reasons why this automation may be desirable. First, automation can relieve the resident of tasks that are repetitive, highly predictable or require little judgment (e.g., dimming lights or changing thermostat settings at specific times). Second, automation can assume responsibility for tasks that would be too difficult for a resident to complete because of cognitive impairments that limit task performance accuracy or safety (e.g., turn off the stove if it has been left on too long). A system that is capable of both providing task guidance and performing independent actions might lend itself to shared performance of tasks. At the appropriate time, or when it senses that the user might wish to perform a task, the system can begin preparing for the task (e.g. turn on lights in the kitchen, preheat the oven) while also guiding the user through his or her part of the task (e.g. taking vegetables out of the refrigerator, stirring a pot). Third, automated systems can be used to create task-specific user interfaces that combine multiple actions into a single command [24].

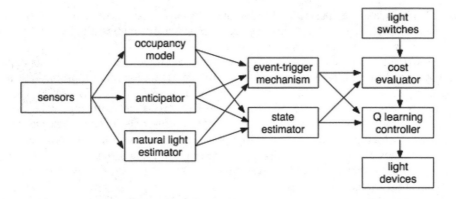

**Fig. 2.** Overview of the ACHE System (adapted from [13])

The Adaptive Control of Home Environments (ACHE) project at the University of Colorado [13, 14] controls the lighting within the house by using an optimal control framework to balance inhabitants' comfort with energy conservation. A *discomfort cost* is calculated based on the inhabitants' actions to manually adjust the lights, and an *energy cost* is calculated based on total energy consumption. The *expected average cost* at time $t_0$, $J(t_0)$, is then:

$$J(t_0) = E\left[\lim_{K \to \infty} \frac{1}{K} \sum_{t=t_0+1}^{t_0+K} d(x_t) + e(u_t)\right]d$$

where $d(x_t)$ is the discomfort cost for environmental state $x$ at time $t$, and $e(u_t)$ is the energy cost of control decision $u$ at time $t$. ACHE's goal is to find a mapping from environmental states to decisions that minimizes the expected average cost.

The architecture for ACHE is shown in Fig. 2. The *Q learning controller* uses reinforcement learning to identify the mapping between the current state and desired lighting level. The *event-trigger mechanism* identifies when events have occurred that require a response from ACHE. The *state estimator* uses the activities of inhabitants and the current level of natural light to categorize the state of the environment.

## 4  Monitoring Behavior and Identifying Emergencies

A dilemma faced by clinicians is reconciling the fact that observations of patients only occur during (infrequent) face-to-face meetings in a clinic or laboratory, while what is really needed are assessments that reflect the patient's capabilities in the real world, where distractions are present and dual-task performance is often required. As such, there is a need for ecologically valid tests, that can provide information about a patient's ability to function in a real-life environment [25]. Sensors integrated into the patient's environment as part of a smart home can allow medical staff to obtain a much clearer view of the patient's condition than is available from short periods of monitoring in the hospital or doctor's office [26].

"Pervasive healthcare technology" offers the potential for continuous measurement, processing and communication of physiological and physical parameters from patients to service providers, family and other support people [27-31]. The appropriate design and integration of different kinds of sensors, as well as the appropriate medical algorithms to process the data could offer new possibilities for preventing health risks [27, 29, 32], managing chronic diseases [27, 29, 30, 33-37], and providing support to elderly and disabled persons living independently [27, 30, 32, 36, 38, 39].

Continuous monitoring may allow smart homes to identify changes in health status more quickly [40] by detecting symptomatic performance failures or deteriorating behavioral patterns. This is particularly important because these patterns often occur only under specific conditions that are not easily replicated in the clinic (e.g., exiting and returning to the kitchen too many times, in confusion, when preparing a meal, because of an idiosyncratic configuration of items in the refrigerator; failing to take medications correctly, but only when the television is on or the telephone rings). These types of subtle failures may be noted most during the early stages of a disease process, or actually remain undetected because the resident is still able to recover from (or mask) the failure. In these situations, family members or other observers must typically serve as informants.

Continuous monitoring may also allow smart homes to document spontaneous compensatory strategies. This is particularly important for individuals who are able to function effectively in the home because it is familiar (e.g., avoiding falls as long as the furniture is never moved), but who may experience difficulty during clinical evaluation. In such cases, information about the conditions under which an individual avoids error, may allow caregivers and clinicians to postpone more disruptive interventions, such as placement in a supervised setting or increasing attendant care. Continuous monitoring may also provide information to caregivers about changes that can be made in the home to promote increased use of compensatory strategies that might not have otherwise been considered (e.g., improving accurate medication compliance by disabling the television until a certain time, or changing the furniture pattern in a room where repeated performance errors are noted, to the pattern in a room where such errors never occur).

The Independent LifeStyle Assistant (I.L.S.A.) [41, 42] passively monitors the behavior of inhabitants and can alert caregivers in the event of an emergency (e.g., a fall). I.L.S.A. is an agent-based system, with separate agents for monitoring medication use, monitoring mobility, providing scheduled reminders, and learning patterns of behavior. Each agent relies on sensors and actuators, which may be shared with other agents, and is responsible for situation assessment within its domain area. Each agent also maintains a library of domain-specific plans for (1) recognizing user intent and (2) choosing system responses.

## 5  Example Scenario of Using Planning Within a Smart Home

Consider the following scenario which contains elements of all three applications of planning within smart homes: task guidance, performing actions and monitoring behavior:

*Irene is a 73 year-old women with mobility and memory impairments who wants to continue living in her community rather than a nursing home. At noon on a given day, the system reminds her that it is time for lunch and, detecting that Irene is in the bedroom, guides her to the kitchen and turns on the lights. Once Irene is in the kitchen, the system asks whether she would like a sandwich or soup. Irene chooses soup, and the system guides her through the process of finding the soup can and pot and warming up the soup. When the soup is ready, the system detects that Irene has left the stove on, and reminds her to turn it off. After eating, Irene puts the dirty dishes in the dishwasher. The system senses this and, knowing that Irene needs to take medication after lunch, directs her to her medication dispenser and instructs her on the appropriate pills to take. When Irene fails to take her medicine, the system notifies Irene's daughter, who lives nearby.*

Leading Irene through the steps involved in making soup, and instructing Irene to take her medication after lunch, are examples of task guidance. To effectively lead Irene through each task, and present the proper information at the proper time, the system must have an explicit representation of each task, along with an appropriate means to convey instructions to Irene. Turning on lights in the kitchen is an example of performing actions Irene would otherwise have to do herself. A smart home could activate lights based on detection of motion, without regard to any plan. However, a smart home that does reason about the user's plans and goals can turn on the light *in anticipation* of the resident's needs, or even use the action of turning on a light as a cue to the resident regarding where they should be. Detecting when Irene has failed to take her medication is an example of monitoring behavior.

Another challenge to successfully integrating planning into a smart home is distinguishing between events that must happen at specific times (e.g., lunch happens at noon) and events that must happen *relative to* other events (e.g., medication is taken half an hour after eating). COACH represents plans as simple sequences of actions. For example, the task of making soup would be represented as:

- *find the soup can;*
- *find the pot;*
- *open the soup can;*
- *pour the soup can into the pot;*
- *place the pot on the stove;*
- *turn on the burner.*

Hence, COACH is well-suited for reasoning about relative events but is poorly-suited for initiating actions at specific times. ACHE, on the other hand, explicitly incorporates time into its reasoning. However, because ACHE's representation of plans is diffused throughout a neural network rather than explicitly represented, actions carried out at an unusual time may not be correctly recognized. Of the three systems examined in this chapter, only I.L.S.A. has sufficient representational flexibility to accommodate both absolute and relative timing of events. The trade-off, however, is the need to develop separate agents for each task.

## 6  Research Issues

### 6.1  User Interface

Smart homes present several challenging interface issues:

- Who should receive information? The inhabitant of the home, family members, caregivers and medical professionals all may have an interest in some of the data collected by the sensors within a smart home.
- What information should each person receive? Data privacy and security, as well as common sense, dictate that data be distributed on a need-to-know basis, but *who* needs to know *what*?
- How should information be presented? Information to the home resident may best be presented using more familiar devices and interfaces, such as a television, radio or telephone. Caregivers may prefer a computer-based interface, but different caregivers may prefer more or less detail.

The goal of the smart home will have a significant influence on the nature of the interface. Systems that provide task guidance have the most difficult user interface issues, since they interact most frequently with the inhabitant across multiple locations and different input and output modalities may be appropriate for specific tasks and locations. For example, an interface that accepts voice commands and provides picture and video output might be most appropriate for guidance in the kitchen, but a purely auditory interface might be more appropriate in the bathroom.

Systems that perform actions for the resident may have no interface at all, or may be designed to provide a single, simplified, task-based interface (rather than multiple device-based interfaces). For systems that focus on monitoring behavior and identifying emergencies, the primary user interface may not be intended for the resident of the home, but rather for a medical professional, family member, or other caregiver. Systems that monitor for instantaneous emergency situations (e.g. a fall or a heart attack) may alert the appropriate emergency personnel, as well as a designated family member (or may try multiple family members until one responds). Other systems could monitor more subtle trends in health status or activity level. A user interface will be needed to report these trends to the appropriate person(s), potentially including the resident and one or more caregivers. Depending on the particular application and the individual situation, the visualization of data must balance clear presentation of the important data with respect for the user's privacy. It is also important to present the most pertinent data in the most succinct fashion; so that the underlying trends (or important outliers) can be quickly seen without having to sort through hours of sensor data.

## 6.2 Plan Recognition

Smart homes that provide task-specific assistance or monitor task-specific behaviors must, necessarily, know what task (or tasks) the resident of the home is engaged in at any given time, which implies that the system must have some way of automatically determining what the resident is doing. Recognizing what a person is doing (or failing to do) based on observations from potentially noisy sensors is called *plan recognition* [43]. Plan recognition plays a critical role in many of the systems described in this chapter.

Performing plan recognition in real world environments with imperfect sensors poses several challenges [43, 44]:

- **Knowledge Representation.** Many factors that affect behaviors (e.g., user preferences and capabilities, constraints imposed by the physical environment) can be difficult to represent within existing probabilistic frameworks.
- **Task and Behavior Overlap.** People often pursue more than one plan at the same time, or use a single action to achieve more than one goal.
- **Multi-Agent Systems.** More than one person may be involved in completing a task, so plan recognition must be performed over multiple agents.
- **Failed Actions.** People sometimes fail to achieve a goal, either because they do the wrong thing or because the right thing to do didn't work.
- **Abandoning Plans.** People sometimes give up on plans altogether, due to forgetfulness, distraction, or a higher priority interruption.
- **Hostile Agents.** Not everyone wants to have all their actions observed and will therefore try to hide some actions.

Based on the above constraints, many smart homes rely on a probabilistic approach to plan recognition, such as Bayesian networks [17] or Hidden Markov Models [43]. A probabilistic approach allows multiple potential plans to be considered simultaneously, accommodates hidden or unobserved data, execution errors and task failures.

### 6.3 Knowing When and How to Prompt the User

Assistance that is unwanted, unneeded, or delivered at an inopportune time, can be worse than no assistance at all [17, 43]. Prompts for tasks that have already been completed, or prompts that interrupt a higher-priority task, will lead to frustration and possibly rejection of the system. If frustration becomes high enough and an "off" button is not easily available, "system rejection" could involve a hammer. Worse, actions that are simply wrong (failing to prompt someone to take medication, prompting someone to take an extra dose of medication, turning off the lights while someone is in the room) could lead to injury or health emergencies. This is especially dangerous if the system works much of the time, leading to a false sense of security and reliance on the system.

An over-reliance on the system may be undesirable even if the system works well. For many users, it is desirable to provide the minimum necessary level of task guidance. This allows the user to exercise their inherent cognitive capacity, and maintain a maximum level of independence [17]. Poorly-delivered assistance can lead to reduced independence, injury, or rejection of the system.

Furthermore, even if assistance is correctly timed, it must be delivered in a way that enhances, rather than interferes with, task performance. This includes such considerations as the frequency of prompts, the modality (e.g. text, pictures, speech, non-speech audio cues), and managing interruptions. Management of interruptions includes controlling how the system responds to external interruptions, controlling when and how the system can interrupt other activities, and controlling when and how the system can coordinate competing internal tasks (e.g. the system is in the midst of a task when a higher priority task becomes active).

Adding to the challenge is the fact that the timing of assistance must take into account previous or future activities. For example, medication must often be timed with meals. Things that the user doesn't do can also effect the value of providing assistance. For example, reminders to drink sufficient amounts of water should become more urgent if previous prompts to drink water have been ignored.

### 6.4  Knowledge Representation

A knowledge-based system must, necessarily, have a method of representing that knowledge. In a smart home, the knowledge representation must satisfy a number of constraints [45]:

1. The representation must provide a computational surrogate for real-world entitles, such as people, sensors, projectors, lights, and appliances.
2. The representation implies a set of *ontological commitments*, which define how the smart home looks at the world. For example, is camera input interpreted as people or as blobs of color being tracked through a room?
3. The representation defines how inferences are made, and determines what kinds of inferences are possible.
4. The representation collects, organizes and links together large quantities of information.

An often-overlooked aspect of implementing a knowledge-based system is the need to acquire the necessary knowledge. In order for a smart home to make use of plans, the smart home must either be given the plans or given the knowledge necessary to construct the plans. Given the variety of activities that occur in the home, creating a complete set of plans by hand can be a daunting task. However, providing the system with enough information to generate its own plans can be even more difficult. In cases where there is no explicit internal representation of plans (e.g., when neural networks are used) then the system must be trained, which can take significant effort.

## 7  Conclusion

Plans and planning have been incorporated into smart homes in a variety of ways to support a range of behaviors. Plans may not be human-readable, or even explicit, and may be hand-generated, machine-generated or learned over time. A knowledge of what a home's inhabitant is supposed to do, and how he or she is supposed to do it, is critical for sharing, guiding or monitoring task execution.    Plans also serve as templates for plan recognition algorithms.  Finally, only smart homes with the ability to plan will be able to respond to unanticipated events.

# References

[1]  D. Smith, J. Frank, and A. Jonsson, "Bridging the gap between planning and scheduling," *Knowledge Engineering Review*, vol. 15, 2000.
[2]  A. Blum and M. Furst, "Fast planning through graph analysis," in *International Joint Conference on Artificial Intelligence (IJCAI)*, 1995.
[3]  S. Russel and P. Norvig, *Artificial Intelligence: A Modern Approach*: Prentice Hall, 1994.
[4]  D. Wilkins and K. Myers, "A multiagent planning Architecture," in *Proceedings of the AIPS*, 1998.
[5]  A. Tate, J. Dalton, and J. Levine, "O-Plan: A web-based AI planning agent," in *National Conference on Artificial Intelligence (AAAI)*. Austin, TX: AAAI Press, 2000.
[6]  H. Geffner, "Perspectives on artificial intelligence planning," in *National Conference on Artificial Intelligence (AAAI)*. Edmonton, CA: AAAI Press, 2002.
[7]  R. J. Firby, *The RAPS Language Manual*. Chicago, IL: Neodesic, Inc., 1999.
[8]  M. Georgeff, A. Lansky, and P. Bessier, "A procedural logic," in *International Joint Conference on Artificial Intelligence (IJCAI)*, 1985.
[9]  M. Burstein and D. McDermott, "Issues in the development of human-computer mixed-initiative planning systems," in *Cognitive Technology: In Search of a Human Interface*, B. Gorayska and J. L. Mey, Eds.: Elsevier Science, 1996.
[10] A. Mihailidis, B. Carmichael, and J. Boger, "The use of computer vision in an intelligent environment to support aging-in-place, safety, and independence in the home," *IEEE Transactions on Information Technology in Biomedicine*, vol. 8, pp. 238-247, 2004.
[11] A. Mihailidis, B. Carmichael, J. Boger, and G. Fernie, "An intelligent environment to support aging-in-place, safety, and independence of older adults with dementia," presented at UbiHealth 2003: The 2nd International Workshop on Ubiquitous Computing for Pervasive Healthcare Applications, Seattle, Washington, 2003.
[12] A. Mihailidis, G. Fernie, and J. C. Barbenel, "The use of artificial intelligence in the design of an intelligent cognitive orthotic for people with dementia," *Assistive Technology*, vol. 13, pp. 23-39, 2001.
[13] M. C. Mozer, "Lessons from an adaptive house," in *Smart environments: Technologies, protocols, and applications*, D. Cook and R. Das, Eds. Hoboken, NJ: Wiley & Sons, 2005, pp. 273-294.
[14] M. C. Mozer, "An intelligent environment must be adaptive," *IEEE Intelligent Systems and Their Applications*, vol. 14, pp. 11-13, 1999.
[15] S. K. Das, D. J. Cook, A. Battacharya, E. O. Heierman, and L. Tze-Yun, "The role of prediction algorithms in the MavHome smart home architecture," *IEEE Wireless Communications*, vol. 9, pp. 77-84, 2002.
[16] R. Levinson, "The planning and execution assistant and trainer (PEAT)," *Journal of Head Trauma Rehabilitation*, vol. 12, pp. 85-91, 1997.
[17] M. E. Pollack, "Intelligent technology for an aging population," *AI Magazine*, vol. 26, pp. 9-24, 2005.

[18] E. F. LoPresti, A. Mihailidis, and N. Kirsch, "Assistive technology for cognitive rehabilitation and compensation: State of the art," *Neuropsychological Rehabilitation*, vol. 14, pp. 5-39, 2004.

[19] J. J. Evans, H. Emslie, and B. A. Wilson, "External cueing systems in the rehabiliation of executive impairments of action," *Journal of the International Neuropsychological Society*, vol. 4, pp. 399-408, 1998.

[20] M. Philipose, K. P. Fishkin, M. Perkowitz, D. J. Patterson, D. Fox, H. Kautz, and D. Hahnel, "Inferring activities from interactions with objects," *Pervasive Computing*, vol. 3, pp. 50-57, 2004.

[21] M. E. Pollack, L. Brown, D. Colbry, C. E. McCarthy, C. Orosz, B. Peintner, S. Ramakrishnan, and I. Tsamardinos, "Autominder: An intelligent cognitive orthotic system for people with memory impairment," *Robotics and Autonomous Systems*, vol. 44, pp. 273-282, 2003.

[22] E. A. Inglis, A. Symkowiak, P. Gregor, A. F. Newell, B. A. Wilson, J. J. Evans, and P. Shah, "Usable technology? Challenges in designing a memory aid with current electronic devices," *Neuropsychological Rehabilitation*, vol. 14, pp. 77-88, 2004.

[23] E. L. Glisky, D. L. Schacter, and E. Tulving, "Learning and retention of computer-related vocabulary in amnesic patients: Method of vanishing cues," *Journal of Clinical and Experimental Neuropsychology*, vol. 8, pp. 292-312, 1986.

[24] C. L. Isbell, O. Omojokun, and J. S. Pierce, "From devices to tasks: Automatic task prediction for personalized appliance control," *Personal and Ubiquitous Computing*, vol. 8, pp. 146-153, 2004.

[25] A. M. Moseley, S. Lanzarone, J. M. Bosman, M. A. van Loo, R. A. de Bie, and L. Hassett, "Ecological validity of walking speed assessment after traumatic brain injury: A pilot study," *Journal of Head Trauma Rehabilitation*, vol. 19, pp. 341-348, 2004.

[26] D. Raskovic, T. Martin, and E. Jovanov, "Medical monitoring applications for wearable computing," *The Computer Journal*, vol. 47, pp. 495-504, 2004.

[27] I. Korhonen and J. E. Bardram, "Guest editorial: Introduction to the special section on pervasive healthcare," *IEEE Transactions on Information Technology in Biomedicine*, vol. 8, pp. 229-234, 2004.

[28] E. Dishman, "Inventing wellness systems for aging in place," *IEEE Computer Magazine*, pp. 34-41, 2004.

[29] A. Lymberis and S. Olsson, "Intelligent biomedical clothing for personal health and disease management: State of the art and future vision," *Telemedicine Journal and e-Health*, vol. 9, pp. 379-386, 2003.

[30] V. Rialle, F. Duchene, N. Noury, L. Bajolle, and J. Demongeot, "Health "smart" home: Information technology for patients at home," *Telemedicine Journal and e-Health*, vol. 8, pp. 395-409, 2002.

[31] P. Cuddihy, "Home assurance system," in *Pervasive Computing*, 2004, pp. 48.

[32] R. Suzuki, M. Ogawa, S. Otake, T. Izutsu, Y. Tobimatsu, S.-I. Izumi, and T. Iwaya, "Analysis of activities of daily living in elderly people living alone: Single-subject feasibility study," *Telemedicine Journal and e-Health*, vol. 10, pp. 260-276, 2004.

[33] J. Woolliscroft and T. M. Koelling, "Guest editorial: Redesigning the management of chronic illness," *Telemedicine Journal and e-Health*, vol. 10, pp. 118-121, 2004.

[34] S. M. Finkelstein, S. M. Speedie, G. Demiris, M. Veen, J. M. Lundgren, and S. Potthoff, "Telehomecare: Quality, perception, satisfaction," *Telemedicine Journal and e-Health*, vol. 10, pp. 122-128, 2004.

[35] D. A. Lankford, "Wireless CPAP patient monitoring: Accuracy study," *Telemedicine Journal and e-Health*, vol. 10, pp. 2004, 2004.

[36] R. Kobb, N. Hoffman, R. Lodge, and S. Kline, "Enhancing elder chronic care through technology and care coordination: Report from a pilot," *Telemedicine Journal and e-Health*, vol. 9, pp. 189-195, 2003.

[37] R. Suzuki, M. Ogawa, Y. Tobimatsu, and T. Iwaya, "Time-course action analysis of daily life investigations in the welfare techno house in Mizusawa," *Telemedicine Journal and e-Health*, vol. 7, pp. 249-259, 2001.

[38] N. R. Chumbler, W. C. Mann, S. Wu, A. Schmid, and R. Kobb, "The association of home-telehealth use and care coordination with improvement of functional and cognitive functioning in frail elderly men," *Telemedicine Journal and e-Health*, vol. 10, pp. 129-137, 2004.

[39] T. Sato, T. Harada, and T. Mori, "Environment-type robot system "Robotic Room" featured by behavior media, behavior contents, and behavior adaptation," *IEEE/ASME Transactions on Mechatronics*, vol. 9, pp. 529-534, 2004.

[40] T. L. Hayes, M. Pavel, P. K. Schallau, and A. M. Adami, "Unobtrusive monitoring of health status in an aging population," presented at UbiHealth 2003: The 2nd International Workshop on Ubiquitous Computing for Pervasive Healthcare Applications, Seattle, Washington, 2003.

[41] L. M. Kiff, K. Z. Haigh, and X. Sun, "Mobility monitoring with the Independent LifeStyle Assistant (I.L.S.A.)," in *International Conference on Aging, Disability and Independence (ICADI)*, 2003.

[42] V. Guralnik and K. Z. Haigh, "Learning models of human behavior with sequential patterns," in *AAAI Workshop on Automation as Caregiver*: AAAI Press, 2002.

[43] L. Liao, D. J. Patterson, D. Fox, and H. Kautz, "Behavior recognition in assisted cognition," in *AAAI Workshop on Supervisory Control of Learning and Adaptive Systems*. San Jose: AAAI Press, 2004.

[44] C. W. Geib, "Problems with intent recognition for elder care," presented at AAAI Workshop on Automation as Caregiver, 2002.

[45] S. Peters and H. E. Shrobe, "Using semantic networks for knowledge representation in an intelligent environment," presented at IEEE International Conference on Pervasive Computing and Communications, Ft. Worth, TX, 2003.

# Temporal Data Mining for Smart Homes

Mykola Galushka, Dave Patterson, and Niall Rooney

Northern Ireland Knowledge Engineering Laboratory (NIKEL)
Shore Road, Newtownabbey,
Co. Antrim, BT37 0QB, Northern Ireland
{mg.galushka, wd.patterson, nf.rooney}@ulster.ac.uk

**Abstract.** Temporal data mining is a relatively new area of research in computer science. It can provide a large variety of different methods and techniques for handling and analyzing temporal data generated by smart-home environments. Temporal data mining in general fits into a two level architecture, where initially a transformation technique reduces data dimensionality in the first level and indexing techniques provide efficient access to the data in the second level. This infrastructure of temporal data mining provides the basis for high-level data mining operations such as clustering, classification, rule discovery and prediction. These operations can form the basis for developing different smart-home applications, capable of addressing a number of situations occurring within this environment. This paper outlines the main temporal data mining techniques available and provides examples of where they can be applied within a smart home environment.

## 1 Introduction

Temporal data mining is a reasonably new area of research in computer science. It has become more popular in the last decade due to the increased ability of modern computerised systems to store and process large quantities of complex data. It is not unusual for modern equipment within a real-time environment to generate megabytes of temporal data, through the constant monitoring of different parameters. Even a simple smart-home sensor can produce an enormous amount of temporal information, which is difficult to analyse without specifically developed temporal data mining techniques.

Researchers have different views on how to structure temporal data types and how to go about temporal data mining tasks. Each individual strategy reflects an individual perspective on this problem. This review presents a summary of various temporal data mining algorithms that have been used in the past or could be applied to the smart home environment.

The rest of this chapter is structured as follows. First, we describe the various temporal data types which can be generated by smart home equipment. Then we discuss the generic concept of a temporal data mining framework, which consists of three main components: a transformation, a similarity metric and a mining operation. A review of a relatively new direction, temporal cased-based reasoning, is also provided and its applicability to smart homes outlined. In the final section a summary is provided along with guidance as to which techniques would be best applied to the smart-home scenario.

J.C. Augusto and C.D. Nugent (Eds.): Designing Smart Homes, LNAI 4008, pp. 85–108, 2006.
© Springer-Verlag Berlin Heidelberg 2006

## 2  Data Types

Conceptually, temporal data types can be considered as belonging to one of two types: sequences or time series.

### 2.1  Sequence

A *sequence is an ordered set of events, frequently represented by a series of nominal symbols* [1]. The simple example in figure 1 explains how real world events can be represented by a sequence data type. Suppose a piece of equipment is monitoring the behaviour of a person in a smart-home environment. A short episode of typical actions on a work day morning may consist of the following: "get up", "take a shower", "drink coffee", "get dressed" and "go to work" (refer to figure 1).

Sequence:

| to get up | to take "a shower" | to drink "coffee" | to dress up | to go "to work" |
|-----------|--------------------|-------------------|-------------|-----------------|
| Event 1   | Event 2            | Event 3           | Event 4     | Event 5         |

time →

**Fig. 1.** Sequence Data Type (Ordered Sequence)

All these events are ordered on a time scale and occur sequentially one after another. However, for some applications it is not only important to have a sequence of these events, but also a time when these events occur. To justify the importance of the time factor, consider another simple situation, which might occur in the smart-home environment. Suppose an elderly person switches on a cooker and then goes to the living room and watches TV. By itself the information contained in this sequence of events, does not raise concern. However with the addition of timestamp details, it can be inferred that a person has not returned to the kitchen within ten minutes of the first event, it potentially can mean that this person has simply forgotten the previous event, which should immediately trigger an alarm. It is obvious that detecting such situations is impossible by using a simple sequence of events. So, a solution is to build in time stamps in the sequence when each new event occurs. An example of a sequence with time-stamps is shown in figure 2.

Sequence:

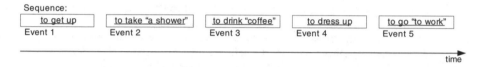

| to get up | to take "a shower" | to drink "coffee" | to dress up | to go "to work" |
|-----------|--------------------|-------------------|-------------|-----------------|
| Event 1   | Event 2            | Event 3           | Event 4     | Event 5         |
| 7:00 am   | 7:10 am            | 7:30 am           | 7:50 am     | 8:15 am    time |

**Fig. 2.** Sequence Data Type (Time-stamped Sequence)

Some researchers tend to define a time stamped sequence as an independent temporal data type [2], but we regard it as just an extension of the basic sequence data type. To avoid any confusion in terminology between these two sequence variations within this chapter, we specifically refer to either *ordered sequence* or *time stamped sequence* to prevent any ambiguity in meaning.

## 2.2 Time-Series

*Time-series is a sequence of continuous real-value elements* [1]. This type of temporal data is usually produced by equipment which constantly monitors certain parameters such as temperature, brightness, vibration, pressure and so on. Each time-series is characterized by a set of specific properties such as its range of potential deviation and its sample rate. Typical time-series data is shown in figure 3.

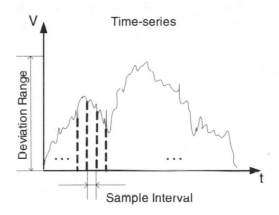

**Fig. 3.** Time-series Data Type

The important characteristic of time-series is the large number of samples (real-value elements are taken periodically through the fix time interval) which have to be stored. Even a simple sensor monitoring a basic parameter such as temperature in a smart-home environment can easily generate megabytes of source data (for example data collected from the temperature sensor during 1 year with the sample rate 1 minute can exceed size equal to 0.5 megabyte). Practically all time series data require preliminary transformation before any actual data mining analysis can take place. Different types of transformations are discussed in section 3.1.

## 3 Temporal Data Mining

The majority of temporal data mining techniques can be described by a two stage workflow as represented in figure 4, where a transformation is applied to the original temporal data in the first stage and a mining operation in the second.

The main goal of the transformation stage is to reduce the complexity (dimensionality) of the original data and represent it in a format suitable for mining operations. The mining operation performs an analysis on the transformed data to discover useful knowledge from it. Since the majority of temporal data mining techniques require a similarity determination between items (for example k-NN, k-means), an important

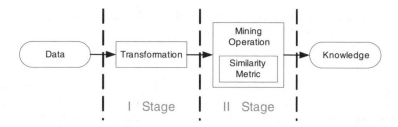

**Fig. 4.** The two stages workflow for temporal data mining

component of this sage is choosing a suitable metric. The optimal choice of transformation, similarity metric and mining operation is determined by the temporal data type and the requirements of the end system.

## 3.1 Transformation

Since temporal data can be characterised as one of two main types: time-series or sequences, it is possible to identify transformation techniques which work equally well for both groups or relevant to one specifically. Six categories (*"No Transformation"*, *"Jagged Time-series"*, *"Point in N-dimensional space"*, *"Language"*, *"Sequence"* and *"Model"*) of the most common transformation techniques are presented in figure 5, where four (*"No Transformation"*, *"Jagged Time-series"*, *"Point in N-dimensional space"* and *"Language"*) are relevant to time-series and the other two (*"Sequence"* and *"Model"*) to both.

Let's look first at the categories of transformation techniques for time series data. The first category *No Transformation* simply represents situations, where no specific transformation is applied to the original time-series data. This is relatively unusual, however for some applications it might be the best choice to perform analysis in the original time domain instead of carrying out preliminary transformations [3], [4], [5], [6]. *Jagged Time-series* transformation combines all techniques which approximate the original time-series and reduce the number of fluctuations making the signal simpler to represent. Examples of this include [7], [8], [9], [10]. *Point in N-dimensional* space transformations include techniques which transform time-series from the time domain to other domains where it can be represented by N-features [11], [12], [13], [14]. An important aspect of using this technique is its ability to significantly reduce dimensionality, where even long and complex signals can be represented as a reasonably small set of features. *Language transformations* represent all techniques, which build language-type descriptions of the original signal, where signal changes are represented as a set of words like "up", "down" and so on [15], [16], [17]. The *Sequence* category represents techniques, which transform data into a sequence of values or events [18], [19], [20]. This category also includes techniques for transforming one sequence into another, where the transformed sequence has less complexity than the original. Such transformations are required when the original sequence is very long and its direct analysis would be inefficient and highly complex. Sequence transformation techniques are quite popular in the temporal data mining community, since they provide a better understanding of the temporal nature of the

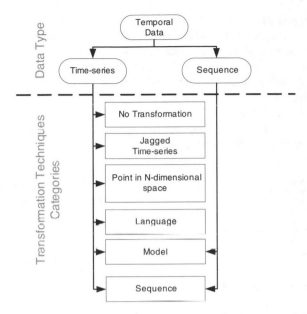

**Fig. 5.** Different type of transformation techniques for temporal data

source information and are suitable for rule discovery. The last category, *Model transformation*, integrates a set of techniques which build a model based on the original time-series or sequential data types, which then can be used for the evaluation of the newly obtained temporal data [21], [22], [23], [2 4].

### 3.1.1 The "No Transformation" Category

Applying a data mining technique to an original time-series signal (such as that generated by a temperature sensor) without any transformation is not a common practice. The primary disadvantage of using such temporal signals directly in analysis is their potential incompatibility. Signals are defined by a number of parameters such as amplitude, phase (shift), and sample rate. It is obvious, that applying a mining algorithm or simple similarity metric to two non transformed time-series signals, each with a different sampling rate for example, is unlikely to produce a reasonable result. However, some techniques were designed to deal with time-series in the original time domain. The technique developed by [3] splits a time-series signal into a number of non-overlapping segments, it then applies a scaling and offset procedure to adjust them to enable sequential comparison of corresponding segments. [4] present a lazy learning algorithm. It is based on k-nearest neighbours, where two different similarity metrics are defined. One is value-distance for calculating a distance between two time-series in the time domain and the other is shape-distance which takes into consideration shape of comparing time-series. All comparisons were performed in the original time domain. [5] introduced a dynamic programming method for spoken word recognition, which was generalised and proposed to the data mining community by Berndt [1994] as Dynamic Time Wrapping (DTW). All these techniques are unified in their ability to operate in the original time domain without any transformation. They are mentioned again in section 3, where we discuss similarity metrics.

### 3.1.2 The "Jagged Time-Series" Category

All transformation techniques, which try to find a piecewise linear function to approximate the original time-series data, fall into this category. A typical example of such techniques is shown in figure 6. As can be seen from this figure, the piecewise approximation removes high frequency fluctuations and replaces them with steady intervals of increasing or decreasing signals on linear segments. Techniques using this concept of transformation find wide recognition in the temporal data mining community. The main challenge in developing such techniques is to establish an algorithm for performing piecewise approximation.

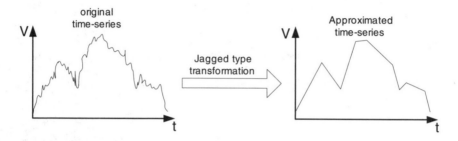

**Fig. 6.** A typical example of "Jagged time-series" transformation

A lot of temporal data mining techniques using piecewise approximation have been developed. Keogh [1997] proposed the robust segmentation technique which copes with one limitation of segmentation techniques, where the number of segments had to be specified in advance. Latter in [8] this approach was improved by introducing a weight vector, which defines the importance of each generated segment. Keogh [2000] proposed a dimensionality reduction technique called Piecewise Aggregate Approximation (PAA). It approximated time-series by splitting it into equal-sized sections and calculating the mean value for these sections. This approach was modified in later work [10], where adaptive piecewise constant approximation was proposed. Each time-series signal in it is represented as a constant number of different sized segments, approximated by the mean value. This approach combines advantages of PAA with the ability to place more segments in areas of the signal with higher activity and fewer segments in areas with lower activity.

### 3.1.3 The "Point in N-Dimensional Space" Category

All the main transformation techniques in this category transform the initial time-series data from the time domain to another domain, where it can be represented by N-features. The typical example of such a technique is shown in figure 7 and describes a transformation of time-series from the time domain to the frequency domain, where it is represented by the first three complex frequency coefficients. Taking into consideration the fact that each complex frequency coefficient consists of two parts, real and imaginary, the total number of dimensions required to store the given time-series in the frequency domain is increased to six. It would therefore be represented as a point with the following coordinates $(r_1, i_1, r_2, i_2, r_3, i_3)$, where $(r_1, i_1)$ is the first frequency coefficient $C_1$, $(r_2, i_2)$ is the second $C_2$, and $(r_3, i_3)$ the third $C_3$ respectively.

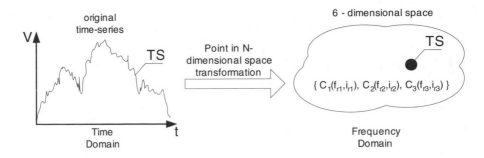

**Fig. 7.** Typical example of a "Point in N-dimensional space" transformation

Time series transformed from one domain to another becomes more manageable through a reduction in dimensionality, which provides increased possibilities to establish a meaningful similarity metric and to more effectively apply data mining operations.

The most popular techniques for transforming time-series are Discrete Fourier Transformation (DFT) [12] and Discrete Wavelet Transformation (DWT) [13]. The former approach transforms time-series data from the time domain to the frequency domain. An important observation with this technique is that for the majority of real world signals its main energy is concentrated within the first few frequencies, which makes this particularly useful for dimensionality reduction purposes. As a consequence of Parseval's theorem [12], the Euclidian distance is preserved in the frequency domain as well as in the time domain. These observations were utilised in [11], where the extracting and storing of the $k$ - first few complex frequency coefficients was proposed in conjunction with their continuous indexing in $k$-dimensional space. Using the last few Fourier coefficients in a distance computation was proposed in [12], due to an important observation, which nearly doubled the efficiency of the algorithm. This observation showed that coefficients at the end are conjugates of coefficients at the beginning, which allows their use with the same level of confidence. Mörchen [2003] proposed, instead of using the first few frequency coefficients, to choose the best coefficient from the set of time series by using Fourier or wavelet transformations. Haar wavelet decomposition was proposed for use in [14] for selecting appropriate features for the classification of time-series.

### 3.1.4  The "Language" Category
All techniques transforming time-series to a language representation format belong to this category. A typical illustration of such a process is shown in Figure 8.

This approach provides the possibility to represent the time-series by a set of definitions, which describe changes in its shape. For example if the value of the time-series constantly increases in a particular segment, the general curve behaviour can be expressed by the term "up". In the opposite scenario when the value decreases, the curve can be described by term "down" and so on. Use of language representation opens the possibility of matching the general behavior of time series without any time consuming preprocessing steps.

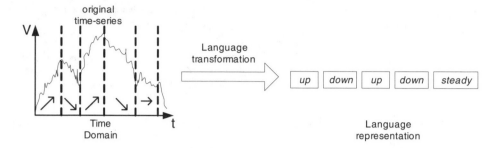

**Fig. 8.** A typical example of "Language" transformation

A number of techniques were proposed to perform language-like transformations. A Shape Definition Language was proposed in [16]. It retrieves objects based on their shapes by using a reasonably easy but quite powerful language, which allows the creation of a large variety of different queries. A significant feature of this language is the performing of a "blurry" match, which focuses on matching overall shape without taking into consideration small details. Transforming time–series into a sequence of symbols was proposed in [16]. The transformation is performed by applying sliding windows, which traverse the whole time-series and divide it into segments. Resulting segments are clustered and each cluster is specified by a letter or a combination of letters. Then the segments in the original time-series are replaced by cluster identifiers. Using this representation creates the possibility of deploying different techniques for rule discovery. Another transformation approach, IMPACT, was proposed in [17]. It transforms a time-series into a string of symbols by mapping the original signal onto a grid type structure, where a letter identifier is associated with each grid cell.

### 3.1.5  The "Sequence" Category
Techniques, which transform time-series data into a sequence format are described in this section. A typical example of such a transformation is shown in figure 9.

In most cases, the task of transforming time-series into a sequence depends on the identification of significant elements (episodes) and their representation in sequential formats: such as an ordered sequence or a timestamp sequence. A general approach

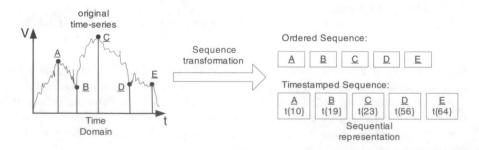

**Fig. 9.** A typical example of a "Sequence" transformation

for change-points detection, implemented in batch and incremental versions was proposed and evaluated on synthetic and real world data in [18]. Keogh et al. [19] introduced a domain independent algorithm for detecting unexpected patterns in time series databases. A new framework for anomaly detection was proposed in [20] which include a mechanism for associating a defined anomaly with a confidence value. An important advantage of episodic discovery on time-series is the significant reduction in data volume. Episodes also provide the possibility to map them on other sequences obtained from different time-series channels for discovering inter-channel relations.

### 3.1.6 The "Model" Category

Techniques belonging to this category transform a collection of original time series data into a model structure (see figure 10).

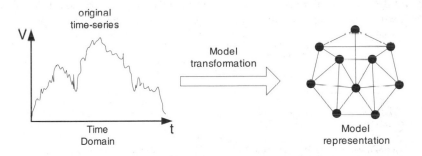

**Fig. 10.** Typical example of "Model" transformation

One advantage of a model representing time-series and sequential data types can be clearly seen during the knowledge discovery process. In general, the model structure tends to extract important elements from temporal data and establishes relations between them, which enables more complex analysis, whereby hidden relationships and interactions can be discovered. A novel approach proposed in [21] built Markov-based Models for time-series data and used a Viterbi-like algorithm [25] for the detection of time-series patterns. A Markov-based module was also proposed to be used as a similarity/distance measure for different sized time-series data in [26].

Another popular model-based approach is the use of Artificial Neural Networks (ANNs). It can be successfully applied to a broad range of different data mining tasks including those, which address temporal data. The use of ANNs was proposed in [23] for forecasting time series data. Since, the neural network does not require a lot of information about the original data, the focus was on selecting optimal parameters for the back-propagation algorithm. A single hidden layer feed-forward neural network was also proposed in [24] for modeling and forecasting using time series data.

Building complex episode models based on single or multiple entry inputs of events is another possibility for structuring temporal data. An approach for recognizing and structuring the frequent episodes in a defined collection of events occurring in specified time intervals was proposed in [27]. A method for finding particular orders for describing relationships between events belonging to a collection of sequences was proposed in [28].

Constructing an inference grammar [29], [30], [31] for temporal data is a promising approach for temporal data analysis. It provides for the possibility to construct a complex grammar model by applying discrete search algorithms to temporal data collections. However, despite increased research attention, it still remains more a theoretical than a practical approach.

## 3.2  Similarity Metrics

Measuring the similarity between two temporal sequences is an important aspect of data mining. During clustering for example some notion of distance is used to identify which cluster a particular time series or temporal sequence belongs to. In classification similarity is used for identifying the closest time-series or temporal sequence to a predefined query, in order to make a prediction. Taking into consideration the variety of temporal data representations, it is possible to identify four main similarity metrics for the following representations: time domain representation, N-point space representation, discrete space representation and model representation (see figure 11).

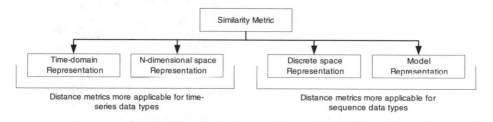

**Fig. 11.** Classification of similarity metrics

### 3.2.1  The "Time-Domain" Similarity Metrics

Measuring distance between two time-series in the time domain is not a particularly efficient and accurate way of defining similarity. This approach often has a number of significant disadvantages such as:  comparing time-series of different lengths, scale and shift incompatibility, differences in sampling rates and dimensionality problems.

However, in some situations, it is possible to apply a direct comparison in the original time domain [4]. The most simplistic measure is the *Manhattan distance* defined by (1):

$$d(\mathbf{x}, \mathbf{y}) = \sum_{i=1}^{N} |x_i - y_i|, \tag{1}$$

where $x_i$ and $y_i$ are the samples of two time-series $\mathbf{x}$ and $\mathbf{y}$ and N the number of samples.

*Euclidian distance* is another popular similarity metric, which also can be used for comparing time-series [4]. Its formal definition is specified by expression (2).

$$d(\mathbf{x}, \mathbf{y}) = \sqrt{\sum_{i=1}^{N} (x_i - y_i)^2} . \tag{2}$$

Both Manhattan and Euclidean measurements suffer from the drawbacks outlined above.

Another approach was proposed in [32]. It consists of finding a linear function, which can map one time series onto another. This approach is advantageous in that it takes into consideration outliers, different scales and sampling rates and thus addresses some of the disadvantages of the previous measures.

A probabilistic approach was proposed in [7], where the main idea was to use the prior probability distribution for transforming a prototype template into the form of a time-series based query. The global time-series shape can be reconstructed by local features, which support some degree of deformation. At the same time stretching and amplitude adjustments are applied to the global time-series.

DTW provides a very robust distance computation [33]. It constructs a distance matrix based on two evaluated time-series. Each cell of this matrix stores a distance between (two sample values for different time series) the $i$-sample value of time-series $X$ and the $j$-sample value of time-series $y$. A search algorithm is then used to identify a path in the matrix, which satisfies certain constraints. One of the disadvantages of this approach is the computational cost required for calculating distances. However, some researchers try to combat this limitation by applying jagged transformations to the original time-series, before deploying DTW calculations [9].

### 3.2.2 The "N-Dimensional Space" Similarity Metrics

Defining similarity between time-series transformed into n-dimensional space is the most exploited area of temporal data mining. This is a consequence of the fact that many techniques which have been developed for conventional (non temporal) data mining domains, can be reused. A lot of similarity metrics try to accurately calculate distance measures between two entities in a high-dimensional space [34], which makes them nearly impossible to be used for time-series data directly. However, nearly every time-series after a transformation becomes a point in n-dimensional space, whose dimensionality is significantly less in comparison to the original data. This enables the direct application of similarity metrics such as Euclidean or Manhattan in the reduced space.

Consider a simple example. After DFT transformation a time-series is trans-formed from the time-domain to the frequency domain, where it is represented by a set of complex frequency coefficients. Give an example of the original feature space size. If the number of frequency coefficients taken into consideration is 5, it is easy to see that the total space required to store this time series, is reduced to 10 (since each complex coefficient is defined by real and imaginary parts). Distance measures like Euclidian or Manhattan can then be effectively applied to this transformed space of frequency coefficients.

### 3.2.3 The "Discrete Space" Similarity Metrics

Similarity measurements with respect to discrete features has received a lot of attention over the last decade, mainly due to significant research intensification in two separate areas, namely that of bioinformatics and internet personalization. Both of these areas focus heavily on sequences of discrete elements, with the objective of defining the degree of similarity between two discrete sequences.

The concept of similarity is based on the sequence alignment concept, where alignment is the correspondence between two sequences. A correspondence is a relation, where an element of one sequence can be mapped to the element of another sequence and where an order of elements in both sequences is maintained.

An important aspect of designing or using discrete similarity measures is to identify an objective function. This provides a practical justification of the similarity. Consider the simple example of two sequences as shown in figure 12.

| Seq. 1: | A | B | B | A |
|---------|---|---|---|---|
| Seq. 2: | B | B | A | B |

| Seq. 1: | A | B | B | A | - |
|---------|---|---|---|---|---|
| Seq. 2: | - | B | B | A | A |

**Fig. 12.** Sequence similarity

Both of these sequences have an equal number of elements (*A* and *B*). If we directly compare these sequences the number of matching elements is 1. However, if we shift the elements in sequence two by 1, the number of matching elements is 3. The question therefore is, is this shift meaningful or is this operation completely inappropriate for this domain?

A *Blurry* match is used for retrieving similar sequences, which are represented by a Shape Definition Language [35]. *Blurry* matches consider sequences as similar according to their overall shape, and where small fluctuations are not considered significant. The performance of *Blurry* match was achieved due to defining a set of operations like: *nomore, noless, precisely* etc., which provide for the possibility to enrich the query language and as a consequence to facilitate an execution of a complex query.

In the IMPACTS method [17], which transforms time-series into symbol strings, similarity is identified by using a suffix tree, where each element of the target string matches against tree nodes during a downwards scanning process.

### 3.2.4 The "Model" Similarity Metrics

In general, a distance measurement for the model representation can be defined by how closely a sequence or time-series fits into the model. For graph-based and deterministic grammar models the similarity is usually characterized by a binary criterion (*yes* or *no*), where "yes" defines situations where the tested sequence or time-series matches a given model, "no" defines the opposite scenario.

For stochastic and mixture models the similarity is defined as a probabilistic measure, which shows the possibility that a sequence or time-series can be generated by a given model [28].

### 3.3 Mining Operation

Temporal data mining, like conventional data mining, encompasses many different techniques and algorithms, that focus on intelligent data analysis and knowledge discovery. From figure 13 it can be seen that these techniques can be categorized into four main groups: *classification, clustering, association* and *prediction*. We will consider each briefly in turn.

**Fig. 13.** Categories of mining operations

### 3.3.1 Classification

Classification techniques represent the most common temporal data mining operation. The main focus of classification operations is to classify an unknown instance into one of a number of fixed class values [36]. A number of different models have been developed to perform classification. Examples of these include: *Perceptrons,* developed as a simple artificial neural network model, which tried to identify a linear decision boundary surface. *Linear descriminat* models focus on searching a linear combination of parameters for the best class separation. *Tree models* provide a partitioning of the instances space to maximize a class purity in each of created branches. *Nearest neighbor* models are the most simplistic and straightforward way of classification, where the k-closest points are defined by a specified distance metric and used for assigning a class to the query. *Logistic discriminate analysis* focuses on solving primarily a binary classification problem by apply regression function, where a probability value obtains from the regression defines belonging of tested instance to the one class or another. *Naive Bayes* models focus on the class-condition distribution and use Bayes theorem for defining classification [36].

The term classification here refers to the situation where a record is assigned a class value based on a finite discrete set of values In the case where the assigned field is defined by a real value, classification is referred to as regression. There is a large overlap in the methods used for regression with those of classification. The biggest challenge in the temporal domain is to modify or develop new techniques, which are able to effectively cope with the high dimensionality of temporal instances.

As was mentioned before nearly all time-series and sequential data types require preliminary transformation. This significantly reduces their dimensionality and complexity, and as a result makes it possible to deploy classification techniques like nearest neighbours or decision trees, ID3, C4.5/C5.0 [36] from the conventional data mining background.

The following is a typical example of using a classification technique for temporal data in the smart-home context. Suppose a blood pressure sensor is attached to a patient to constantly monitor their health. All measurements are continuously transferred from the attached device to a database, which is integrated into the smart-home environment. Over a fixed period of time (time-window) measurements are evaluated, and classified into two classes: "normal state" and "alarming state". Using the DFT transformation method, described in section 3.1.3, the obtained time-series measurements contained in the observation time- window are transformed into a set of complex frequency coefficients. These coefficients can be passed into a classifier such as C5, which will make the appropriate classification.

Taking into consideration the fact that a number of different transformations and similarity metrics can be applied to the original temporal data, a large variety of different classification approaches can be synthesized. The selection of the most appropriate transformation and similarity metric is usually made by considering a combination of several factors such as the format of the input temporal data, its complexity, the number of input channels, the expected level of accuracy and efficiency and so on.

Often, even after transformation the data can still contain quite a high number of dimensions, which can prohibit the direct use of some classification techniques. In this situation, feature selection process can be applied in conjunction with transformation, to reduce the number of features further. Typical examples of such techniques are described in [37].

### 3.3.2 The "Clustering" category

Techniques which group items together, based on some form of distance measure generally belong to this category. There are 2 types of clustering – supervised and unsupervised. In supervised clustering the algorithm is given examples (training set) of the different types of classes found in the data. It then uses this information to segment the unseen data into the appropriate classes. This has drawbacks in that if the training data is poor, for example if a class was omitted from the training data, then the clustering process will be poor. In unsupervised clustering no examples are provided and the algorithm naturally discovers or learns the classes or groups based on the features of the data only. Often the only input to this type of algorithm is the number of groups to form. Both forms rely heavily on the distance metric used to segment the data. Semi-supervised clustering involves a mixture of instances with known and unknown class labels.

The result of using clustering techniques usually provides a better understanding of a dataset structure and gives useful information for further analysis. K-Means [38], CLUSTER/2 [39], COBWEB [40] are typical representatives of clustering techniques.

There are two main approaches for clustering data: partitional and hierarchical. The partitional clustering approach [36] tries to split all entities in the dataset into $K$ disjoint segments (clusters), where entities within a segment are as homogeneous as possible. The number of segments (clusters) $K$ can either be identified automatically or specified by an expert. Homogeneity of entities within a cluster is defined by a score function, which aims to minimize the distance between entities assigned to the cluster and its centroid. The centroid is the representative point of the cluster, which is usually defined as the average of all entities belonging to it. The most typical example of a partitioning clustering algorithm is $K$-means [38]. It splits the dataset into $K$ clusters using a recursive algorithm. In the first stage all entities are randomly distributed across $K$ clusters and centroids are calculated. Then each entity is re-evaluated, by calculating the distance between itself and each centroid. Finally the entity moves to the cluster whose centroid it is closest to. The whole process is repeated until no more moves are possible (equilibrium) or acceptable homogeneity is reached as defined by a score function.

The hierarchical clustering approach [36] uses a different strategy in that it forms clusters recursively based on the data. This can be either done agglomeratively or divisively. In agglomerative clustering data points that are most similar are joined into a larger cluster. These clusters are then joined together into larger clusters and so on until one large cluster remains. With divisive clustering the opposite occurs in that the data is split into clusters, each of which is themselves split into sub-clusters and so on (see figure 14). In this way all entities are gradually grouped into a hierarchical tree structure. Similar to classification techniques, it is important to identify appropriate transformation and similarity techniques, as these have a direct impact on the performance of the clustering algorithm.

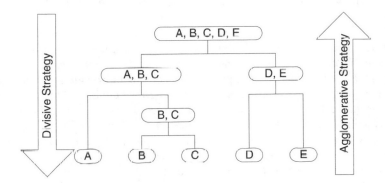

**Fig. 14.** Agglomerative and divisive clustering strategies

Clustering techniques have received some attention in smart home research. An example of using clustering was presented in [41], where a Task-based Markov Model was proposed (TMM) and integrated with k-means clustering to discover higher level activities. The clustering algorithm takes many parameters into consideration for the clustering process, such as, the number of actions involved in the individual task, the time-length of the task performance, and the number of devices used during the task. This method was used to provide a prediction of the next high–level task-type.

Another example of how clustering could be used is in the identification of the different life styles of the different inhabitants within the smart-home environment. This task is highly important since the smart-home has to adapt and react differently to the behavioral patterns of its inhabitances. A typical task in this context could be the clustering of inhabitants into different activity groups. Clustering can be done by observing motion sensor data over time. For some inhabitants the level of activity will be higher than for others and clustering could be used identify distinct groups. Then the smart-home could use the profile for each of these groups for making further decisions.

### 3.3.3 The "Pattern and Rule Discovery" Category

These techniques have been widely used in commercial environments in order to discover buyer patterns and customer behaviors in supermarkets and on-line. However, these techniques have shown a clear applicability to other areas such as the discovery of behavior patterns in smart home environments.

Association rule or pattern discovery techniques [36] are usually applied to transactions where each transaction consists of a set of items. The aim is to discover all associations among the items where the presence of one set of items in a transaction implies the presence of some other items.

Approaches related to pattern analysis quite often are based on the *apriori*-algorithm. The main idea behind this algorithm is to generate candidate item-sets from a sequence of actions or events and then to identify frequent item-sets by using a *support* factor, which has to be greater than the user defined minimum. Typical approaches which use *apriori*-algorithm are Parallel Apriori [42], DIC [43], DHP [44], Q2 [45] , Itemset Clustering [46] and Hybrid Distribution [47].

A simplistic rule discovered can be presented as: *if event A occurs then event B occurs (support 75%)*. This means that when A is observed B is also observed 75% of the time. However, taking into consideration a temporal aspect in the rule discovery, the previous example can be presented as: *if event A occurs then event B occurs within time T* (support 75%). Temporal rules contain information, which not only identify the consequent action or event for a predefined condition, but also have the time within this action or event occurs. The process of discovering these temporal rules is sometimes referred to as *sequence discovery*.

An example of applying pattern analysis can be in Episode Discovery (ED), proposed in [41] for identifying significant episodes in event histories. By a significant episode here we mean an ordered, partially ordered or unordered set of events occurring within a regular interval or as a response to spatial *triggering* event. The process of ED uses a sliding window to split event histories into segments. Then an analyzing algorithm evaluates events within the sliding window by using a minimum description length (MDL) approach [48].

### 3.3.4  The "Prediction" Category

This category includes all techniques, which focus on the reconstruction of a time-series pattern. Originally these techniques were developed to facilitate research in two main areas: a financial prediction [49] and weather forecasting [50]. However, with the rapid development of areas such as smart-homes and health care, the need for such techniques has increased.

The workflow of prediction techniques can be split into two stages. A number of time-series which are similar to the query are retrieved in the first stage. The retrieval process may also utilize elements of techniques from other data mining categories such as clustering and classification, which can help identify similar time-series. In the second stage a spatial algorithm analyses the retrieved temporal entities and generates a summary shape from them. The task of generating time-series based on retrieved samples is not straightforward. It has received a lot of attention in the past, and still remains a high priority for the temporal data mining community, due to the large number of open issues.

An example of where prediction can be used in the smart home is in movement tracing. Previous research has shown the possibility of creating a smart-floor [51]. This smart-floor receives information about a person's movement through specially designed sensitive tiles. Let's suppose that an elderly person gets up from the sofa in the living room and starts to move. Each step is continuously monitored through the intelligent environment. Using information obtained from their initial steps, the algorithm identifies similar examples in the history database. These patterns are used to predict the potential courses for the person within their environment. This information can then be used by other equipment, for example turning on lights, or music in another room.

# 4  Temporal Case-Based Reasoning

Taking into consideration the variety of different scenarios, which can occur in a smart-home, it is practically impossible to specify beforehand a set of fixed rules that cover even the most probable situations. This is why the data mining techniques described so far are so important especially when considering that circumstances change over time and that old rules may become invalid and new ones need to be discovered. This leads to the classical problems associated with rule based systems in terms of their brittleness and maintenance. Additionally all rules need to be verified before they are used, which is an enormous overhead on designated experts.

Case-Based Reasoning [52], [53], which is described in more detail in chapter (*Cases, Context, and Comfort: Opportunities for Case-Based Reasoning in Smart Environments*), may provide a reasonable solution for these drawbacks within the smart-home environment as its knowledge engineering overheads are widely regarded to be lower.

Temporal CBR (TCBR) is a topical subject at present in CBR circles as evidenced by the fact that the number of publications in this area have increased in the last two years (Two entire workshops were dedicated to this new field at the International Conference on CBR in 2003 and the European Conference on CBR in 2004, entitled "Applying case-based reasoning to time series prediction"). Despite the increased affordability and the importance of utilising temporal data in problem solving, there has been very little work done in TCBR to date. Some research has been carried out on initial work in the area by Jaczymski [54], who proposed a framework for the design of CBR systems, to enable retrieval of cases with time-oriented features, Malek [55], who designed the COBRA approach for predicting user actions on the WEB based on previous navigation experiences and Anamodt [56], who used temporally enabled cases to predict problems that are likely to occur in oil drilling platforms based on a history of previous events that led to problems. No work has been done for applying TCBR to the smart-home up to now.

The main drawback of applying the conventional CBR methodology to the temporal domain is the lack of a reliable TCBR methodology within the time dimension. Traditionally a case in CBR is characterized by a set of static (non temporal) values. In a dynamic environment such as the smart-home, a case can be defined as a combination of static values, sequences and time-series data types.

Ultimately to enable CBR systems to operate optimally in a temporal environment changes in the CBR methodology [57] are required, where processes and knowledge containers can be adapted to cope with temporal cases. A potential modification to the conventional CBR methodology is shown in figure 15.

Three preprocessing steps are required to be integrated into a TCBR methodology: transformation, episode discovery and case association. The transformation simplifies input information in a format suitable for the episode discovery. This step is also necessary to reduce data dimensionality. Then the episode discovery step performs an analysis on the simplified data to produce a set of episodes or scenarios. The case association module constantly monitors all existing cases and defines either the discovered episode as part of an already existing case or as a newly emerging one. If the episode is part of an existing ongoing case, the association module updates it and passes it on for further processing. Conversely, if the discovered episode is a new entity, the association module creates a new case.

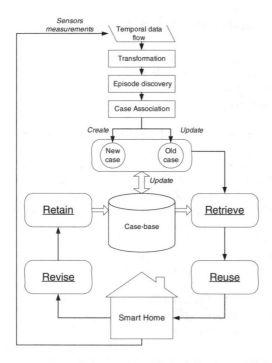

**Fig. 15.** One of the potential modifications to the CBR cycle for handling temporal cases

An updated or newly created case is used by the *retrieval* process to search for similar temporal cases in the past, where the important feature of the *retrieval* process in the real–time system is the search time. Since data dimensionality is significantly reduced during the transformation step, it is often possible to use indexing techniques from conventional CBR background such as k-d-tree, Grid File, BT-tree, R-tree [58], D-HS [59] to speed up the *retrieval* process. In the next step the *reuse* process generates a solution for the new problem by analyzing retrieved temporal cases. Taking into consideration the large variety of different data types and prediction tasks it is difficult to specify an adaptation strategy in advance. As with conventional CBR this may have ultimately to be carried out manually. However, in general the adaptation algorithms focus on two main prediction products: the sequence of oncoming events (actions) or the shape of the time-series. The evaluation step is performed by the *revise* process. During this step the CBR system deploys the solution and evaluates the performance. Depending on the result of this, the *retain* process updates the case-base and other knowledge containers or sends it for further repair.

## 5  The Smart-Home Scenario

A possible use of temporal data mining techniques within a smart-home environment is described in this section. Let's assume that the smart home data analysis environment has been operational for some time and useful information has already been mined and stored by the system.

The smart-home layout is shown in the Figure 16, which consists of four main spaces: a living room, a kitchen, a bedroom and a bathroom. Each of these spaces has a motion sensor, according to the plan presented above. Taking into consideration that only three spaces (a living room, a kitchen and a bedroom) are used in this scenario, only three motion sensors are considered: ML – a motion sensor in the living room, MK – a motion sensor in the kitchen and MB – a motion sensor in the bedroom. Also two other sensors take part in the scenario, where KS is a cooker "switch on/off" sensor and BP is a pressure sensor, which measures if anybody is lying in bed.

All showing sensors constantly monitor the surround environment and generate nominal values "on"/"off" through the fix time interval $\Delta t$ (which in this case is equal to 1 minute). The time diagram in Figure 17 shows the changing of sensor values during the observation period, which lasts 34 minutes.

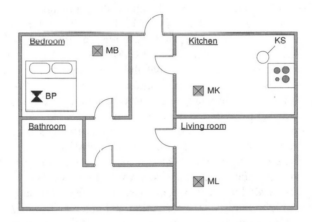

**Fig. 16.** The smart-home layout

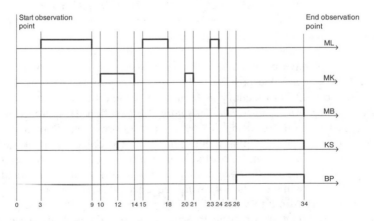

**Fig. 17.** Time diagram of the observation period

This diagram represents the following scenario. A person $P$ came from a hospital and the system started to monitor $P$ movements. On the $3^{rd}$ minute of the observation $P$ entered the living room and spent 6 minutes there. Then $P$ entered the kitchen and on the $12^{th}$ minute $P$ switched on the cooker. After staying in the kitchen 4 minutes $P$ came back to the living room, where they spent 3 minutes and returned to the kitchen again for a quick look. Staying in the kitchen no more than 1 minute, person $P$ returned to the living room and straight after went to the bedroom. Person $P$ lay down on the bed at the $26^{th}$ minute, and spent 8 minutes there, until the last observation point.

Obviously, the scenario presented shows reasonably normal behavior for an average person. However, a potential alarming situation lays in the fact that person $P$ switches on the cooker and goes to bed. If person $P$ in the next few minutes comes back and checks the cooker no alarm needs to be raised. Otherwise if the person forgets about the cooker and stays in bed the alarm should be initiated.

Consider the following possible design of an intelligent system for handling this scenario. The first consideration requires defining an appropriate *data type* (see section 2). All five input channels (ML, MK, MB, KS and BP) generate nominal values (on/off) every minute. It means that the most appropriate data type for this scenario is the *stamped sequence* (see section 2.1). A justification for using this particular data type is a requirement to not only be able to order events, but also to store the time when events occur and their duration.

The next step is to define a suitable *transformation* (see section 3.1). This particular example is very simple and all information obtained during the observation can be easily stored directly in the database, but for a real smart-home system the volume of information generated can easily exceed the storage limit. It means a transformation is required for a real system. Despite the fact of using a very simplified example it is possible to apply a transformation technique to it. The *frequent episode discovery* (see section 3.1.5) is one example of a transformation approach which can be used in this scenario. Consider the sequence of events, where the person continuously moves between the living room and the kitchen. It is clearly seen that the episode (living room -> kitchen) can be classified as being frequent and replaced by a spatial marker. This trivial discovery can dramatically simplify further data mining processes and save a lot of storage space.

After transforming data the next step is to identify *data mining operations* (see section 3.3), which have been carried out on the data and an appropriate *similarity metric* (see section 3.2). One possible solution is to deploy the *Task-based Markov Model* (see section 3.2.2) to identify general tasks, which the person $P$ performs and then to use a *Temporal Case-based Reasoning* (see section 4) approach to form a solution. A justification for using TMM is that information about the person's movement does not say anything about the person's objective (task). However knowledge about the task being performed can contribute considerable weight to the prediction process. Suppose $P$ cooks a dinner. This information can be identified by using TMM. This may involve the following sequence of events, $P$ puts a meal on the cooker, spends a little time to watch it, and then checks it again before going for a little rest. The important information to be mined out of this sequence is that the person is preparing dinner and the meal is cooking at the same time that the person is lying on the bed. Now, the important issue, which has to be addressed is how the smart-home environment reacts to this situation, whether this is normal behaviour for the person cooking dinner or whether it is not and should cause concern.

One possible solution is to deploy TCBR. The great advantage of using TCBR is the flexibility to obtain an intelligent adaptation to the ongoing situation, instead of using hard coded rules. TCBR can extract a set of similar cases from the past and compare them against the current situation. If in the past person $P$ displayed a similar behavior type, where finally they came to the kitchen and switched off the cooker, no alarm is required. In the opposite scenario, if the person has previously forgotten about cooking, an alarm has to be raised.

This example shows the potential of temporal data mining techniques to the smart home environment. It is up to an engineer to determine the combination of transformations, similarity metrics and mining operations, which satisfy the requirements of the designed system.

# 6 Conclusion

Temporal data mining is one of the major building blocks for creating robust, intelligent and efficient smart-home applications. Despite a large variety of different perspectives on how to present and classify temporal data mining, it is possible to identify two main aspects, data and methods.

In this paper we propose three main data types are used for handling temporal information namely: an ordered sequence, a time-stamp sequence and time-series. The first two data types represent sequences of discrete events which are either independent or dependent from time. The third data type represents continuously changing values over a fixed period of time.

A two levels architecture is proposed for handling temporal data, where transformations are applied in the first level and indexing in the second. Transformation reduces the dimensionality of the original data and indexing facilitates efficient access to it.

These transformation and indexing methods provide infrastructural support for high-level mining operations such as clustering, classification, rule discovery and prediction. All these operations are the building blocks for developing a sophisticated smart home environment, which is capable of quickly and intelligently reacting to the majority of real-world situations.

# References

1. Antunes, C. and Oliveira, A.: Temporal data mining: an overview, (2001) 1-13
2. Roddick, J. and Spiliopoulou, M.: A Survey of Temporal Knowledge Discovery Paradigms and Methods: IEEE Transactions on Knowledge and Data Engineering, IEEE Educational Activities Department, Piscataway, NJ, USA, 14(4), (2002) 750-767
3. Agrawal R., K.-I.Lin, Sawhney H., and K.Shim K: Fast similarity search in the presence of noise, scaling, and translation in time-series databases: VLDB Conference, (1995) 490-501
4. Illa J., Alonso J., and Marre S. :Nearest-Neighbors for time series: Kluwer Academic Publisher, Applied Intelligence, USA, (20), (2004) 21-35

5. Sakoe, H and Chiba, S.: Dynamic programming algorithm optimization for spoken word recognition: Trans. on ASSP, 26, (1978) 43-49
6. Berndt D. and Clifford J.: Using dynamic time wrapping to find patterns in time series: Seatte, Washington, AAAI94 Workshop on Knowledge Discovery in Databases (KDD-94), (1994)
7. Keogh E. and Smyth P.: A probabilistic approach to fast pattern matching in time series databases: AAAI Press, In Proc third international conference on knowledge discovery and data mining, Menlo Park,California, USA, (1997) 24-30
8. Keogh E. and Pazzani M.: An Enhanced Representation of Time Series Which Allows Fast and Accurate Classification, Clustering and Relevance Feedback: In proceedings of the 4th Int'l Conference on Knowledge Discovery and Data Mining, New York, NY, (1998) 239-241
9. Keogh E., Chakrabarti K., Pazzani M., and Mehrotra S.: Dimensionality Reduction for Fast Similarity Search in Large Time Series Databases: Knowledge and Information Systems, 3(3), (2000) 263-286
10. Keogh E., Chakrabarti K., Pazzani M., and Mehrotra S.: Locally adaptive dimensionality reduction for indexing large time series databases: In  proceedings of ACM SIGMOD Conference on Management of Data, (2001) 151-162
11. Agrawal R., Faloutsos C., and Swami A.: Efficient Similarity Search In Sequence Databases: Proceedings of the 4th International Conference of Foundations of Data Organization and Algorithms (FODO), (1993)
12. Rafiei D. and Mendelzon A.: Efficient Retrieval of Similar Time Sequences Using DFT: Proceedings of 5th Intl. Conf. on Foundations of Data Organizations and Algorithms (FODO '98), Kobe, Japan, (1998)
13. Mörchen, F.: Time series feature extraction for data mining using DWT and DFT: Technical Report No. 33, Departement of Mathematics and Computer Science Philipps-University Marburg, (2003)
14. Zhang H., Ho T., and Lin M.: A Non-Parametric Wavelet Feature Extractor for Time-Series Classification: In  proceedings of the 8th Pacific-Asia Conference on Knowledge Discovery and Data Engineering (PAKDD), Sydney, Australia, (2004)
15. Agrawal R., K.-I.Lin, Sawhney H., and K.Shim K.: Fast similarity search in the presence of noise, scaling, and translation in time-series databases.: VLDB Conference, (1995) 490-501
16. Das G, Lin K., Mannila H., Renganathan G., and Smyth P.: Rule discovery from time series: In proceedings of the 4th Int'l Conference on Knowledge Discovery and Data Mining, New York, NY, USA, (1998) 16-22
17. Huang Y. and Yu P.: Adaptive query processing for time-series data: ACM Press, Proceedings of the fifth ACM SIGKDD international conference on Knowledge discovery and data mining, New York, NY, USA, (1999) 282-286
18. Guralnik V. and Srivastava J: Event detection from time series data: Proceedings of the fifth ACM SIGKDD international conference on Knowledge discovery and data mining, San Diego, California, US, (1999) 33-42
19. Keogh E., Lonardi S., and Chiu B.: Finding surprising patterns in a time series database in linear time and space: ACM Press, Proceedings of the eighth ACM SIGKDD international conference on Knowledge discovery and data mining, New York, NY, USA, (2002) 550-556
20. Ma J. and Perkins S.: Online novelty detection on temporal sequences: ACM Press, Proceedings of the ninth ACM SIGKDD international conference on Knowledge discovery and data mining, New York, NY, USA, (2003) 613-618
21. Ge X. and Smyth P.: Deformable Markov model templates for time-series pattern matching: ACM Press, Proceedings of the sixth ACM SIGKDD international conference on Knowledge discovery and data mining, New York, NY, USA, (2000) 81-90

22. Qian Y., Jia S, and Si W.: Markov model based time series similarity measuring: International Conference on Machine Learning and Cybernetics, (2003) 278-283
23. Kolarik T. and Rudorfer G.: Time series forecasting using neural networks: ACM Press, Proceedings of the international conference on APL : the language and its applications: the language and its applications, New York, NY, USA, (1994) 86-94
24. Medeiros M., Teräsvirta T., and Rech G.: Building neural network models for time series: A statistical approach: Paper provided by Stockholm School of Economics in its series Working Paper Series in Economics and Finance with number (2002) 508
25. Forney G.: The Viterbi algorithm: Proceedings of IEEE, (1973) 268-278
26. Qian Y., Jia S, and Si W.: Markov model based time series similarity measuring: International Conference on Machine Learning and Cybernetics, (2003) 278-283
27. Mannila H., Toivonen H., and Verkamo A.: Discovering frequent episodes in sequences: Proc. Intl. Conf. on Knowledge Discovery and Data Mining, (1995)
28. Mannila H. and Meek C.: Global partial orders from sequential data: ACM Press, Proceedings of the sixth ACM SIGKDD international conference on Knowledge discovery and data mining, New York, NY, USA, (2000) 161—168
29. Honavar V. and Slutzki G.: Grammatical Inference.: Springer, In Lecture Notes in Artificial Intelligence, (1998) 1433
30. Miclet L. and Higuera C.: Grammatical Inference: Learning Syntax from Sentences: Springer. In Lecture Notes in Artificial Intelligence, (1996) 1147
31. Oliveira A. Grammatical Inference: Algorithms and Applications: Springer, In Lecture Notes in Artificial Intelligence, (2000) 1891
32. Das G, Gunopulos D., and Mannila H.: Finding Similar Time Series: Springer-Verlag, Proceedings of the First European Symposium on Principles of Data Mining and Knowledge Discovery, London, UK, (1997) 88—100
33. Kruskall J. and Liberman M.: The symmetric time warping algorithm: Fromcontinuous to discrete: In Time Warps, String Edits and Macromolecules: The Theory and Practice of String Comparison. Addison-Wesley, (1983)
34. Bellman R.: Adaptive Control Processes: Princeton University Press, (2005)
35. Agrawal R., Psaila G., Wimmers E., and Zaït M.: Querying Shapes of Histories: Morgan Kaufmann Publishers Inc., Proceedings of the 21th International Conference on Very Large Data Bases, San Francisco, CA, USA, (1995) 502-514
36. Hand D., Mannila H., and Smyth P.: Principles of Data Mining: A Bradford Book, The MIT Press, Cambridge, Massachusetts; London, England, (2001)
37. Kira K. and Rendell L.: The feature selection problem: Traditional methods and a new algorithm: In Tenth National Conference on artificial intelligence, (1992)
38. MacQueen J.: Some methods for classification and analysis of multivariate observations: In Proceedings of the Fifth Berkeley Symposium on Mathematical Statistics and Probability, eds L. M. Le Cam & J. Neyman, Berkeley, CA: University of California Press, (1), (1967) 281-297
39. Michalski R. and Stepp R.: Learning from observation: conceptual clustering: Tioga Publishing Company, In R.S. Michalski, J.G. Carbonell, and T.M. Mitchel, editers, Machine Learning: An Artificial Intelligence Approach, (1983) 331-363
40. Fisher D.: Knowledge acquisition via incremental conceptual clustering: Machine Learning, 2, (1987) 139-172
41. Cook D., Youngblood M, Heierman E., III, Gopalratnam K., Rao S., Litvin A., and Khawaja F : MavHome: An Agent-Based Smart Home: First IEEE International Conference on Pervasive Computing and Communications, (2003) 521

42. Agrawal R. and Shafer J. (1996) Parallel mining of association rules: IEEE Transaction on Knowledge and Data Engineering, 8(6) 962-969

43. Brin S., Motwani R., Ullman J., and Trus S.: Dynamic itemset counting and implication rules for market basket data: In Proceedings of the ACM SIGMOD International Conference on Management of Data, (1997) 255-264

44. Park J., Chen M.-S., and Yu P.: An effective hash-based algorithm for mining association rules: SIGMOD Record, 25(2), (1995) 175-186

45. Buchter O. and Wirth R. (1998) Discovery of association rules over ordinal data: a new and faster algorithm and its application to basket analysis: In X.Wu, R. Kotagiri, and K. Korb, editors, Proceedings of the Second Pacific-Asia Conference on Knowledge Discovery and Data Mining, Melbourne, Australia, 36-47

46. Zaki M., Parthasarathy S., Ogihara M., and Li W.: New algorithms for fast discovery of association rules: In Proceedings of the Third International Conference on Knowledge Discovery and Data Mining, Newport Beach, California, (2005) 283-286

47. Han E.-H., Karypis G., and Kumar V.: Scalable parallel data mining for association rules: In Proceedings of the ACM SIGMOD International Conference on Management of Data, (2005) 277-288

48. Heierman E. and Cook D.: Improving home automation by discovering regularly occurring device usage patterns: Proceedings of the International Conference on Data Mining, (2003)

49. Kimoto T., Asakawa K., Yoda M., and Takeoka M.: Stock market prediction system with modular neural networks: In Proceedings of IJCNN-90, San Diego, (1990)

50. Bourbeau L., Carcagno D., Goldberg E., Kittredge R, and Polguère A.: Bilingual Generation of Weather Forecasts in an Operations Environment: International Committee on Computational Linguistics, Proceedings of the 13th. International Conference on Computational Linguistics, Helsinki, Finland, (1990) 318-320

51. Kidd C., Orr R., Abowd G., Atkeson C., Essa I., MacIntyre B., Mynatt E., Starner T., and Newstetter W.: The Aware Home: A Living Laboratory for Ubiquitous Computing Research: In Proceedings of the Second International Workshop on Cooperative Buildings, Pittsburgh, PA, USA, (1999)

52. Kolodner J.: Case–Based Reasoning: Morgan Kaufmann Publishers, Inc., San Mateo, CA, USA, (1993)

53. Leake D.(editor): Case-Based Reasoning: Experiences, Lessons & Future Directions: MIT Press, MA, USA, (1996)

54. Jaczynski M.: A framework for the management of past experiences with time extended situations: In Proceedings of CIKM'97, Las Vegas, USA, (1997) 32-39

55. Malek M. and Kanawati R.: COBRA: A CBR-Based Approach for Predicting Users Actions in a Web Site: In Proceedings of International Conference on CBR, (2001) 336-346

56. Aamodt A. and Skalle P.: Representing temporal knowledge for case-based prediction. Advances in case-based reasoning: European Conference, ECCBR'02, Aberdeen, Lecture Notes in Artificial Intelligence, LNAI 2416, Springer, (2005) 174-188

57. Aamodt A. and Plaza E.: Case-based reasoning: Foundational issues, methodological variations, and system approaches: AI Communications, 7(1) , (1994)

58. Gaede V. and Günther O.: Multidimensional access methods: ACM Computing Surveys, 30(2), (1997) 170-231

59. Patterson D., Rooney N., and Galushka M.: Efficient Similarity Determination and Case Construction Techniques For Case-Based Reasoning: Proceedings of the 4th European Conference on Case-Based Reasoning (ECCBR-02), Aberdeen, Scotland, (2002) 292-305

# Cases, Context, and Comfort: Opportunities for Case-Based Reasoning in Smart Homes

David Leake, Ana Maguitman, and Thomas Reichherzer

Computer Science Department, Indiana University, Lindley Hall 215
150 S. Woodlawn Avenue, Bloomington, IN 47405, U.S.A.
{leake, anmaguit, treichhe}@cs.indiana.edu

**Abstract.** Artificial intelligence (AI) methods have the potential for broad impact in smart homes. Different AI methods offer different contributions for this domain, with different design goals, tasks, and circumstances dictating where each type of method best applies. In this chapter, we describe motivations and opportunities for applying *case-based reasoning* (CBR) to a human centered approach to the capture, sharing, and revision of knowledge for smart homes. Starting from the CBR cognitive model of reasoning and learning, we illustrate how CBR could provide useful capabilities for problem detection and response, provide a basis for personalization and learning, and provide a paradigm for home-human communication to cooperatively guide performance improvement. After sketching how these capabilities could be served by case-based reasoning, we discuss some design issues for applying CBR within smart homes and case-based reasoning research challenges for realizing the vision.

## 1 Introduction

Smart home environments have the potential for extensive impact on occupant comfort, convenience, and safety. Serious accidents can occur in the home because residents are distracted or overwhelmed by ongoing events, and natural age-related declines in mobility and cognitive abilities may exacerbate problems, with occupants requiring monitoring and assistance [1]. For eldercare, smart home technology offers the prospect of a more independent life style in a private home compared to high-cost assisted living alternatives, or increased support and efficiency in group settings. Consequently, smart home technology may help alleviate the looming health-care crisis resulting from steady increases in health care cost and a rapidly aging population [2, 3, 4]. Even for those who do not need special assistance, smart homes can facilitate daily tasks and provide an added measure of security by detecting and responding to emergencies.

Artificial intelligence (AI) methods for smart homes may provide both the flexibility to adapt to changing circumstances and the reasoning capabilities required to interpret events within the home and to make the right choices at the right times. In the introductory chapter to this volume, Augusto and Nugent argue for the promise of smart homes as an AI domain, both because of the potential payoff for AI methods and because the constrained task environment of smart homes facilitates application of AI solutions [5]. This chapter focuses on the use of case-based reasoning as an approach to enable smart

J.C. Augusto and C.D. Nugent (Eds.): Designing Smart Homes, LNAI 4008, pp. 109–131, 2006.

homes to learn from observation of and direct interaction with their residents, to be adaptable to new tasks and to particular individuals' needs.

One of the inspirations for a CBR-based approach to smart homes comes from *human-centered computing* (HCC), which focuses on the computer-human team. HCC dictates going beyond simply requiring that the home attempt to "do the right thing" to requiring that the home can interact effectively with its residents, sharing the burden with them in whatever ways will maximize overall performance. When the home can provide capabilities that the human lacks, or can increase efficiency, it should do so; when the human has unique capabilities or prefers to act independently, the home should defer and support the human's preference. This suggests that smart homes should support the *explanation* of their decisions, (1) to help an informed and capable occupant trust the home enough to accept its judgments and determine when to relinquish control, and (2) as background for an informed and capable resident to directly adjust the home—reducing the burden of autonomous-only learning, and making it feasible to refine system behavior more rapidly and reliably. To further explanation and adjustment, the home should support a *simple and transparent learning process*, making it easy to revise system behaviors. These desiderata suggest exploring methods which learn in a way that people find understandable and offer simple processes for capturing new information.

One of the inspirations for case-based reasoning comes from cognitive modeling of human reasoning and learning (e.g., [6, 7]). Experience with fielded CBR systems suggests that humans are comfortable receiving information in the form of cases, and experiments show the usefulness of cases for explaining system reasoning [8]. Likewise, CBR provides a simple, easily comprehensible learning process. This chapter sketches how CBR could support smart homes tasks such as responding to and learning from expectation failures, helping residents, caregivers and relatives to identify problems, and interacting with residents/caregivers through examples, to explain and adjust the homes' behaviors.

The chapter begins with a synopsis of case-based reasoning, including the role of cases in human understanding, reasoning, and learning, the pragmatic motivations for applying case-based reasoning, and a sketch of a formalization of CBR foundations. As observed by Watson [9], case-based reasoning is a general approach, rather than a single technology; it provides an overarching framework which can be instantiated in multiple ways, drawing on technologies as needed for a specific problem. Consequently, rather than focusing on specific underlying technologies, the chapter focuses on identifying types of smart homes tasks for which the CBR approach has special promise and sketching how CBR could be applied to them. It closes by discussing special CBR challenges for realizing this vision of smart homes which reason and learn from experiences.

## 2   A Synopsis of CBR: Cases for Understanding, Learning, and Problem-Solving

One of the early foundations for case-based reasoning was Schank's study of human *reminding* during understanding, which gave rise to Schank's Dynamic Memory Theory

([10]; summarized in [11]). Dynamic Memory Theory addresses the relationship of human understanding, learning, and memory, with a central focus on how knowledge is structured, organized and revised based on experience. This approach is of interest to smart home development for three reasons. First, a fundamental need for smart homes is recognizing events and predicting following steps. Second, no smart home can be perfect: Smart homes will need to adapt to experience. Third, the use of human-like learning methods may help residents to understand and interact with the smart home, increasing its acceptance.

In Dynamic Memory Theory, standard event sequences (such as the events involved in hosting a party—sending invitations, preparing food, welcoming guests, offering them food, etc.) are characterized by sequences of basic components, called *scenes*, which normally describe events which take place in a single location, with a single purpose, and in a single time interval. These sequences are captured in knowledge structures called Memory Organization Packages, or "MOPs". They are hierarchical, with shared structure enabling lower-level components to be shared by a number of MOPs.

A central focus of Dynamic Memory is the process by which an understander refines its knowledge structures, to improve future predictive power—a process of great importance to smart homes as well—and the role of remindings in that process. Each MOP provides certain expectations, which provide top-down guidance for understanding. If these expectations are not borne out, an expectation failure occurs. For example, with RFID tags, a smart house might detect an impaired resident picking up a toothbrush, leading to the expectation for toothpaste to be picked up next. If, instead, the resident picked up a tube of shoe polish, an expectation failure would occur—and would require a warning.

A tenet of Dynamic Memory Theory is that failure episodes are stored under the processing structures in effect at the time of the failure, making them accessible as remindings when another similar failure occurs. Dynamic Memory Theory and later work in its tradition (e.g., [12, 13, 14]) developed indexing vocabularies aimed at capturing the features needed for computer models to generate the types of remindings observed in humans. If we accept the general ability of people to generate useful remindings, we can expect that analogous remindings may be pragmatically useful for a smart home to generate, as a surrogate memory for the home's residents. These remindings provide a starting point for case-based reasoning by either the human or the home.

Beyond the immediate usefulness of remindings to aid current tasks (e.g., by warning of a possible mistake or suggesting a useful past solution), such remindings can provide data for future generalization to generate new schemas. For example, the first time a patient confuses shoe polish with toothpaste, a warning may be sufficient, but if this happens often, the smart house may determine that the patient will reach for anything available, and might need to guide a visiting nurse to remove any potentially dangerous objects when preparing the house for the night. Likewise, case data may be useful to refine responses such as warnings (e.g., whether a nurse should be called or an audible warning generated with a speech synthesizer is sufficient, and what volume warning is needed).

For a system trying to explain a resident's behavior, having access to cases for prior experiences provides a number of potential benefits. First, the cases focus attention on scenarios which actually *have happened* for the particular subject. Second, cases augment the system's built-in knowledge. Third, remindings can carry solutions or predictions which applied in the past, and which may be useful again. If the last time a subject overslept, he skipped breakfast, the home might not turn on the coffee maker, but instead could start warming up the car. If the heat is on, but the home does not become warm, a reminding that the same problem occurred when a door was left ajar, and was fixed by closing it, might provide a solution. Third, the case provided by the reminding may contain lessons from both successes and failures.

This process provides a first-pass suggestion of a framework for how smart homes may combine general schemas with cases to understand actions, predict the actions to follow—in order to support them—and note deviations in order to explain, react, and learn. For example, the schema for a daily routine might include getting up, dressing, eating breakfast, and so on. If a home's resident fails to get up when the alarm goes off one morning, the anomaly might prompt remindings of other similar instances, for example, a case of prior illness.

In general, a case-based reasoning system exploits remindings to help interpret new situations or to solve new problems. When faced with a new problem, a CBR system retrieves prior cases for similar problems and adapts their solutions to fit new circumstances. When faced with a new situation to interpret, a CBR system retrieves prior cases for similar situations and compares and contrasts them to the current situation to form a new interpretation. The steps of the CBR process include situation assessment, to describe a situation in a vocabulary commensurate with the indices used in memory, then retrieval and similarity assessment of candidate cases, then adaptation to fit the case to the new situation and evaluation of the results (first by internal reasoning and then by application of the case to the new problem, providing real-world feedback). If problems are detected, the adaptation/evaluation cycle may be continued, until the final result is stored in the case base. Figure 1 sketches this process. Additional variations and extensions are possible—for example, drawing on multiple cases to provide parts of a solution. For a more in-depth overview, see, for example, [15, 16, 17].

Flexible processes for situation assessment, similarity assessment, and case adaptation enable cases to be applied in new contexts and despite imperfect matches to past

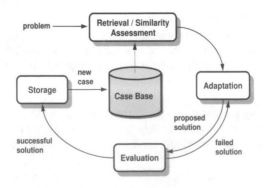

**Fig. 1.** The CBR cycle

events. In smart homes, it might seldom be true that two tasks were performed exactly the same way and in the same context. To realize the full potential of CBR, a CBR system must generalize its indices—even as it keeps the cases themselves specific— to enable potentially relevant cases to be retrieved, must be able to assess similarity of differing situations, and must be able to adapt solutions to new needs. In practice, CBR applications will address these to different levels. Depending on the granularity of sensor information, for example, different amounts of indexing information will be needed.

The CBR literature presents a number of practical motivations for using CBR (see [17] for one more detailed treatment):

1. **Knowledge acquisition by example:** Providing knowledge in the form of cases can seem more natural to subjects than attempting to distill knowledge into general rules. Cases only need to be captured for situations that actually arise in practice, and the system can be fielded with a small set of "seed cases," acquiring more cases as needed. However, more traditional knowledge acquisition problems may arise in case engineering or capturing supporting knowledge such as similarity or adaptation knowledge.

2. **Learning from both successes and failures:** Case acquisition not only accumulates successful cases as future guidance, but also failure cases which can serve as warnings of problems.

3. **Inertia-free learning:** Cases provided to the system may immediately be applied, without any need for re-training of the system or learning period during which the system responds incorrectly until more evidence is acquired.

4. **Simple and lazy learning:** Case acquisition to cover new problems can improve system coverage with a very simple learning process, and small initial cost. Effort to generalize cases, etc., need only be applied if similar circumstances arise in the future, only need to be done to the extent required by the new situation, and can immediately be tested with the feedback of that situation.

5. **Ability to draw on multiple types of knowledge:** What domain knowledge is available can be integrated into many parts of the CBR process, to improve indexing or ease adaptation.

6. **Problem-solving efficiency:** Case-based reasoning can be combined with other methods, such as rule-based or model-based reasoning, to provide speedup learning by reusing results of past reasoning rather than requiring them to be derived from scratch.

7. **Ability to function in poorly-understood domains:** When a domain is poorly understood, cases that have worked in similar situations may implicitly capture important factors that would not be captured in rules reflecting current understanding.

8. **Ability to provide operational and contextualized guidance:** Because cases are kept at an operational level rather than generalized, they may be easier to apply (e.g., a cooking plan could be stored including the specific places to look for an ingredient in a household, etc.).

9. **User acceptance:** Cases capturing similar prior situations can provide effective explanations for why a system performed as it did [8].

## 3   Requirements for CBR

Whether case-based reasoning is appropriate for a particular task domain depends both on characteristics of the problem domain and the ability to endow the system with knowledge to guide the CBR process. To clarify the issues involved, this section sketches a formalization adapted from our work in [18]. Its description simplifies the process by omitting some issues and refinements; a detailed survey of current approaches is available in [19].

*Formalizing the basic CBR process:*  We can describe a case-based problem-solving system as processing problems presented to the system from a problem space $P$, whose solutions are elements of a solution space $S$. Cases are pairs $(p, s) \in C = P \times S$, the set of all possible cases. The system begins with a finite "seed" case base $B_0 \subseteq C$. As the system is used, it processes a sequence of problems $Q = p_1, p_2, \ldots, p_j$, where each $p_k \in P$ for $k = 1, \ldots, j$.

In the basic CBR process, learning occurs after each problem is processed and the resulting solution has been evaluated, with a case reflecting the new problem and solution added to the case base. Each problem $p_k$ is processed using the case base $B_{k-1}$. This results in a sequence of case bases, with $B_k = B_{k-1} \cup (p_k, s_k)$, for $k = 1, \ldots, j$. If the system cannot correctly solve a problem itself, it may store an externally-provided solution or a record of the failed solution and its outcome. When a failure case is retrieved, it serves as a warning which can be used to anticipate potential difficulties.

*How problem distance guides retrieval:*  To predict which case or cases will be most relevant to the input problem, a CBR system may use a "problem distance" function $PDist : P \times C \rightarrow [0, \infty)$ to measure the distance between a new problem and the problem description of a stored case. $PDist(p, c)$ is zero if $p$ is the same problem solved by $c$. Given a new problem, the CBR system may retrieve the case closest to that problem according to $PDist$. (CBR functions for problem closeness may be either "distance functions" or "similarity functions;" similarity increases as distance decreases.) In the simplest retrieval approach, nearest neighbor retrieval, the $PDist$ distances from the current problem are computed for all stored cases to identify the most similar cases. In large-scale applications, other methods are used to enable retrieving promising candidates more efficiently (e.g., by organizing cases in discrimination trees according to their feature values).

Part of the effectiveness of the CBR system depends on whether the distance function accurately reflects the usefulness of retrieved solutions. For example, if the adaptation time required to generate a new solution is important, "real distance" might be measured in terms of estimated adaptation time [20, 21] (and the distance function might not be symmetric); if reliability of adaptation is an issue, "distance" could estimate how reliably a case could be adapted to a new problem, regardless of adaptation time.

*Problem-solution regularity:*  In an ideal CBR system, $PDist$ would always select the most appropriate case; in practice, $PDist$ is generally an approximation. The extent to which $PDist$ has this property is formalized as *problem-solution regularity*, which calculates the probability that a case returned as optimal by the similarity function will actually be within a non-negative $\epsilon$ of an optimal case. Problem-solution regularity relates to the information retrieval notion of precision (note that for CBR systems which reason from a single most similar case, the IR notion of *recall* is not relevant). One requirement for high problem-solution regularity is that the task domain is regular, i.e., that the lessons of similar prior experiences are likely to be useful. Everyday experience leads us to expect that this will hold for the smart homes domain. The ability to exploit this regularity with CBR involves knowledge engineering: it must be possible to engineer an appropriate distance function for the domain.

*Problem-distribution regularity:* The benefit a CBR system accrues from learning depends on whether new problems will tend to resemble the problems addressed in previous cases (either in the seed case base, or in cases learned during prior processing). This property is *problem-distribution regularity*. If it is possible to define a distance function providing high problem-solution regularity, retrieved cases will be useful; when problem-distribution-regularity is high, the CBR system will either be able to cover a sufficient set of problems based on the initial case base, or by learning when addressing similar problems.

## 4    Opportunities for CBR in Smart Homes

Case-based reasoning has been widely applied to advisory tasks, including the selection of assistive technology for smart homes [22]. However, to our knowledge the direct application of CBR to the internal function of smart homes remains unexplored. As many strands of CBR research have potential applications to smart homes, this section will outline the reasons for applying CBR to this domain and avenues for its application.

The characteristics of CBR suggest four motivations for applying CBR as an AI methodology within smart homes. First, case learning provides a simple method for refining and personalizing a smart home over time by storing cases for new event sequences, to be generalized into new schemas, and for learning appropriate responses. Second, CBR's ability to reuse prior reasoning—regardless of the original reasoning process—can increase efficiency for expensive reasoning tasks within smart homes, such as generating abductive explanation of observed anomalies [23]. Third, the use of CBR can facilitate human-system interactions by enabling humans to provide unanalyzed examples (or provide feedback on examples) as a means of training the smart home. Fourth, references to cases provide an intuitive way for smart homes to explain their behaviors to people [8, 24, 25].

In the remainder of this section, we illustrate the potential usefulness of CBR to support selected smart home tasks. In this discussion, we will assume that the smart home is equipped with the array of sensors described in the introduction to this volume, providing capabilities to monitor properties such as the locations of residents, on/off states of appliances, and vital signs of residents. We also assume that raw sensor data will be transformed and mined to provide information in a more summarized form suitable for use by a CBR component (for example, using techniques such as discussed by [26] in this volume).

## 4.1   Monitoring, Problem Detection and Response

An essential capability for smart homes is the ability to monitor household events and resident state. This monitoring may serve two purposes. One is to recognize instances of routine patterns, to enable the home to anticipate and satisfy standard needs (e.g., to turn on the coffee maker after the occupant gets up, or to guide an impaired resident through normal steps of daily life). Another is to recognize unusual and potentially hazardous situations and respond. Case-based methods can be useful for both.

Comparison to past cases can help to detect situations which require action, and to suggest responses. For example, cases from prior emergencies could be indexed by predictive features, in order to warn of problems and suggest responses when they are retrieved. A case indexed by "resident falls to the floor" (as determined by the change in location of a sensor worn by the patient), could identify falling as a potential emergency condition. That case could contain the prior response (e.g., making an urgent call to a nursing station, broadcasting to the resident that help has been requested, and turning on house lights), for potential reuse. If the case was captured in highly similar circumstances (e.g., at the same nursing home), the response could provide not only a general outline, but a rich set of useful details (e.g., telephone numbers).

Likewise, cases associated with particular residents can be useful to personalized monitoring. Cases captured during routine activities may provide a vehicle for assessing whether a situation is routine (e.g., by comparing heart rate while climbing stairs), for making predictions in order to provide aid (e.g., to turn on the bedroom light if the resident is preparing for bed), and for forming generalized schemas for routine events.

Cases could also be used for proactive aid in less critical situations. For example, a smart home might be equipped with RFID readers enabling it to monitor which ingredient packages are removed from the refrigerator and cabinets. If the ingredients flour, sugar, butter, eggs, vanilla and chocolate chips are gathered, those ingredients might be used as indices to retrieve a stored case, captured from a cookbook, for making chocolate chip cookies. Based on the recipe, the home could set the oven to the

| Problem description: | Anomaly: Oven cannot hold temperature |
|---|---|
| Additional features: | – Oven status (on)<br>– Recency of last on/off status change<br>– Oven door status (open)<br>– Recency of last door status change<br>– Oven temperature setting<br>– Recency of temperature setting<br>– Actual oven temperature |
| Solution: | Warn resident with audible message; turn off oven if no action within time limit. |

Fig. 2. Sample features and solution for case for oven door left open

proper temperature, broadcasting an audible message to inform the resident that it was preheating the oven to the temperature for the chocolate chip cookie recipe.

Figure 2 illustrates some components of a sample case for kitchen monitoring and response. The case captures an episode in which an impaired resident has left the oven door open with the oven turned on after removing an item from the oven. Cases for problem-solving tasks, such as response to anomalies, include a *problem description* describing the problem to address, which serves the primary index for retrieving the case. They may also include additional features—for this example, oven attributes, attributes of the oven contents, and external sensor readings—which may be relevant to assessing similarity between cases for similar problems. Such features may be drawn from any of the data captured by smart home sensors, as well as any derived features. However, not every feature is relevant to the indexing of every case. For example, while the readings of indoor room sensors that measure room temperature or identify hot spots in the room may be useful for retrieving a fire-response case, such sensor readings might be ignored in determining the applicability of cases for other tasks.

*CBR for anytime response:* For problem response, a useful characteristic of CBR is its potential for tailoring problem response speed to problem urgency. When emergency conditions require very rapid response (e.g., when a heat sensor detects a fire), it may be crucial to begin actions without extensive reasoning, suggesting the use of anytime algorithms [27], which can be terminated at any time while still providing a meaningful answer, and which can return answers whose quality improves with increased processing time. Riesbeck points out that CBR has "anytime" properties, because the solution of a prior case provides a basis for immediate action even while the system continues to search for possibly more on-point cases and possible adaptations as time permits [28]. Different types and levels of alarms could suggest different points at which to harvest the intermediate results of CBR.

For example, given a fire, the system might immediately find a case for another fire involving turning on sprinklers, turning off room power and calling for emergency services, all of which can be applied directly from a prior case. Other aspects of the case, such as how to notify the resident's relatives, would require adaptation, perhaps depending on time-consuming additional effort. Applying anytime CBR requires methods for rapidly estimating the severity of the situation and the applicability of the current case without adaptation.

## 4.2 Personalizing Smart Home Responses

A smart home guided by standard schemas can provide stereotyped responses, but will not reflect the differing needs of different users. Building up personalized sets of cases for different users addresses that problem. For example, suppose that a window was left open on a cool summer night, with the air conditioner left on, but not running because the house was cool. If, the next morning, the house becomes warm enough for the air conditioner to start, two different residents might favor different courses of action. One person might close the window (favoring maintaining a pleasant temperature), while another might turn off the air conditioner (favoring fresh air). A case supporting the second resident's preferences is sketched in Figure 3.

| Problem description: | Window open and house temperature exceeds air conditioner setting. |
|---|---|
| Additional features: | Inside temperature, outside temperature, window sensor status (open/shut), resident |
| Solution: | Turn off air conditioner and notify resident with audible message. |

**Fig. 3.** Sample features and solution for case for turning off air conditioner rather than closing window, reflecting resident preference

| Differences | Context | Adaptation to solution |
|---|---|---|
| Asleep | Non-emergency | Replace case's audible notifications with a stored summary to be presented at rising time. |
| Asleep | Emergency | Trigger strobe light and audible alarm as first step of the response. |
| Hearing-impaired | All | Increase warning volume. |
| Absent | Non-emergency | Delete requests for user response before system action, immediately perform automatic fallback actions, and save summary to present upon resident return. |
| Absent | Emergency | Replace notifications to resident by notifications to central monitor. |
| | | Immediately perform automatic actions. |
| Present | Non-emergency | Add notifications before automatic actions. |

**Fig. 4.** Sample adaptations for warning messages, based on differences between the resident in the retrieved case and the current situation

Adaptation may help to adjust cases to individual preferences and needs. Figure 4 illustrates a set of possible adaptations for cases which warn a resident of problems. The first column of the table describes the difference between new situation and prior cases necessitating adaptation to the case's proposed solution (e.g., the resident is asleep rather than awake). The second summarizes contextual features affecting the selection of adaptations. For example, when the resident is sleeping and a non-urgent situation arises, it is reasonable to adapt the prior response to suppress notifications untill the resident awakens, but in a dangerous situation, the system should add steps to awaken the resident.

Developing personalized CBR systems requires replacing the task-centric view—that there is a single solution for each problem—with a user centric view that supports multiple solutions, based on the user as well as the problem situation [29]. This can be addressed by modeling the user as well as the task, and using both types of information to guide CBR at many levels. Routine adaptations, such as the adaptation for hearing-impaired occupants from Figure 4, provide a first basic step, but much richer adaptations can be performed.

Again, different CBR processes can play different roles. For example, a secondary CBR process can be used to directly support the personalization process [30], to classify a new individual based on individuals already classified; this can be an index provided to the main CBR process to reflect different users during retrieval, adaptation, evaluation and storage. Augmenting case descriptions with user properties can improve the system ability to identify useful solutions.

## 4.3   Enabling Personalized Levels of Smart Home Autonomy

Not all advice is useful, and not all aid is desired; different individuals have varying needs and tolerances. Likewise, it may be desirable for a system to balance user preferences against general policies (e.g., comfort vs. energy costs [31]). Consequently, a smart home should provide *adjustable autonomy* [32], furnishing different levels of support depending on its own capabilities, user preferences, user needs, and general policies. Thus another useful type of personalization would consider potential actions and decide which should actually be performed for a particular resident, or how to adapt them to make them more acceptable.

Decisions about whether to act depend on many factors, such as the user's physical and mental condition, the user's tolerance of system intervention, system's confidence in its assessment of a situation, the cost of action, the potential risk of failure to act, and so on. Because of the complexity of weighing these conflicting factors, it may be desirable either to rely on experience, using CBR to asking what this user or similar users have favored in similar situations, or to exploit CBR to retrieve and adapt the results of prior calculations performed by other AI methods for similar prior problems.

## 4.4   Personalization of Information Presentation

In addition to deciding when to present information, a smart home must decide how to present it, choosing from a plethora of interface options. For example, one direct presentation approach is implemented in the REA system [33], a virtually embodied interface agent that advises customers on real-estate purchases and uses a variety of verbal and non-verbal input modalities when interacting with its customers. Alternatively, ambient display technologies exist in the periphery of subjects' perception and only appear if subjects choose to interact, thereby contributing to a calm environment [34]. Examples of such technologies include Hello.Wall, which facilitates communication by presenting unobtrusive digital light patterns to individuals as they walk by, to alert them of new messages which can be accessed through a PDA if desired [35]. Ambient display technologies remove restrictions of traditional keyboard-mouse-based human-computer interaction, which require users to be located in a single spot and to explicitly initiate each interaction. Likewise, spoken-dialogue systems with a variety of input and output modalities allow for spontaneous interaction between humans and the system. Cases may be used to capture the presentation preferences of particular users, for particular types of information.

## 4.5  Explanation of System Decisions

It has long been recognized that increased user understanding of system reasoning may increase user confidence in an intelligent system's decisions (e.g., [36]). The ability of a system to explain its decisions may also be helpful to support user-assisted refinement of system function.

CBR systems' cases provide a natural vehicle for explanation. Unlike more opaque methods such as neural networks, CBR outputs can be explained in an intuitive way, by presenting the specific prior cases on which decisions are based. Users can then compare the current situation to the prior cases, to assess their applicability. If the resident of a smart home considers the system's case choice incorrect, the resident could manually override (e.g., by setting the oven to a lower temperature if making chocolate chip bars instead of cookies), and—based on sensor input—the system could capture the changes, to store a new variant case labeled by the user (e.g., as "chocolate chip bars"). If more than one case might apply, given current information, a query proposing the alternative cases may enable the resident to provide guidance (e.g., "It appears you are making chocolate chip cookies or chocolate chip bars. Which preheat temperature should I set?").

Early CBR work sometimes considered the case alone to be a sufficient explanation; recent work is developing a richer view (for a sampling of recent work, see [25]). In addition to providing arguments for the relevance of a case and a conclusion (e.g., in the form of comparisons and contrasts [37]), current research is examining how to explain other facets affecting system conclusions, such as how features of a case contribute to similarity calculations [38]. Each of these explanations in turn provides a point to which a user might provide feedback accounting for an erroneous conclusion and enabling system refinement.

## 4.6  Providing Task-Relevant Reminders from Captured Cases

Elderly or infirm patients may have difficulty following normal task sequences. Consequently, the ability to capture and provide task guidance could be valuable. More generally, memory augmentation, in the form of environment-aware systems which can use context to disambiguate requests for information, could provide valuable services in smart homes—from guiding tasks to providing recipes to more general questions.

Considerable research has already been done on intelligent reminder systems, and many tools have been developed to augment human memory through context-based proactive assistance in homogeneous and regulated environments. Much of this work centers on the desktop paradigm, where tasks are often limited to editing, searching, entertainment and communication [39, 40, 41, 42]. Within this paradigm, case-based systems have already been applied to tutoring systems which monitor an individual's progress in a simulated environment, tracking behavior to detect potential problems and present video clips of cases with "remindings," warning about potential pitfalls [43]. While smart home environments would present many challenges beyond simulated ones, this work provides a general outline for the approach. An additional issue will be the need to aid more general tasks and provide smooth integration, by being delivered using the right modality, at the right time, and at the right location. In general, making this determination may be a daunting task, making it appealing to gather examples, which may be combined with general rules for deciding where and when to provide guidance.

Systems that offer guidance as the individual completes daily activities have been developed primarily to assist the cognitively impaired. Some of these systems, such as Autominder [44], are general purpose tools. They operate by monitoring the individual's task and perform schedule management functions that otherwise would require human assistance. Others have as a goal to assist more specific tasks. An example of such a system is COACH [45], a tool developed to assist in the hand washing process by providing needed reminders. A primary motivation for exploring CBR for these tasks would be their capability for simple and lazy learning, and their ability to function in new domains by providing them with additional examples, making them especially suitable to adapt to diverse situations, without the need for a predefined plan of daily activities.

### 4.7    Enabling User Instruction of Smart Homes

No smart home will be perfect; the home must learn. One form of learning is simply for the system to observe the user's actions. If the system mis-sets the morning temperature and the user adjusts it, the system can adapt the outcome of its stored case, replacing its initial choice with the user's corrected one. Observing and learning from user settings alone is a promising vision, but also has limitations in that few cues may be directly available to the system [31]. In addition, if the smart home learns by methods requiring much training data, the system may continue in its old behavior for some time after the user's behavior changes, prompting user frustration.

The more sophisticated inferences a home requires, the more it may be difficult for a system to autonomously select appropriate behaviors and learn from the limited information that may be available by observation. Consequently, it may be desirable to enable users to choose to share some of the burden in exchange for faster learning or better performance. CBR provides a potential avenue for this. If cases are captured in a comprehensible form and made available to users for interactive case adaptation, users can refine cases to directly reflect the conclusions they find appropriate. Numerous avenues for interaction with CBR systems have been explored [46], and this continues to be an active research area.

An interesting extension of these approaches would be to provide new paradigms for interacting with cases, such as monitoring user actions in the home to automatically gather case information (e.g., using RFID tags to track ingredients used in a recipe). Because cases encode episodes, which may be presentable in an intuitive way, case presentation and editing interfaces might provide general-purpose methods to enable sophisticated users to adjust system behavior themselves through case editing. For example, some CBR research has pursued using concept maps [47] as the basis for browsable and editable cases [48, 49].

## 5    Putting it into Practice: Tasks for Case Generation and Access for Smart Homes

Building any CBR application requires developing methods for the core CBR tasks of Section 2, as described in sources such as [50, 51]. This section focuses on the key tasks of generating the system's initial case base and developing methods for accessing the cases based on information available from the home.

## 5.1    Generating Case Bases

CBR systems are only as good as their cases. Consequently, case capture and engineering are central issues in fielding CBR applications, and a first step is determining the case representation. As discussed by Kolodner and Leake [16], a case is *a contextualized piece of knowledge representing an experience that teaches a lesson fundamental to achieving the goals of the reasoner.* Cases must contain a *problem/situation description*, describing the state of the world when the episode recorded in the case occurred, a *solution* or *interpretation*; and the *outcome* of applying the solution. The solutions/interpretations that cases provide may take different forms, ranging from simple textual advice to a resident (e.g., "Are you forgetting to take out the garbage?") to rich structured representations (e.g., the plan for a recipe). The preferred representation will depend on the task, in light of a tradeoff between easy generation (e.g., for textual cases) and the ability for cases to support further reasoning (e.g., for a recipe, for which the home might suggest how to revise the recipe when substituting for an unavailable ingredient).

In order for a CBR-based system to be useful as soon as it is fielded, developers must "jump start" the system with initial knowledge capturing the events, actions, and behaviors of individuals in the home relevant to system tasks. For a CBR system which monitors and predicts behaviors, one option would be to base initial processing on generalized schemas; another would be for developers to manually identify prototypical or critical events and activities for the system to handle, such as common, regular activities and behaviors (e.g. when people get up in the morning, when they leave the house, etc.), or to analyze automatically generated cases to determine which to store. For example, plans generated by a planner for standard tasks could be evaluated by hand and stored for future use, or plans generated on the fly and their effects in practice could be stored for future use, for speedup learning and to anticipate and avoid plan failures. A detailed description of planning for smart homes is provided in this volume [52].

Cases may be useful if their history suggests that they would be frequently used in the home, if they would help solve critical problems (e.g., for emergencies), if they would fill gaps in the system problem coverage, or if they would be easily adaptable, increasing system flexibility. The result is an initial case base with a representative set of cases capable of adapting to the specific requirements. Given the range of CBR processes that may apply within a smart home, multiple case bases may be needed, e.g., for monitoring resident vital signs, monitoring home conditions, etc.

## 5.2    Information Sources and Situation Assessment

Accessing the right cases requires methods for retrieving relevant cases, based on information from the smart home. Work on pervasive computing for smart homes has developed sensor technologies and smart appliances to monitor individuals and their physical environment, and has built middleware to provide services and facilitate communication among the different components. A number of research projects have focused on developing an infrastructure to deal with context in smart home environments (e.g., the Aware Home Research Initiative [53, 54]), providing a foundation on which case-based smart home applications could build.

Generally, a pervasive computing architecture for smart homes can be broken down into a physical layer, a middleware service layer, and an application layer, which together provide a platform delivering high-level information abstracted from the sensors, detectors, actuators, smart appliances and wired or wireless communication devices to integrate new technologies and services in smart homes (examples include the Gator Tech Smart House [55] and MavHome [56]). The CBR layer, like other AI methods for smart homes, can be integrated into the pervasive computing architecture, to process a comparatively high-level information stream.

Existing projects address many component issues for deriving a number of types of information which might be useful for a CBR system to generate indices for retrieval. For example, the Pfinder project studies tracking individuals in a smart room [57], and the Sociometer project studies how to track people's interaction with others [58], potentially providing a basis for generating more abstract indices.

To facilitate humans interactively providing the system with supplementary information (e.g., by a resident simply telling the system that he or she wants to bake a cake), information provided to situation assessment could also be based on human-like input and output modalities such as speech, body postures, eye movements and other non-verbal gestures. All such interactions must be able to feed into the CBR system, and their interpretation may itself require considerable AI processing to provide the information used in indexing. For example, the Trips system [59], a spoken-dialogue computer system for planning, parses human language into practical dialogues that capture what the user meant by an utterance, applies domain-independent problem-solving models, and domain-specific task models and is capable of recognizing user intentions, which could then become part of the context used by CBR retrieval.

### 5.3 Capturing Context and Context-Based Indexing

In order to access the right cases, cases must be organized; the *indexing problem* is the problem of assuring that a case is accessed whenever appropriate [16]. The CBR system's situation assessment process must be able to generate suitable indices. A number of general indexing vocabularies have been developed for tasks such as indexing explanations of anomalies [13], and could be exploited in the smart homes setting. However, for smart homes, contextual factors will play a key role in indexing as well, and the range of potential information is extensive. For example, Dey proposes that "Context is any information that can be used to characterize the situation of an entity. An entity is a person, place, or object that is considered relevant to the interaction between a user and an application, including the user and applications themselves" [60]. Capturing context for reasoning in smart environments is challenging because of the need to determine relevant classes of features and how they can be recognized based on numerous heterogeneous sources. If sensors only provide on/off device information, the informativeness of each individual sensor's information may be fairly small—determining useful information may depend on the context of other sensor readings and sensor changes over time.

It is difficult to determine in advance which aspects of a situation are important to include in context-based indices, because feature relevance will change from situation to situation. However, general vocabularies can be developed to capture fundamental properties. For example, Gross and Specht [61] propose including dimensions for *identity* (information about user's short and long term needs, interests, preferences, knowledge, etc.) as also discussed in Section 4.2, *location*, *time* (while tracking time is simple, using temporal information for planning and decision-making poses several challenges; see the discussion of temporal reasoning in smart homes in this volume [26], and *environment and activity*, describing the artifacts and the physical location of the current situation. Awareness of the environment beyond the house could be relevant to issue recommendations or alerts. For example, during a rainy day a smart home could remind the resident to carry an umbrella. Efforts to develop suitable vocabularies can draw on considerable active research on context modeling (for a sampling, see [62]).

A smart home system makes predictions from its observations based on current system knowledge and the current state of the environment. A discrepancy between a prediction and the actual outcome may suggest the need for updates to system knowledge, to learn from a new situation. A difficult problem for both prediction and learning is that effects may depend on hidden context, causing smart home systems to make incorrect recommendations or to generate false alerts due to incomplete information. Thus an important goal for smart home systems is to detect context changes without being explicitly informed about them and to quickly recover from context changes, adjusting their hypotheses to fit the new context. Approaches to this problem as it relates to concept learning may also be valuable for smart home systems [63].

The situation assessment and indexing problems are open-ended. Developing vocabularies for describing fairly specific features, such as patient vital signs, will be straightforward. Developing principled methods to derive highly abstract features is still an open challenge for long-term research (e.g., to recognize that an occupant is having a bad day).

## 6    Some Research and Practical Issues for Realizing the Vision

While CBR provides an appealing methodology for smart homes, many specific issues must be addressed to fully realize its promise. This section highlights a few which may be especially salient for the smart homes domain.

*Case Engineering:* In broad outline, CBR simplifies knowledge acquisition by alleviating the need to develop rules (for a rule-based system) or to acquire extensive training data (e.g., for neural network approaches). However, CBR requires its own knowledge sources, such as indexing and similarity knowledge and knowledge to adapt cases to fit new needs. While it may be possible to develop, e.g., standardized types of indices for the smart homes domain (following the example of standardized indexing vocabularies of [12, 13, 14]), enabling multiple projects to leverage this research, a major effort would be required to develop indices or similarity criteria covering a wide range of scenarios.

*Integrating similarity judgments with additional information sources:* In the basic CBR model, each problem is addressed by identifying the most similar case and adapting its solution to the new situation. However, in problem detection tasks, it may not be desirable to predict problems whenever the most similar case was a problem case, due to the risk of false alarms. Addressing this issue may require combining case-based prediction with other reasoning methods. For example, CBR could provide candidate predictions which could then be further scrutinized by Bayesian methods (e.g., based on patient history, probabilities of particular events, etc.) as part of the case evaluation process.

*Case adaptation:* Automated case adaptation has long been recognized as a key challenge for case-based reasoning [17, 64, 65]. Although many methods exist, building on methods such as rule-based reasoning or constraints (see [19] for a recent survey), it can still be difficult to capture the needed case adaptation knowledge. A number of systems have explored interactive adaptation methods (e.g., [66]), including methods in which system adaptation is augmented by the user as needed (e.g., [67]). With appropriate interfaces, such methods might enable competent residents and care-givers to guide the application of prior cases as needed, in conjunction with methods to allow traces of their adaptations to themselves be captured and reused by CBR, as in (e.g., [68]).

*Case-base maintenance:* As CBR systems have received extended use, maintenance of CBR systems has become an active CBR research area (e.g., [69]). In smart homes, changes in the home and residents (e.g., during the course of a terminal disease) would require methods to address both the volume of new cases and the changing circumstances which might render old cases or similarity functions obsolete [18, 70].

*Event mining for case generation:* The monitoring processes of smart homes will provide a rich stream of information to mine for cases. However, distilling and segmenting these into meaningful cases—both indices and responses—may be difficult to automate. Some CBR research has considered mining cases from sources such as database records (e.g., [71]) and has considered issues in capturing and controlling continuous phenomena through CBR [72]. However, this area remains largely unexplored.

*Exploiting multiple case sources:* As already mentioned, CBR systems for smart homes must function even during early use, when little experience is available. If the smart home system begins with an initial set of standard schemas, those schemas will provide a basis for initial processing, but will not reflect special individual needs.

An interesting alternative is case-based experience sharing. Many opportunities to support human decision making can come from other people's experiences. When an individual encounters a situation that is novel to him or her, but potentially successful solutions can be collected from the experiences of other individuals, CBR can empower the individual with the ability to make more informed decisions. Collective case memories provide the knowledge that a single individual may lack.

Approaches such as *multi-case-base reasoning* (MCBR) [73] are designed to address gaps in a single reasoner's case base by drawing on external case bases and adapting externally provided cases to reflect differences in task and user characteristics. Applying

MCBR requires developing adaptation methods not only for particular tasks, but also for differences in user characteristics. In the smart homes domain, MCBR approaches might also need to address instances of cases which simply conflict, by choosing between a range of alternatives for handling a particular situation.

It may also require addressing potential differences in the vocabularies in which cases are captured. Otherwise, cases and events may fail to match simply due to differences in terminology between case descriptions and event descriptions. For example, an event *stove-turned-on* cannot trigger the selection of a case describing the same event as *range-turned-on*. This vocabulary issue is well known in AI, and can be overcome by using ontologies [74] to provide standardized representations (e.g., an ontology could simply specify that *stove-turned-on* and *range-turned-on* are equivalent). In addition, ontologies may capture the information required to facilitate further reasoning about cases or to enable their adaptation to new circumstances.

*Internal system confidence:* The smart homes domain has a marked difference from many CBR applications. Many CBR systems are advisory to an expert, who makes the final decisions; autonomous systems making judgments about health and safety questions must address substantial risk issues. Recent research examines how CBR systems can assign confidence levels to their solutions [75]. However, this is only a first step towards assuring the needed system reliability.

*Trust:* Related to internal confidence is external trust in the quality of system decisions. Regardless of the objective performance of a CBR system, its practical use depends on those with authority over the smart home having sufficient trust to place certain tasks under system control. As mentioned previously, presentation of cases may itself constitute a useful form of explanation, helping to build user trust in a recommendation. Current CBR research is augmenting this type of explanation with new methods (see [25] for a collection of this work). Special challenges for building trust may arise if CBR systems are fielded with a limited set of cases, to be augmented as needed in response to failures. In that case, a certain level of failure will be expected during the learning process.

*Privacy, security, and control:* For smart home technology to gain wide acceptance, issues of privacy, security, and control are of great importance. Occupants must feel in control of the information collected—they must be assured that their privacy is protected, that information is secure from illegal access, and that it is shared and disseminated only to appropriate parties, for the occupants benefit. For example, for eldercare, any abnormalities in a person's behavior that may indicate a serious change in health or well being may need to be shared with relatives and caretakers, while daily routines and more personal choices need to be private. Thus, the smart home environment must provide a flexible security system to adapt to the privacy and security needs of its residents. One strategy for alleviating privacy issues as cases are shared might be to aggregate cases from a number of users before distribution [76].

In agent-based systems, issues of privacy and security control have been addressed by the use of *policies* [77, 78]. These may restrict what agents can do, and may determine what they must do, allowing system developers to specify a "legal" framework within which agents operate. Applying a CBR approach to control privacy and security has the advantage of not requiring a full "legal" framework to fully function. For example, an initial case base may include the most important restrictions and obligations that the system must follow for privacy and security protection. Subsequently, the CBR system may acquire additional cases derived from interactions with residents that model exceptions to an initially more restrictive and generic framework. However, the use of such cases raises additional issues—for example, security of case sources and reliability of case selection procedures.

# 7   Conclusion

The previous sections have discussed three main areas in which the use of case-based reasoning may provide benefits for smart homes: supporting personalization, supporting interactive adjustment of the system by the user, and facilitating customization and knowledge acquisition by the developer. The connections of CBR to human reasoning make cases a promising way to communicate knowledge and to explain system actions, potentially increasing trust. This is important because the success of smart homes will rest not only on their ability to fulfill human needs, but on the willingness of residents or caregivers to entrust themselves or their charges to the home's care.

Case-based methods promise to be applicable to many different processes within smart homes, and case-based methods can be combined with other approaches to exploit their strengths and capture their results for efficient reuse. Likewise, case-based smart home installations may be designed to share experiences with other smart homes, to assure their competence not only for common cases, but for rarely-occurring emergencies. Thus smart homes offer a rich potential area for the application of CBR.

# References

1. Craik, F.I.M., Salthouse, T.A.: The Handbook of Aging and Cognition, 2nd Ed. Lawrence Erlbaum, Mahwah, NJ (2000)
2. Mann, C.W., Helal, S.: Pervasive computing research on aging, disability and independence. In: Proceedings of the 2004 International Symposium on Applications and the Internet Workshops (SAINTW'04), Tokyo, Japan, IEEE Computer Society (2004) 244–248
3. Mynatt, E., Essa, I., Rogers, W.: Increasing the opportunities for aging-in-place. In: Proceedings of the ACM Conference on Universal Usability, Arlington, VA, USA, ACM (2000) 65–71
4. Pollack, M.: Intelligent technology for an aging population: The use of AI to assist elders with cognitive impairment. AI Magazine **26**(2) (2005) 9–24
5. Augusto, J., Nugent, C.: Smart homes can be smarter. In Augusto, J., Nugent, C., eds.: Designing Smart Homes: The Role of Artificial Intelligence. Springer, Berlin (2006)
6. Kolodner, J.: From natural language understanding to case-based reasoning and beyond: A perspective on the cognitive model that ties it all together. In Schank, R., Langer, E., eds.: Beliefs, Reasoning, and Decision Making: Psycho-Logic in Honor of Bob Abelson. Lawrence Erlbaum, Hillsdale, NJ (1994) 55–110
7. Leake, D.: Cognition as case-based reasoning. In Bechtel, W., Graham, G., eds.: A Companion to Cognitive Science. Blackwell, Oxford (1998) 465–476

8. Cunningham, P., Doyle, D., Loughrey, J.: An evaluation of the usefulness of case-based explanation. In: Case-Based Reasoning Research and Development: Proceedings of the Fifth International Conference on Case-Based Reasoning, ICCBR-03, Berlin, Springer-Verlag (2003) 122–130

9. Watson, I.: Case-based reasoning is a methodology not a technology. Knowledge-Based Systems 12(303-308) (1996)

10. Schank, R.: Dynamic Memory: A Theory of Learning in Computers and People. Cambridge University Press, Cambridge, England (1982)

11. Schank, R., Leake, D.: Natural language understanding: Models of Roger Schank and his students. In: Encyclopedia of Cognitive Science. Nature Publishing Group, London (2002) 189–195

12. Domeshek, E.: Do the Right Things: A Component Theory for Indexing Stories as Social Advice. PhD thesis, The Institute for the Learning Sciences, Northwestern University (1992)

13. Leake, D.: Evaluating Explanations: A Content Theory. Lawrence Erlbaum, Hillsdale, NJ (1992)

14. Schank, R., Osgood, R., Brand, M., Burke, R., Domeshek, E., Edelson, D., Ferguson, W., Freed, M., Jona, M., Krulwich, B., Ohmayo, E., Pryor, L.: A content theory of memory indexing. Technical Report 1, Institute for the Learning Sciences, Northwestern University (1990)

15. Aamodt, A., Plaza, E.: Case-based reasoning: Foundational issues, methodological variations, and system approaches. AI Communications 7(1) (1994) 39–52 http://www.iiia.csic.es/People/enric/AICom.pdf.

16. Kolodner, J., Leake, D.: A tutorial introduction to case-based reasoning. In Leake, D., ed.: Case-Based Reasoning: Experiences, Lessons, and Future Directions. AAAI Press, Menlo Park, CA (1996) 31–65

17. Leake, D.: CBR in context: The present and future. In Leake, D., ed.: Case-Based Reasoning: Experiences, Lessons, and Future Directions. AAAI Press, Menlo Park, CA (1996) 3–30 http://www.cs.indiana.edu/ leake/papers/a-96-01.html.

18. Leake, D., Wilson, D.: When experience is wrong: Examining CBR for changing tasks and environments. In: Proceedings of the Third International Conference on Case-Based Reasoning, Berlin, Springer Verlag (1999) 218–232

19. Mantaras, R., McSherry, D., Bridge, D., Leake, D., Smyth, B., Craw, S., Faltings, B., Maher, M., Cox, M., Forbus, K., Keane, M., Aamodt, A., Watson, I.: Retrieval, reuse, revise, and retention in CBR. Knowledge based systems (2006) In press.

20. Smyth, B., Keane, M.: Adaptation-guided retrieval: Questioning the similarity assumption in reasoning. Artificial Intelligence 102(2) (1998) 249–293

21. Leake, D., Kinley, A., Wilson, D.: Linking adaptation and similarity learning. In: Proceedings of the Eighteenth Annual Conference of the Cognitive Science Society, Mahwah, NJ, Lawrence Erlbaum (1996) 591–596

22. Wiratunga, N., Craw, S., Taylor, B., Davis, G.: Case-based reasoning for matching SMART-HOUSE technology to people's needs. Knowledge based systems 17 (2004) 139–146

23. Leake, D.: Focusing construction and selection of abductive hypotheses. In: Proceedings of the Eleventh International Joint Conference on Artificial Intelligence, San Francisco, Morgan Kaufmann (1993) 24–29

24. Kolodner, J.: Improving human decision making through case-based decision aiding. AI Magazine 12(2) (1991) 52–68

25. Leake, D., McSherry, D.: Explanation in Case-Based Reasoning. Kluwer (2005) Special issue of *Artificial Intelligence Review*, In press.

26. Patterson, D., Rooney, N., Galushka, M.: Learning by data mining. In Augusto, J., Nugent, C., eds.: Designing Smart Homes: The Role of Artificial Intelligence. Springer, Berlin (2006)

27. Dean, T., Boddy, M.: An analysis of time-dependent planning. In: Proceedings of the seventh national conference on artificial intelligence, San Mateo, CA, Morgan Kaufmann (1988) 49–54

28. Riesbeck, C.: What next? The future of CBR in postmodern AI. In Leake, D., ed.: Case-Based Reasoning: Experiences, Lessons, and Future Directions. AAAI Press, Menlo Park, CA (1996) 371–388

29. Leake, D.: Personalized CBR: Challenges and illustrations. In: ECCBR: Workshop on Case Based Reasoning and Personalization, Aberdeen, Scotland (2002)

30. Blanzieri, E.: A cognitive framework for personalization of the CBR cycle. In: ECCBR Workshop on Case Based Reasoning and Personalization, Aberdeen, Scotland (2002)

31. Mozer, M.: Lessons from an adaptive house. In Cook, D., Das, R., eds.: Smart environments: Technologies, protocols, and applications. Wiley, Hoboken, NJ (2005) 273–294

32. Musliner, D., Pell, B., eds.: Agents with Adjustable Autonomy. AAAI Press, Menlo Park, CA (1999) Technical Report SS-99-06.

33. Cassell, J.: Embodied conversational agents. AI Magazine 22(4) (2001) 67–83

34. Weiser, M.: The computer for the 21st century. Scientific American 265(3) (1991) 94–104

35. Streitz, N., Röcker, C., Prante, T., van Alphen, D., Stenzel, R., Magerkurth, C.: Designing smart artifacts for smart environments. Computer 38(3) (2005)

36. Buchanan, B., Shortliffe, E.: Rule-Based Expert Systems: The MYCIN Experiments of the Stanford Heuristic Programming Project. Addison-Wesley, Reading, MA (1984)

37. Ashley, K., Rissland, E.: Compare and contrast, a test of expertise. In: Proceedings of the Sixth Annual National Conference on Artificial Intelligence, San Mateo, CA, AAAI, Morgan Kaufmann (1987) 273–284

38. Massie, S., Craw, S., Wiratunga, N.: A visualisation tool to explain case-base reasoning solutions for tablet formulation. In: Proceedings of the 24th SGAI International Conference on Innovative Techniques and Applications of Artificial Intelligence, Berlin, Springer-Verlag (2004)

39. Rhodes, B., Starner, T.: The remembrance agent: A continuously running automated information retrieval system. In: Proceedings of The First International Conference on The Practical Application of Intelligent Agents and Multi Agent Technology (PAAM '96), London, UK (1996) 487–495

40. Budzik, J., Hammond, K.: Watson: Anticipating and contextualizing information needs. In: 62nd Annual Meeting of the American Society for Information Science, Medford, NJ (1999)

41. Rhodes, B.J.: Margin notes: Building a contextually aware associative memory. In: The Proceedings of the International Conference on Intelligent User Interfaces (IUI '00). (2000)

42. Budzik, J., Hammond, K., Birnbaum, L.: Information access in context. Knowledge based systems 14(1–2) (2001) 37–53

43. Burke, R., Kass, A.: Retrieving stories for case-based teaching. In Leake, D., ed.: Case-Based Reasoning: Experiences, Lessons, and Future Directions. AAAI Press, Menlo Park, CA (1996) 93–109

44. Pollack, M.E., Brown, L., Colbry, D., McCarthy, C.E., Orosz, C., Peintner, B., Ramakrishnan, S., Tsamardinos, I.: Autominder: An intelligent cognitive orthotic system for people with memory impairment. Robotics and Autonomous Systems 44(3-4) (2003) 273–282

45. LoPresti, E.F., Mihailidis, A., Kirsch, N.: Assistive technology for cognitive rehabilitation: State of the art. Neuropsychological Rehabilitation 14(1-2) (2004) 5–39

46. Aha, D., Munoz, H.: Interactive Case-Based Reasoning. Volume 14. Kluwer (2001) Special issue of *Applied Intelligence*.

47. Novak, J., Gowin, D.: Learning How to Learn. Cambridge University Press, New York (1984)

48. Cañas, A., Leake, D., Wilson, D.: Managing, mapping, and manipulating conceptual knowledge. In: Proceedings of the AAAI-99 Workshop on Exploring Synergies of Knowledge Management and Case-Based Reasoning, Menlo Park, AAAI Press (1999) 10–14
49. Leake, D., Wilson, D.: A case-based framework for interactive capture and reuse of design knowledge. Applied Intelligence **14** (2001) 77–94
50. Kolodner, J.: Case-Based Reasoning. Morgan Kaufmann, San Mateo, CA (1993)
51. Watson, I.: Applying Case-Based Reasoning: Techniques for Enterprise Systems. Morgan Kaufmann, San Mateo, CA (1997)
52. Simpson, R., Schreckenghost, D., LoPresti, E.F., Kirsch, N.: Plans and planning in smart homes. In Augusto, J., Nugent, C., eds.: Designing Smart Homes: The Role of Artificial Intelligence. Springer, Berlin (2006)
53. Dey, A., Abowd, G., Salber, D.: A context-based infrastructure for smart environments. In: Proceedings of the 1st International Workshop on Managing Interactions in Smart Environments (MANSE '99). (1999) 114–128
54. Meyer, S., Rakotonirainy, A.: A survey of research on context-aware homes. In: CRPITS '03: Proceedings of the Australasian information security workshop conference on ACSW frontiers 2003, Darlinghurst, Australia, Australian Computer Society (2003) 159–168
55. Helal, S., Mann, W., El-Zabadani, H., King, J., Kaddoura, Y., Jansen, E.: The gator tech smart house: A programmable pervasive space. Computer **38**(3) (2005)
56. Cook, D.J., Youngblood, M., Heierman, E.O., Gopalratnam, K., Rao, S., Litvin, A., Khawaja, F.: Mavhome: An agent-based smart home. In: Proceedings of the IEEE International Conference on Pervasive Computing and Communications, IEEE Computer (2000) 521–524
57. Pentland, A.: Smart rooms. Scientific American **274**(4) (1996) 68–76
58. Choudhury, T., Pentland, A.: Sensing and modeling human networks using the sociometer. In: Wearable Computers (ISWC 2003), IEEE Press (2003) 216–222
59. Allen, J.F., Byron, D.K., Dzikovska, M., Fergusion, G., Galescu, L., Stent, A.: Toward conversational human-computer interaction. AI Magazine **22**(4) (2001) 27–37
60. Dey, A.: Understanding and using context. Personal Ubiquitous Computing **5**(1) (2001) 4–7
61. Gross, T., Specht, M.: Awareness in context-aware information systems. In: Proceedings of Mensch & Computer, Wiesbaden, Teubner Verlag (2001) 221–232
62. Roth-Berghofer, T., Schulz, S., Leake, D., eds.: Modelling and retrieval of context: Second International Workshop, MRC 2005. Springer Verlag (2006)
63. Widmer, G., Kubat, M.: Learning in the presence of concept drift and hidden contexts. Machine Learning **23**(1) (1996) 69–101
64. Barletta, R.: A hybrid indexing and retrieval strategy for advisory CBR systems built with ReMind. In: Proceedings of the Second European Workshop on Case-Based Reasoning, Chantilly, France (1994) 49–58
65. Mark, W., Simoudis, E., Hinkle, D.: Case-based reasoning: Expectations and results. In Leake, D., ed.: Case-Based Reasoning: Experiences, Lessons, and Future Directions. AAAI Press, Menlo Park, CA (1996) 269–294
66. Smith, I., Lottaz, C., Faltings, B.: Spatial composition using cases: IDIOM. In: Proceedings of First International Conference on Case-Based Reasoning, Berlin, Springer Verlag (1995) 88–97
67. Gervasio, M., Iba, W., Langley, P., Sage, S.: Interactive adaptation for crisis response. In: Proceedings of the AIPS-98 Workshop on Interactive and Collborative Planning. (1998)
68. Leake, D., Kinley, A., Wilson, D.: Learning to improve case adaptation by introspective reasoning and CBR. In: Proceedings of the First International Conference on Case-Based Reasoning, Berlin, Springer Verlag (1995) 229–240
69. Leake, D., Smyth, B., Wilson, D., Yang, Q., eds.: Maintaining Case-Based Reasoning Systems. Blackwell (2001) Special issue of *Computational Intelligence*, 17(2), 2001.

70. Zhang, Z., Yang, Q.: Towards lifetime maintenance of case base indexes for continual case based reasoning. In: Proceedings of the 1998 International Conference on AI Methodologies, Systems and Applications (AIMSA-98), Berlin, Springer Verlag (1998) 489–500
71. Yang, Q., Cheng, S.: Case mining from large databases. In: Case-Based Reasoning Research and Development: Proceedings of the Fifth International Conference on Case-Based Reasoning, ICCBR-03, Berlin, Springer-Verlag (2003) 691–702
72. Ram, A., Santamaria, J.: Continuous case-based reasoning. In: Proceedings of the AAAI-93 Workshop on Case-Based Reasoning, Washington, DC, AAAI (1993) 86–93 AAAI Press technical report WS-93-01.
73. Leake, D., Sooriamurthi, R.: Case dispatching versus case-base merging: When MCBR matters. International Journal of Artificial Intelligence Tools 13(1) (2004) 237 254
74. Gruber, T.R.: A translation approach to portable ontologies. Knowledge Acquisition 5(2) (1993) 199–220
75. Cheetham, W., Price, J.: Measures of solution accuracy in case-based reasoning systems. eccbr 2004. In Funk, P., González, P., eds.: ECCBR-2004: Advances in Case-Based Reasoning, Berlin, Springer Verlag (2004) 106–118
76. Smyth, B., Balfe, E., Freyne, J., Briggs, P., Coyle, M., Boydell, O.: Exploiting query repetition and regularity in an adaptive community-based web search engine. User Modeling and User-Adapted Interaction 14 (2005) 383–423
77. Schreckenghost, D., Martin, C., Thronesbery, C.: Specifying organizational policies and individual preferences for human-software interaction. In: Proceedings of AAAI Fall Symposium on Etiquette for Human Computer Work, Technical Report FS-02-02, North Falmouth, Massachusetts, AAAI (2002) 32–39
78. Barett, R.: People and policies: Transforming the human-computer partnership. In: Proceedings of the 5th IEEE International Workshop on Policies for Distributed Systems and Networks (POLICY 2004), Yorktown Heights, NY, IEEE Computer Society (2004) 111–116

# Application of Decision Trees to Smart Homes

Vlado Stankovski and Jernej Trnkoczy

Department of Construction Informatics, Faculty of Civil and Geodetic Engineering,
University of Ljubljana, Jamova 2, SI-1000, Slovenia
Vlado.Stankovski@fgg.uni-lj.si
http://www.fgg.uni-lj.si

**Abstract.** This chapter aims to illustrate a possible way of using decision trees to make Smart Homes smarter. Decision trees are popular modelling technique, and the corresponding models are both predictive and descriptive. We formulate the modelling problem by defining the generic question "Is the undergoing activity or event in the Smart Home usual?" Then we explain how it is possible to gather appropriate data from the sensors and pre-process these data to form appropriate input for a decision tree algorithm. We further explain the mainstream approaches in decision trees algorithms rather then analysing them in detail, and we give short overview of available software. Finally, we explain some measures for quantitative and qualitative evaluation of the induced decision tree models (e.g. expert opinion, cross-validation, statistical tests etc.).

## 1 Introduction

Decision trees, similarly to other approaches in Artificial Intelligence, may be considered as tools for classifying instances in groups [1]. They provide an effective structure within which it is possible to define attributes of an instance. Then it is possible to investigate the possible outcomes when these attributes are assigned specific values. Decision trees may be also helpful in forming a balanced picture of the positive and negative outcomes associated with possible courses of action.

When a piece of software needs to make a decision automatically, based on several factors (attributes), a decision tree could help identify which factors to consider and how each factor has historically been associated with different outcomes of the decision. It is generally considered that decision trees provide an effective method of decision making because they:

- Provide a framework to quantify the values of outcomes and the probabilities of achieving them.
- Clearly describe the problem so that all possible outcomes can be investigated.
- Allow humans to analyze the possible consequences of a decision.

Decision trees are considered helpful when trying to make the best decisions on the basis of existing information and best guesses.

Could decision trees be also helpful to create an environment, which is capable to react 'intelligently' by anticipating, predicting and taking decisions with signs of autonomy? The answer will be provided by investigating the applicability of decision trees to Smart Homes.

J.C. Augusto and C.D. Nugent (Eds.): Designing Smart Homes, LNAI 4008, pp. 132–145, 2006.
© Springer-Verlag Berlin Heidelberg 2006

In our Smart Home case study, we collect data describing the whereabouts of the person, her/his interaction with appliances, and the duration of specific events. A decision tree algorithm is then used to create a model as either a graphical tree or a set of text rules that can define the 'normal' setting leading to a particular event in the Smart Home. Any event occuring outside the normal setting should lead to various degrees of awareness/alarm/alert in the system or to some sort of automatic behaviour.

## 1.1 Decision Trees as a Modelling Technique

A decision tree is a model which is developed through a learning process, based on data collected for the domain of investigation. The model is called a decision tree because it is presented in the form of a tree structure (see Figure 1.). Obviously, decision tree is both predictive and descriptive model.

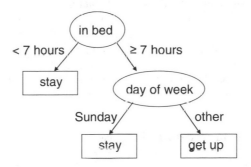

**Fig. 1.** Tree structure of a decision tree model

The visual presentation makes the decision tree model easy to understand, so, it is suitable for human inspection as well as for making automated decisions. Consequently, the decision tree approach is frequently used data mining technique. Decision trees are commonly used for classification (predicting what group an instance belongs to), but can also be used for regression (predicting a specific real value).

The outcome of a decision tree algorithm is a decision tree model, or shortly decision tree. The training process that creates the decision tree is called induction. Induction requires a certain number of passes through the training dataset. This makes the algorithm less efficient than Naive-Bayes algorithms [2], which require only one pass, but significantly more efficient than neural networks, which typically require a large number of passes through the learning set of examples [3]. More precisely, the number of passes required to build a decision tree is no more than the number of levels in the tree.

The number of levels in the decision tree is not predetermined or limited. The complexity of the tree is measured by the depth and breadth of the tree, and it generally increases with the number of independent variables (also called attributes) [3].

A decision tree can be viewed as an arrangement of tests [4]. The first test is prescribed at the root of the tree, the next test is prescribed at the first lower level, and so on until a leaf of the tree is reached. Decision trees classify instances by sorting them beginning from the root node to some leaf node. The leaf provides the classification of the instance. Each node in the tree specifies a test of some attribute of the instance, and each branch descending from that node corresponds to one of the possible values for this attribute.

An instance is classified by starting at the root node of the decision tree, testing the attribute specified by this node, then moving down the tree branch corresponding to the value of the attribute. This process is then repeated at the node on this branch and so on until a leaf node is reached. A nonleaf node of the tree could have more than two branches. This usually depends on the algorithm used and on the set of values which are allowed for the specific attribute that is tested.

The result of the induction process (i.e. the decision tree model) can be easily visualized and interpreted by human experts (see Figure 1). This is particularly important in the healthcare domain, where rationale for the automatic response is usually expected. Visual inspection of the induced model(s) may reveal inconsistencies with previous experience and/or exisiting knowledge.

Decision trees have been applied mostly to data that is void of any explicit notion of time. This covers many application areas where the data is about populations of the same entities, but may not always be suitable for cases where there is a temporal relation among the data. Temporal decision trees are particularly interesting in the area of Smart Homes, when we are gathering data about a single system over time. A recent research report shows that it could be possible to modify existing decision tree algorithms to make time explicit and generate temporal rules and decision trees [5].

## 2  Research Agenda in Smart Homes

Research in Smart Homes is actually a part of a broader area of research called Ambient Intelligence. This is one of the hottest buzzwords in multiple research disciplines at the moment. See for example the public deliverables of the ongoing project AMIGO: Ambient intelligence for the networked home environment [6]. The vision of the AMIGO project is to calmly and unobtrusively support human-to-human or human-to-information interaction without having to deal with typical user interfaces. The vision is that the computer as we know it, will disappear into the environment, still being proactive, sensing how it could serve us. However, for a Smart Home System to effectively support us in our home environments, we must take great care to build trusted platforms that protect our intimate data, and still allow easy access to it. Also, people might be hesitant to accept services that an intelligent ambient home environment offers, if issues of control or privacy are involved [6].

The partners in the AMIGO project consider use-cases from three general domains:

- Home Care and Safety
    - o Voice command based home, Software component based household appliances domotic controller, A Multimedia Telemedicine Home Platform
- Home Information and Entertainment
    - o Interactive Background Portal, EasyLiving: Technologies for Intelligent Environments, Gemini: Accumulating Context for Play Applications, Context Aware Information Retrieval in the Home, Context Aware Multimedia Browsing
- Extended Home Environments
    - o Design Meeting, Tele Worker, Mirror Space and other application areas.

The technical requirements are prompting a wide range of new research and development problems. The work in progress may be classified in the following areas:

- Context collection, aggregation, and prediction
- Adaptive methodologies
- User modelling and profiling
- Awareness and notification
- Content provision, selection and retrieval
- User interfaces
- Security and privacy

Decision trees modelling techniques may prove applicable in few of the above mentioned research areas. This chapter focuses on context aware homes rather than context aware appliances. The decision trees example that we follow in this chapter would generally fit in the context collection, aggregation, and prediction research area.

In order to be successful in the modelling process, we need to carefully follow some general methodology, which is suitable for the decision trees approach, e.g. [9], [10]. The propsed methodology has several distinctive phases: *'Smart Homes' use case problem formulation, data gathering , data pre-processing, hypotheses generation by induction of decision trees*, and *quantitative and qualitative evaluation*. The proposed methodology is illustrated in detail in the following sections.

## 3  Problem Formulation and Data Gathering from the Sensors

Let us assume that the subject of our investigation, a person living in a Smart Home, has currently entered the bedroom and is about to get in bed. The question is whether this is a 'common' and 'normal' activity? After lying in bed for 3.5 hours, our subject gets up and goes to the kitchen. We are interested to find out if s/he stayed in bed for 'too long'?

Actually, we would like our computer system to constantly ask questions whether the activities or events that we explicitly measure from the sensoring system (e.g. in bed for 3 hours, cooker on for 4 hours etc.) are normal in given circumstances (in relation to other measured attributes describing the present state of the Smart Home). In case the undergoing activity is not normal then the system has to raise some level of alarm or initiate automatic activity. For instance, if the person turned on the cooker before going to bed and he stayed in bed for more than 2 hours time, s/he could be automatically alarmed and if this is not successful then the cooker should be automatically switched off.

In order to formulate our problem more precisely we assume that data from the sensors are automatically collected and stored in a local information system. These data are then pre-processed to get information about the (i) whereabouts of the person (ii) her/his interaction with appliances and (iii) the duration of events.

The decision trees approach requires that the attributes (describing the state of the Smart Home) have finite value sets. For example, the attribute "cooker" can get a finite number of values (e.g. on for 30 minutes, on for 40 minutes, and on for more than 50 minutes). Some activities which are longer than 24 hours should clearly be handled as exceptions in the system. E.g. the light in the living room remains on for more than 24 hours, or the cooker is on for more than 24 hours or the person remains in bed for more than 24 hours. For practical reasons, it might also prove helpful to include some attributes such as the 'day of week' in the learning process. In such case, the system should be able to induce that an alarm should not be raised, if the cooker is turned on for more than 3 hours on Saturday, because, this is the usual time when the person is cooking a cake for a Sunday party.

Let us now consider the following example: When the person entered the kitchen, he turned the light on, he stayed there for 30 minutes and then left the kitchen forgetting to turn the light off. So, the light remains on for more than 2 hours.

This could be mapped to the following sequence of events:

```
at living on
at living off
at reception on
at reception off
at kitchen on
Kitchen light on
cooker on
at kitchen off
at reception on
at reception off
at bedroom on
inbed on
...
```

The current state would correspond to the following attribute-value pairs:

| Attribute | Value |
|-----------|-------|
| at living on | false |
| at reception on | false |
| at kitchen on | false |
| kitchen light on | true for 2 hours |
| cooker on | true for 2 hours |
| at reception on | false |
| at bedroom on | true for 1.5 hours |
| inbed on | true for 1.5 hours |

Following is the new state in two hours time:

| Attribute | Value |
|-----------|-------|
| at living on | false |
| at reception on | false |
| at kitchen on | false |
| kitchen light on | true for 4 hours |
| cooker on | true for 4 hours |
| at reception on | false |
| at bedroom on | true for 3.5 hours |
| inbed on | true for 3.5 hours |

The system should obviously raise an exception, as the cooker is on for 4 hours, and this is not normal (for the particular user!). Additional useful information could be encompassed by introducing the 'time from end of event' concept. So, instead of noting that the lights in the living room are off, we also note that they are off for 4 hours already. For simplicity, we use only real values here. So, the number "2" corresponds to the following definition "the event is taking place already for 2 hours". The number "-2" means that "the event/action ended before 2 hours". Consider the following table, which forms a complete learning example:

| Attribute | Value |
|---|---|
| at living on | - 4<br>(meaning: false, already for 4 hours) |
| at reception on | - 4 |
| at kitchen on | - 4 |
| kitchen light on | 4<br>(meaning: true, already for 4 hours) |
| cooker on | 4 |
| at reception on | - 3.5 |
| at bedroom on | 3.5 |
| inbed on | 3.5 |

Let us now reconsider the the prediction problem that we posed in the beginning of this section. For someone it would be logical to ask if it is normal that the person is in bed for 3.5 hours, and for another person, it would be more logical thing to ask, if it is normal that the cooker is on for more than 4 hours? For a third person it would seem strange that the lights in the living room have not been on for more than 4 hours. So, all of these undergoing actions or expired events could be normal or problematic! That is why we have to reformulate the prediction problem by asking a more generic question: *"When do the specific events expire or end?"*

Decision trees could help us analyze whether certain actions are happening too long and what is the usual duration of the events, given the specific circumstances.

This could be based on the assumption that all events that usually happen in the Smart Home may be considered as 'normal events'. So, the training data set describes large amount of 'normal events'. The induced decision tree(s) will therefore describe the normal state of the Smart Home. Each new event in the Smart Home may be analyzed by inspecting the corresponding decision tree. The decision tree may reveal that the event is not usual or typical, and will therefore raise some degree of awareness, alert or alarm.

Let us reiterate at this point that the decision tree approach is generally best suited to problems with the following characteristics:

- Instances are represented by attribute-value pairs.
- Instances are described by a definite set of attributes (e.g., 'at living on'), but their values could also be continuous.
- The typical situation for decision tree learning is when each attribute takes on a smaller number of possible values that are disjoint.
- Modifications of the basic learning algorithm allow for handling real-valued attributes as well (e.g., a real value for the time), and handling temporal data.
- The decision tree has discrete values in the leaves, but it could also have real values in case a modification of the basic algorithm is used.
- By using a decision tree it is possible to classify instances.

- The training data may contain errors. Decision tree learning methods are robust to errors - both errors in classifications of the training examples and errors in the attribute values that describe these examples (i.e. can handle noise data).
- The training data may contain missing attribute values, which is not typical for the Smart Home. Such a situation could arise if a sensor is broken and thus not capable of supplying relevant data.

## 4   Data Pre-processing

Next step of our process is to define a table containing the learning examples i.e. instances (see Table 1). Basically, we define one table as input for the induction process of one decision tree. The table has the form $(x_1, x_2, ..., x_M, y)$, where $x_i$ are the values of M independent variables (that could be discrete or real), which we call attributes and y is the value of the dependent variable, which we also call a class.

**Table 1.** Illustration: pre-processed data ready for the induction process

| $x_1$ (kitchen light on) | $x_2$ (in bed on) | ... | y (cooker on) |
|---|---|---|---|
| 4 | 3 | ... | 3.5 (yes) |
| 4.5 | 3.5 | ... | 4 (yes) |
| ... | ... | ... | ... |
| 5 | 0 | ... | -0.5 (no) |

In our particular case, y is the value of the 'outcome' that we would like to model with a decision tree, e.g. we shall try to model the 'normal' circumstances under which the cooker is on and predict the value of this attribute. For simplicity, we may assume that the dependent variable has only two possible values {yes, no}. Later, we shall see that it is also possible to use the regression trees approach that assumes real values of the dependent variable.

Basically, our aim is to model an arbitrary number of events or actions happening in the Smart Home. Each time, we select one attribute and make it a dependent variable and we consider all remaining variables as independent. Then our aim is to induce many decision tree models – each model defines the values of the selected dependent variable under the given circumstances (i.e. given values of the independent variables). Computer storage and processing power are much cheaper now then they were several years ago, so, there are no technological limitations preventing us from inducing a forest of decision tree models. In other words, we may decide to induce one decision tree model for each particular event monitored by the sensoring system. Even if the number of possible events is in the degree of hundreds this does not pose computational problems. Also, the Smart Home environment may evolve with time, therefore, the decision trees induction process should be frequently repeated to adapt to the changing environment. Thus, an attempt to address all possible scenarios within the Smart Home environment obviously involves increasing complexity.

Later, when we have actually induced a forest of decision tree models based on the learning examples, we may constantly ask the generic question: "Is the undergoing activity/event normal?" The context for answering this question shall be given by the instance vector (i.e. vector of current values of independent variables) and the answer to the question shall be given by the decision tree corresponding to the particular dependent variable that is under investigation (e.g. 'cooker on'). For example, another typical question that the decision tree model should help us answer is: "Which are the usual i.e. normal cases when the cooker is on for more than 3 hours?"

Further complexity in the system may be introduced if two or more presons are living in the same Smart Home environment. Obviously, the automated system will need to accommodate for the widely different needs and habits people may have. This may be achieved by applying techniques for user modelling and profiling [6], and also use these information in the decision trees induction process.

## 5  Induction of Decision Trees

There are a number of algorithms that can be exploited to induce decision tree models from data. Our aim here is not to make an extensive coverage, but to explain a possible (mainstream) approach.

### 5.1  Top-Down Induction of Decision Trees (TDIDT/ID3) Algorithms

One of the most popular algorithms for induction of decision trees is the TDIDT/ID3 algorithm [7]. There is some gowing evidence that this algorithm may be suitable for the application area of Smart Homes [8], however, there is still a lack of comprehensive stud ies in real-world settings. Following is a brief description of the TDIDT/ID3 algorithm.

In order to induce a decision tree, the set of learning examples is divided according to the values of a chosen attribute into subsets and further at lower levels of the tree into smaller subsets until a stopping criterion is reached. In general terms, the stopping criterion holds when the examples in the current subset have sufficiently similar class values. For example, if we follow the Smart Home example from the previous section, the stopping criterion could be reached when all learning examples have exactly the same or a predominant value for the 'cooker on' class. Then a leaf is created and the class value at that leaf is defined to be the predominant value of the class of the examples falling in the leaf. In our Smart Home use case we have only two possible values of the class, therefore, the value of the leaf can be either 'yes' or 'no'.

Each node of the decision tree could also be viewed as a hypothesis about the observed data [9], [10] (see Figure 2). Given the specific circumstances that are defined in upper levels of the decision tree, the value of the attribute 'kitchen light on' (specifically 0.2 hours) can be used to split the data set in two subsets. The predicted class value in the left leaf is 'no' and in the right leaf is 'yes'.

The following approach offers a possibility to evaluate the statistical significance of the generated hypothesis. First, the set of all examples is divided into two disjoint (independent) subsets, where each of the subsets has approximately 50% of the examples (training and test sets). The training set (consisting of 35 examples) is used to generate the decision tree, and the test set (also consisting of 35 examples) is used to statistically test the generated hypothesis. For the Smart Homes domain it could be possible to employ different statistical tests such as the Student t-test, one-way

analysis of variance and other tests as appropriate. We tested the statistical significance of the generated hypothesis by using the Student t-test ($p \leq 0,05$). This actually
means that the split into two subsets based on the value of the attribute 'kitchen light
on' is statistically significant.

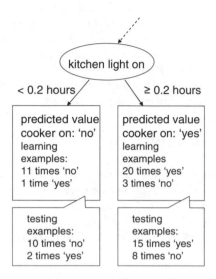

**Fig. 2.** A part of a decision tree induced from 35 examples (training set) and tested on 35
previously not used examples (test set)

It should be noted that it would be a mistake to use the same data for hypothesis
induction as for statistical testing of induced hypotheses, since we need a in independent data set for statistical testing. The point of splitting the available data 50:50 into
the training and the test set, is precisely the independence of these two sets.

ID3 maintains only a single current hypothesis as it searches through the space of
decision trees. However, by determining only a single hypothesis, ID3 loses the capabilities that follow from explicitly representing all consistent hypotheses. For example, it does not have the ability to determine how many alternative decision trees are
consistent with the available training data, or to pose new instance queries that optimally resolve among these competing hypotheses.

ID3, in its pure form, performs no backtracking in its search (it is a so called
greedy algorithm). Once it selects an attribute to test at a particular level in the tree, it
never backtracks to reconsider this choice; it is susceptible to the usual risks of hill-
climbing search without backtracking. ID3 converges to locally optimal solutions that
are not globally optimal. In the case of ID3, a locally optimal solution corresponds to
the decision tree it selects along the single search path it explores. However, this
locally optimal solution may be less desirable than trees that would have been encountered along a different branch of the search.

ID3 uses all training examples at each step in the search to make statistically based
decisions regarding how to refine its current hypothesis. This contrasts with methods
that make decisions incrementally, based on individual training examples. One advantage of using statistical properties of all the examples is that the resulting search is

much less sensitive to errors in individual training examples. ID3 can be easily extended to handle noisy training data by modifying its termination criterion to accept hypotheses that imperfectly fit the training data. However, reduced sensitivity to errors as well as possibility to handle noisy training data may not prove useful for the Smart Homes domain. In the Smart Homes use case (see Section 3) the information collected from the sensors is exact i.e. noisy input from the sensors is not anticipated and at the same time, we would like to achieve greater best fit with the training data.

To recapitulate, ID3 algorithms:

- perform complete search of the hypotheses space.
- search incompletely through the space of all possibilities; initially, the tree has only one leaf-node, then it is developed from simple to complex hypotheses, until its termination condition is met (eg. until it finds a hypothesis fully consistent with the data).
- their inductive bias is based on the ordering of hypotheses by its search strategy (ie. it follows from its search strategy).
- trees that place high information gain attributes close to the root of the decision tree are preferred by the ID3 algorithm over those that do not. Approximate inductive bias of ID3 is that shorter trees are preferred over larger trees.

## 5.2 Pre- and Post-pruning Techniques

Exploring a decision tree model may reveal nodes or subtrees that are undesirable because of overfitting, or the decision tree may contain rules that we might feel are inappropriate. Pruning is a common technique used to make a tree more general. Pruning changes nodes into leafs of the tree, and it deletes the corresponding subtrees. With such algorithms, users will want to experiment to see which pruning rule parameters result in a tree that predicts best on a test dataset. Usually, algorithms that build trees to maximum depth will automatically invoke pruning (pre-pruning). Some software products allow the users to prune the tree interactively.

Given that some pruning is usually a good idea, how does the pruning algorithm determine where to prune the tree? For example, a possible parameter that could be used is the computed difference between the resulting nodes, which may fall below a threshold and is threfore considered insignificant. There are also several other algorithms, but one that some researchers find interesting is to use a control sample with known and verified relationships between the independent and dependent variables [8,9,10,11]. By comparing the performance of each node (as measured by its accuracy) to its subtree, it will be obvious which splits need to be pruned to attain the highest overall accuracy on the control sample.

After generating a tree to maximum depth, it is possible to generate a large number of subtrees in the pruning phase and then automatically compute the accuracy of each on a test dataset. So, we should be able to choose a subtree that contains fewer number of nodes, yet has the highest accuracy. This approach is an effective way to eliminate overfitting with a decision tree.

Pre- and post-pruning techniques are used to generalize the decision tree model, however, in our Smart Homes use case this shall almost certainly reduce the ability of the induced decision tree to detect unusual events happening in the Smart Home.

Depending on the application scenario, it might prove useful to use pruning techniques only to a limited extent and aim at minimizing the prediction error only, which is discussed in the following sub-section.

## 5.3 Quantitative Evaluation: Analysis of Prediction Error

In order to evaluate the accuracy of the induced models, the k-fold cross-validation method can be used. It is possible to choose k=10, 30 or similar, as it is usual in machine learning experiments. This means that the set of all available examples (i.e. instances) is divided into 10 (or 30) disjoint subsets and induction/testing cycle is repeated, say, 10 or 30 times. Each time a different subset is selected as a test set, all the remaining subsets are used for the induction of a decision or regression tree and the induced tree is evaluated on the test set. So, the prediction error is computed 10 (or 30) times. An average of the errors obtained in this process is reported as the final estimate of the prediction error on new data.

## 5.4 Qualitative Evaluation: Understanding the Output

The distinctive output from a decision tree algorithm makes it easy to recognize its descriptive or exploratory value. In an exploratory mode the user is interested in outputs that facilitate insight about relationships between the independent variables and the dependent variable.

One of the inherent benefits of a decision tree model is its ability to be understood by human experts. Graphical presentation of a decision tree model, along with the ability to interactively explore the model, have become standard features supported by many decision tree software vendors. For instance, the popular Weka toolkit includes a decision tree visualizer.

Decision tree output may also be presented as a set of rules, which are concise and, particularly when the tree is large, are often easier to understand. Decision trees have obvious value as both descriptive and predictive models. We have seen that prediction can be done on an instance-by-instance basis by navigating the generated trees. More often, prediction is accomplished by processing multiple new instances through the tree or set of rules automatically and generating an output file with the predicted value or class appended to the record for each instance. Many implementations offer the option of exporting the rules to be used externally or embedded in other applications.

## 5.5 Other Modelling Approaches

Decision trees graphically display the relationships found in data. Certain software products are also able to translate the tree-model to text rules such as `If 'in bed' = -4 and 'kitchen light on' > 1 Then 'cooker on' = yes`. Actually, decision tree algorithms are similar to rule induction algorithms which produce rule sets without a decision tree. Once a decision tree has been constructed, it is a simple matter to convert it into an equivalent set of rules.

Another possibility is to place a regression function in the leaves of the tree instead of the predicted value [10]. In such case, the induced decision tree is called a "regression tree.

There are many modalities of the basic decision trees algorithm, which have been studied in detail elsewhere [1], [4], [5], [7], [11]. In the following sub-section we outline some of the key differences between algorithms for induction of decision trees.

### 5.6 Overview of Available Software

While all decision tree algorithms have basic elements in common, they have some important differences as well. Given the same training data all algorithms will not necessarily produce the same decision tree. The distinguishing features between algorithms include [1]:

- Dependent (Class) Variables: Most decision trees algorithms require that the dependent variable is categorical. An exception to this is the CART algorithm, which directly handles continuous dependent variables.
- Splits: Many algorithms support only binary splits, that is, each parent node can be split into at most two child nodes. Others generate more than two splits and produce a branch for each value of a categorical variable.
- Rule Generation: Some software includes methods to generalize rules associated with a tree; by doing so, it is possible to remove redundancies. Yet, another software simply accumulates all the tests between the root node and the leaf node to produce the rules.
- Split measures: Different algorithms support different and sometimes multiple measures for selecting which variable to use to split at a particular node. Common split measures include gain criterion, gain ratio criterion, gini criterion, chi-squared, and entropy [8][9][10].

Beyond the basic algorithmic differences, users will find that different implementations of the same algorithm provide additional useful features which are too numerous to mention here.

Decision tree algorithms and products are rapidly evolving. Within the last years, C5.0 was released by RuleQuest Research [12]. Algorithm C5.0 implements 'boosting', a technique that combines multiple decision trees into a single classifier. Silicon Graphics, in the 2.0 release of MineSet, has an Option Tree algorithm, in which multiple trees (or subtrees) coexist as 'options' [16]. Each option makes a prediction, and then the options vote for a consensus prediction. The C5.0 algorithm is also used in the latest release of Clementine [17]. Boosting and option trees are techniques to get around sub-optimization problems resulting from the 'greedy' aspect of the decision tree algorithm. Weka [1] and Orange [18] are open source solutions for various data mining approaches. For example, Weka contains the following decision trees algorithms: ADTree, DecisionStump, ID3, J48, LMT, MSP, NBTree, RandomForest, RandomTree, and few others. Most recent efforts in this area are towards execution of these kind of algorithms in grid computing environments [19].

## 7 Conclusion

Although there is some experimental evidence that decision tree algorithms, like TDIDT/ID3, may be particularly suitable for Smart Homes [8], we should be cautious in drawing premature conclusions. Only when we witness a number of experimental and real-world Smart Homes settings, where decision trees are used, we may be able to provide assessment of the decision trees approach and comparison with other existing techniques.

We showed that decision trees, as both predictive and descriptive models, could be used to satisfy some of the key technical requirements (section 2) posed by various Smart Homes use cases. However, decision trees may never be successful in the modelling process, if some appropriate methodology is not used [9], [10]. The methodology proposed here has several distinctive phases: Smart Homes use case problem formulation, data gathering , data pre-processing, hypotheses generation by induction of decision trees, and quantitative and qualitative evaluation.

In the attempt to illustrate a possible way of using decision trees in the area of Smart Homes, we formulate the modelling problem by defining a generic question "Is the undergoing activity or event in the Smart Home usual?" This could help us identify unusual events and raise certain level of awareness, alert or automatic activity in the Smart Home setting.

The Smart Home can not function properly without a human-controlled monitoring centre. In case an exception is raised in the system caused by unusual events or activities in the Smart Home this should be brought to the attention of the specialized personnel working in such centre. Specialists could then visualize the decision tree corresponding to the event and try to identify whether the event is "slightly unusual" or "very unusual" and in the later case they could react accordingly.

# References

[1] Witten, I.H., Frank, E.: Data Mining: Practical Machine Learning Tools and Techniques with Java Implementations. Morgan Kaufmann (1999)

[2] Kononenko, I.: Comparison of Inductive and Naive Bayesian Learning Approaches to Automatic Knowledge Acquisition. Current Trends in Knowledge Adquisition (1990) 190-197

[3] Fausett, L.: Fundamentals of Neural Networks. Prentice-Hall (1994)

[4] Murthy, S.K.: Automatic Construction of Decision Trees from Data: A Multi-Disciplinary Survey. Data Mining and Knowledge Discovery. 2(4) (1998) 345-389

[5] Karimi, K., Hamilton, H.J.: Temporal Rules and Temporal Decision Trees: A C4.5 Approach. Technical Report CS-2001-02. Department of Computer Science, University of Regina. (2001)

[6] AMIGO: Ambient intelligence for the networked home environment. http://www.hitech-projects.com/euprojects/amigo/

[7] Mitchell, T.: Decision Tree Learning, in T. Mitchell, Machine Learning, The McGraw-Hill Companies, Inc. (1997) 52-78

[8] Brdiczka, O., Reignier, P., James L.: Crowley Supervised Learning of an Abstract Context Model for an Intelligent Environment. Joint sOc-EUSAI conference. Grenoble (2005)

[9] Stankovski, V., Bratko, I., Demšar, J., Smrke, D.: Induction of Hypotheses Concerning Hip Arthroplasty: A Modified Methodology for Medical Research. Methods Inf. Med. 40 (2001) 392-396

[10] Stankovski, V., Debeljak, M., Bratko, I., Adami , M.: Modelling the population dynamics of red deer (Cervus elaphus L.) with regard to forest development. Ecol. model. 108(1-3) (1998) 145-153

[11] Murthy, S.: On Growing Better Decision Trees from Data. PhD Thesis. (1997)

[12] Quinlan, R.: Top Down Induction of Decision Trees. Mach. Learn. 1 (1986) 81-106

[13] Myers, R., Walpole, R.: Tests of Hypotheses, in R. Myers, R. Walpole, Probability and Statistics for Engineers and Scientists, Second Edition, Macmillan Publishing Co., Inc., New York, NY (1978) 268 – 273

[14] Hand DJ. Data mining: statistics and more. The American Statistician (1988) 52:112-118

[15] Winston, P.: Learning by Building Identification Trees, in P. Winston, Artificial Intelligence, Addison-Wesley Publishing Company (1992) 423-442

[16] Brunk, C., Kelly, J., Kohavi, R.: MineSet: An Integrated System for Data Mining. Proceedings of the Third International Conference on Knowledge Discovery and Data Mining (Eds. David Heckerman, Heikki Mannila, Daryl Pregibon and Ramasamy Uthurusamy). AAAI Press, Menlo Park, California (1997) 135-138

[17] Clementine, Web site: http://www.spss.com/clementine/

[18] Orange, Web site: http://magix.fri.uni-lj.si/orange/

[19] DataMiningGrid: Data Mining in Grid Computing Environments, Web site: http://www.datamininggrid.org/

# Artificial Neural Networks in Smart Homes

Rezaul Begg[1] and Rafiul Hassan[2]

[1] Centre for Ageing, Rehabilitation, Exercise & Sport,
Victoria University, Melbourne VIC 8001, Australia
Rezaul.begg@vu.edu.au
[2] Department of Computer Science & Software Engineering,
The University of Melbourne, VIC 3010, Australia
mrhassan@csse.unimelb.edu.au

**Abstract.** Many wonderful technological developments in recent years have opened up the possibility of using smart or intelligent homes for a number of important applications. Typical applications range from overall lifestyle improvement to helping people with special needs such as the elderly and the disabled to improve their independence, safety and security at home. Research in the area has looked into ways of making the home environment automatic and automated devices have been designed to help the disabled people. Also, possibilities of automated health monitoring systems and usage of automatic controlled devices to replace caregiver and housekeeper have received significant attention. Most of the models require acquisition of useful information from the environment, identification of the significant features and finally usage of some sort of machine learning techniques for decision making and planning for the next action to be undertaken. This chapter specifically focuses on neural networks applications in building a smart home environment.

## 1 Introduction

Home automation has been the topic of interest for researchers since the 1940s. The major aim has been to automate control of the appliances and systems within the home environment that can work independently [1]. Home automation can be useful, especially for people living alone at home and also for those who need constant monitoring. Advances in technology have facilitated the usages of an increased number of automated devices in our home environment to make the daily tasks easier [2]. However, as more and more devices are used in the home, the problem of controlling and managing these devices increases exponentially. Unlike humans, devices do not have the inherent understanding of the environmental condition and also do not know what actions are to be selected under which situations [3]. Automated control of these devices is, therefore, a demanding research domain and is receiving significant attentions.

An intelligent environment or smart space can be thought of having many highly interactive and embedded devices, and is able to control these devices automatically in order to meet the demands of the environment or space [4]. Another key objective in a smart home environment is to be able to control and manage the home devices (e.g., AC system, TV, fan, security system, cooking devices, etc) from a distance or even over the

J.C. Augusto and C.D. Nugent (Eds.): Designing Smart Homes, LNAI 4008, pp. 146–164, 2006.

internet [5]. Such an environment would apparently carry out tasks that are commonly done typically by a housekeeper and through other support services. Several protocols and architectures have been proposed in the literature that could potentially offer similar benefits to the inhabitants of a smart home. Furthermore, with the elderly populations growing fast around the globe [6, 7], smart homes environment could potentially provide a better alternative for our elders, and also for the disabled people to enjoy the comfort and independence of their own homes without the need to go to the nursing homes. It has been estimated that about 43% of the Americans over the age of 65 years need to enter a nursing home for at least one year [8].

Recently, there have been many fresh interests into building smart homes. For example in 2002, *Intel* launched the proactive health research project [9], while in 2000, *Sun Microsystems* and *Invensys* announced the development of "smart home" infrastructure to accelerate the delivery of services to wired appliances in the home [10]. Also, *C.P. Technology* [11] has used IBM's web sphere and developed the high tech "smart home" for marketing from the year 2004 [12]. All these initiatives are directed at building smart home spaces for people to live independently at home and to allow for remote surveillance of the well-being and healthcare needs of the people. Various computational intelligence techniques have been proposed and tried to support the needs of the smart homes such as, neural networks [30, 31], Fuzzy logic [13], Hidden Markov Models [14, 15], Bayes Classifier [16], etc.

All of these techniques have their own merits and limitations when applied to a smart home premise. For example, before using a Fuzzy logic appropriate rules and membership functions have to be defined based on prior expert knowledge about the solution of a problem. This might be a quite challenging task, especially when the prior expert knowledge is either limited or not available [17]. Although a Bayes Classifier model might seem simple and fast, it's performance depends on the independence of the input features and the selection of the initial distribution for the model. Hence, the Bayes classifier might not be suitable for devices in smart home that would require an automated crisp and perfect solution [18]. Hidden Markov Models (HMM) can result into very complex networks, and although a HMM can be quite useful for situations such as behavioral monitoring [19], its application would be limited in a smart home due to its inefficiency while dealing with a large number of sensors [36].

In contrast, an Artificial Neural Network (ANN) is relatively simple to apply to most problems in the real world environment. In addition, its better adaptability with the problem makes it more suitable to be used in controlling and automating the smart home devices. Despite some obvious limitations (e.g., optimal architecture for a problem, local minima), the ANN has been used successfully for several problems in smart homes. The reader is referred to Section 4 that specifically deals with some of these applications.

In this chapter, following a brief description of the ANNs, we provide an overview of the major applications involving ANNs in a smart home environment. Finally, we discuss how an ANN based model may be used to address some of the important issues and needs in a smart home environment.

# 2  Artificial Neural Networks

## 2.1  Overview

An Artificial Neural Network (ANN) or alternatively known as Neural Network is a computational tool, which follows the activities of a biological brain. The basic processing unit of ANNs is a neuron [20], which has similarity with a biological neuron, first described by Cajal in 1911 [21]. ANNs learn relationships between the inputs and outputs from examples presented to the networks without any prior knowledge about the underlying relationships that exist within the data sets. This important 'adaptive' attribute of the ANNs makes it suitable for many applications where there is very little or no information available regarding the input-output relationships or the underlying transfer function among the data [22].

There are many standard texts [cf. 23 & 24] that describe the history of ANNs and the links that exist between the operations of the biological and artificial neurons. An ANN is usually characterized by: i) the way the neurons are connected to each other, ii) the method that is used for the determination of the connection strengths or weights and iii) the activation function that is used to process the data. Some basic features of ANNs are briefly described below:

## 2.2  Model of a Neuron

As already stated a neuron is the fundamental unit of the ANN. A neuron takes a number of inputs and after some mathematical processing it produces an output. Each neuron is connected to the other neurons by means of links that have weights, which represent strengths of the connections. Figure 1 compares a computational (artificial) neuron and a biological neuron. The inputs to the neuron signify activities of the

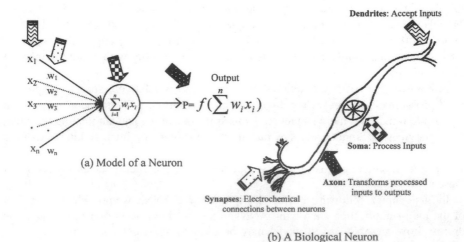

Fig. 1. Activity similarities between (a) a computational neuron and (b) a biological neuron

*dendrites* of a biological neuron. The weights on the edges represent the activities of *synapses,* the mathematical equation shown in the circle is a representation of the *soma,* and the calculation of the output of each neuron signifies the *axon.*

Generally, a neuron in an ANN has more than one input nodes but only one output. The weights shown on each connection line represent information to be used in processing the input signals to build the ANN model of the problem. The mathematical function used by each neuron to calculate the output is called the activation function. There are different types of activation functions used for processing the incoming signals, some of which are briefly discussed in section 2.6.

## 2.3  Network Architecture

The way the neurons are connected to each other can be visualized using the network architecture. Depending on the position of the neurons in an ANN three layers are defined: *input layer, hidden layer* and the *output layer.* There may be none or more than one hidden layer in an ANN which primarily depends on the complexity of the problem. Researchers have proposed different types of network architectures that are suitable for solving their own particular problem. However, the most popular and widely used network architectures include: feed-forward fully connected neural network, recurrent neural network and time-delay neural networks.

### 2.3.1  Feed-Forward Architecture
In a feed-forward neural network (Figure 2(a)), the neurons of each layer are connected to the next layer only in the forward direction, i.e., neurons are connected in unidirectional way and there is no backward connection among the neurons. Figure 2(a) illustrates the structure of a three layer feed-forward fully connected neural network. Feed-Forward ANN has a relatively simple architecture to map the input-output relationship to automate devices (e.g., face recognition, temperature control, fire alarm, etc), which can be applied in a smart home environment.

### 2.3.2  Recurrent Neural Network
The structure of a recurrent neural network (RNN) is the same as the feed-forward ANN except that, there is connection between neurons that feeds back the output of that neuron to the input of the previous neuron. Figure 2(b) illustrates the structure of a RNN. Here the outputs are fed back into the hidden layer, thus the structure representing a RNN. A RNN is normally efficient for dealing with sequential problem where the current state depends on past states of the same variable (e.g., human behavior prediction in a smart home).

### 2.3.3  Time-Delay Neural Network
A time delay neural network (TDNN) or also known as Tapped Delay Line (TDL) is a temporal network where the input pattern is fed into the network by introducing a delay in time. The successive representation of input data sequences facilitates the network to adapt to the temporal behavior of the problem (e.g., daily activities of smart home inhabitant). TDNN can be quite useful for those problems where both the

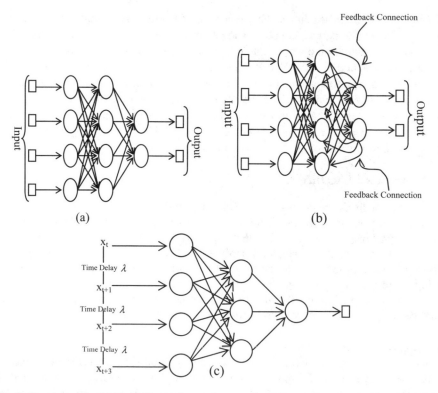

**Fig. 2.** Structure of a (a) Feed-Forward neural network (b) Recurrent neural network, RNN (c) Time-Delay neural network, TDNN

temporal information and the relationship between the input/output data sequences are important. Figure 2(c) illustrates the architecture of a TDNN, here the successive inputs have been delayed by $\lambda$.

## 2.4 Learning Process

One of the main characteristics that make ANNs unique from other mathematical processing methods is that it can learn from the characteristics of the data and adapt parameters of the network according to the underlying structures in the training dataset. The process is known as learning. As defined by Haykin [20], "*Learning is a process by which the free parameters of a neural network are adapted through a continuing process of stimulation by the environment in which the networks is embedded. The type of learning is determined by the manner in which the parameter changes take place*".

Depending on the learning environment there can be fundamentally two different learning paradigms: supervised learning and unsupervised or self-organized learning. As the name suggests, in a supervised learning paradigm the ANN is trained under some guided supervision, i.e., there is target output(s) that the ANN aims to achieve during the learning/training process. On the contrary, in unsupervised learning there is no external supervisor to facilitate ANN's learning: the distribution of the data and the structural similarities amongst the dataset are used as the basis for learning.

Over the years researchers have proposed many rules for training the ANNs that follow the learning technique. Some of the widely used supervised learning rules include:

1. Perceptron Learning rule
2. Error-Correction/ Delta rule
3. Hebbian Rule [27]

Among these rules, the Delta rule is the most widely used one, and a brief description of it is provided below:

## 2.5  Error Correction (Delta) Rule

In error correction rule, the weights that connect the nodes are modified by calculating the difference between the desired output and that produced by the node as shown in Figure 1(a).

Error at the node$= \dfrac{1}{2}$ * (Desired Output, $O$ - Produced Output, $P)^2$

The modified weight at edge connecting from input $x_i$

$$= learning \ \ rate*error \ \ at \ \ the \ \ node*x_i + old \ \ weight$$

Mathematically, the error $(E)$ for each input vector is calculated as follows:

$$E = \sum_s E_s \tag{1}$$

$$\text{where, } E_s = \frac{1}{2}\sum_i (O_i - P_i)^2 ,$$

Where, $O_i$ is the desired output vector in response to the input vector representing the input sequences $x_1, x_2, \ldots , x_n$; and $w_1, w_2, \ldots , w_n$ are the weights connecting the input to the node/neuron. Therefore, the initial output, $P_i$ created by the neuron is given by (Figure 1a).

$$P = f (\sum_{i=1}^{n} w_i x_i) \tag{2}$$

Where, $f(.)$=activation function which we discuss later

According to the delta rule the modified weight at each edge is obtained using the following equation:

$$w_i (new) = w_i (old) + \partial w_i \tag{3}$$

$$\text{where, } \partial w_i = \eta E_i x_i \ (\eta = Learning \ \ rate )$$

These steps are executed iteratively until a minimum acceptable error between the desired and generated output is found. The technique of minimizing the above error with respect to the network parameters is known as *gradient descent* method [25][26].

## 2.6 Activation Function

The output of a neuron in the ANN architecture is generated using a mathematical function, which is known as activation function. Most often a nonlinear function is used as activation function so that the ANN structure becomes suitable to adapt to nonlinear problems. Two of the most popular nonlinear activation functions are:

- Sigmoidal function
- Signum function

Details of these functions can be found in [20]. Now we proceed to the algorithms that employ learning rules described in sections 2.4 and 2.5 in order to train the ANN.

## 2.7 Learning Algorithms

There are several learning algorithms proposed in the literature that can be used to determine the appropriate weights of the ANNs. Some well known learning algorithms include:

- Back propagation
- Radial Basis Function
- Hopfield Algorithm

Among the many learning algorithms, the back-propagation algorithm is widely used involving majority of the applications in a smart home environment (refer to Table 1). In a back propagation algorithm, the weights are modified first by calculating the error via some suitable error function. If a differentiable function is chosen as an error function, gradient descent on such a function will naturally lead to a learning rule. Historically, several researchers have proposed this idea [e.g., 28]. Eventually, Rumelhart et al. [29] developed practical techniques that gave us a powerful engineering tool. The back-propagation technique follows the delta rule while modifying the network weights.

# 3   Applications of Neural Networks in Smart Home Environment

In the above sections we have briefly discussed the operation and algorithms of ANNs. In the context of smart homes, ANN has been used for classification, control and automated home appliances, next step/action prediction, etc. In the following, we review some of the significant applications involving ANNs approaches in smart home environment. A chronological list of the major developments in the area is presented in Table 1.

Chan et al. [30] appear to be the first to use ANN to help develop a smart home automation system for use by the elderly and disabled people. Altogether twelve rooms were included as part of the system where sensors were deployed in the rooms to collect information representative of the behaviors of the inhabitants. ANNs were trained using the acquired data to classify normal and abnormal behaviors.

The first comprehensive application involving ANNs in smart home environment was undertaken by Mozer [31] in 1998. It was named ACHE which stands for *Adaptive Control of Home Environments*. The system was able to alter the environmental system (e.g., air heating, lighting, ventilation, water heating) in line with the residential needs and comfort levels. Thus the home environment was in tune with the lifestyle and requirements of the residents. ACHE had two main goals. It was able to anticipate the inhabitants' needs such as lighting, air temperature, hot water, and ventilation by studying the patterns of adjustments made by the inhabitants. These settings acted as training signals for ACHE so that after some time it was able to anticipate the needs of the resident. The second objective was to conserve energy, i.e., meeting the inhabitant's demand with less energy consumption. To satisfy these two objectives the author introduced a cost function to optimize the comfort level of the resident with least possible amount of energy being consumed. Feed-forward ANNs trained with back propagation algorithm were reported for data analysis and controlling the home appliances.

Jorge and Goncalves [32] focused on automated health monitoring of elder citizens' everyday life using artificial intelligence tool. They used ubiquitous computing devices to collect data from the elderly relating to neurological disorders (e.g., loss of motor, sensorial and cognitive problems). The authors emphasized the usage of artificial intelligence to learn patterns from data produced by ubiquitous computing devices and then to use them to predict next activities. For instance, for patients requiring constant medical monitoring should be considered differently as they might need special needs and care. So, the challenge for the system is to take a decision whether someone should be classified under this group or not based on the available information. For such a problem, the rules and patterns that are inferred by the system should be unique and individual-specific, and in this regard an artificial intelligence tool like the ANN technique could potentially play a significant role in decision-making.

Pigot et al. [33] proposed a theoretical as well a practical framework with a view to minimizing risks that may arise due to the actions undertaken by the elderly in a physical environment. In this framework, the computer infrastructure of the smart home system consisted of three layers: The application layer, the middleware layer and the hardware layer. The hardware layer included electrical equipment, e.g. sensors [34]. The middleware connected the devices in the hardware layer with the application layer. The application layer was the decision making layer which took decision about the action to be undertaken in the next step. Tele-monitoring module was one of the application modules in the decision-making process to detect abnormal behaviors of the monitored person. The authors emphasized the advantage of applying ANNs along with other mathematical models to help in the detection of patterns associated with a risk.

Cook et al. [35] developed a project called *MavHome*. This project focuses on the creation of an environment that acted as an intelligent agent. The main operations of *MavHome* included the control of temperature, electric appliances, TV, video, robot, etc. The *MavHome* was organized into an architecture, which connected the agent and

**Table 1.** Applications of neural networks in smart home at a glance; ANN – Artificial neural networks; AI – Artificial Intelligence

| Authors | Objectives | Inputs | Outputs | Types of ANN | Results/Comment |
|---|---|---|---|---|---|
| Chan et al. (1995) | To develop a smart house automation system for use by the elderly and the disabled. | Living habits and behaviors of the elderly extracted from twelve rooms. | - Person identification -Behavior discrimination -Room temperature control -TV On/Off | Back-propagation Feed-forward ANN (5-18 to 26-1) | 90-100% convergence rate reported |
| Mozer (1998) | To control basic residential comfort systems & to conserve energy. | Status of lights, fans, temperature (gas furnace, water heater, electric space heater etc), sound level etc. | Control of on/off status and intensity of: light banks, ceiling fans, water heater, gas furnace and speakers in each room. | Back-propagation Feed-forward ANN (Architecture not known) | Implemented successfully |
| Jorge et al. (2001) | To study feasibility of using ubiquitous computing for short and medium- term applications in older adults with loss of motor, sensorial and cognitive skills. | Medical data for monitoring (e.g., heart rate, blood pressure, diabetics, etc) and data collected by an implant on the brain, etc. | - Automatic call dispatch to ambulance or hospital in case of emergency - Relay command to the appliances - Help to recollect memory about daily activities | AI techniques including ANN to infer rules and classify data. | Not implemented. |

**Table 1.** (*continued*)

| Authors | Objectives | Inputs | Outputs | Types of ANN | Results/Comments |
|---|---|---|---|---|---|
| Pigot et al. (2003) | -To provide a secure and safety home to help older people especially for those with risk related to gravity and health (falls, inappropriate drug ingestion), etc. | - Activity (movement) information of subject - Physiological information (blood pressure or weight) - Environmental information (smoke, home temperature, hygrometry, etc.). | - In case of any abnormalities in subject's daily behavior or any danger in health status the system immediately reports to the relatives. -Predicts and helps the subject to do his daily tasks in a safe way. | A framework was proposed for detecting abnormal behaviors of person & comment was made to use ANN along with other mathematical models. | Sketched a pervasive infrastructure and applications. |
| Cook et al. (2003) | The project named *MavHome* aims to provide an environment to give comfort to daily life of the home inhabitant. | The daily activities of the inhabitants including their movement, multimedia adaptability and other activities. | Controls devices used to provide comfortable environment depending on the prediction of inhabitant's next action. | Back-propagation ANN & other prediction algorithms. | Further testing of *MavHome* was proposed using data from complex environment. |
| Illingworth et al. (2005) | To develop an environment with embedded ambient intelligence to help older people by providing care & assistance to their daily life activation | Activities of daily living (ADL), human behaviour, status of light, temperature, pressure, etc. | Activity (e.g., sleeping, computer work, eating, listening music, etc.) identification, behaviour recognition and behavioral anomaly detection. | RNN hybridized with ART and Fuzzy ART. | On average, 78-89% activities could be accurately detected. |

the technologies within each agent. The decision layer was one of these four layers. This layer selected actions for the agent to be executed based on information supplied from the other layers. *MavHome* has been defined as a unique agent, which combined technologies from artificial intelligence, machine learning, databases, mobile computing, robotics, and multimedia computing. To acquire and recognize the activities of the inhabitants within the *MavHome* a number of prediction algorithms were employed in parallel: the SHIP prediction algorithm, Active LeZi (ALZ) online algorithm, and a data-mining algorithm known as Episode Discovery. In the final decision phase the MavHome developed a metapredictor called Predict to select one of the predicted actions obtained from the aforementioned predictors. In predict algorithm, a back propagation ANN was applied to learn the confidence value for each of the prediction algorithms based on the gathered data, the accuracy strength of each of the predictors and the meta features (i.e., amount of data, number of devices, etc).

R-Illengworth et al. [36] presented a novel connectionist embedded agent architecture to recognize daily life behaviors. A number of unobtrusive and relatively simple sensors were used in this architecture. Different high-level daily routine activities (e.g., sleeping, eating) were recognized with the help of a constructive algorithm with temporal capabilities. Consequently, abnormal behaviors were also identified using this algorithm. The focus of the task was the development of some connectionist approach which would overcome the difficulties of adapting neural network to the continuous changes in the smart home, and eliminate the requirement of retraining the ANN to take into consideration the newly added input/output nodes (if any). The authors used adaptive neural architecture, first proposed by Kasabov [37], known as EcoS (Evolving Connectionist System), which was found suitable for the environmental data. A memory layer was added to the model to handle temporal component i.e., to detect abnormalities in the sequence, frequency and duration of the activities. Being RNN in nature, there were feedback connections between the two layers (memory and hidden layers) that followed the architecture proposed in [38]. The authors applied this model, in conjunction with 18 sensors, for activity recognition and to identify abnormalities inside a dormitory room at the University of Essex (see Table 1).

# 4   ANNs for the Control of Smart Home Devices and Appliances

People have defined smart homes from different contexts. Smart homes have been designed with the primary aim of helping people with special needs, adapt to meet the user's limitation and also to improve the general lifestyle of the inhabitants. Accordingly, the use of devices within the home environment and the associated models vary. Some application examples of smart homes might be for people with movement disabilities that may require assistance with mobility [39-42], for elderly people to help with balance problem [40-44,46,47], and for people with low hearing and vision requiring specialized communication and lighting devices [45]. Furthermore, smart homes are designed with a focus towards minimizing caregiver support for the people who would like to live independently at home. Table 2 lists some of the main items that might require automation and control in a smart home.

**Table 2.** List of some of the main devices that require automation in smart home

| Major Areas | Items that need automation |
| --- | --- |
| Entertainment | TV on/off, Channel/ movie selection, Daily exercise |
| Security and Safety | Intruder detection, Fire alarm, Automatic door lock, Kitchen equipment control, etc. |
| Caregiver | Eating, Taking bath, Cooking, Shopping, Cleaning, Washing, Housekeeping, Bill payment, etc. |
| Health Monitoring | Medication, Falls and balance, ECG/Heart beat, Blood pressure monitoring, Body temperature monitoring, Pressure sores, Dementia, Alcohol use, etc. |
| Behavior monitoring | Inconsistency in sleeping pattern detection, etc |
| Environment | AC Control, Heating control, Water temp control, Light control, etc |

## 4.1 Entertainment

There are different kinds of equipment that may need automation to provide entertainment to the inhabitants in a smart home. Examples include the provision of an automated TV control that may need turning on and off according to the daily routine of the inhabitant. A trained ANN can be utilized to make this action automated via information collected from various sources (e.g., time/day and activity of the inhabitant such as morning exercise, etc). Chan et al. [30] has already demonstrated the usefulness of ANNs in the control of TV in their smart home. ANNs can also be programmed to expand the controls of TV/Video/DVD during any time of the day by feeding the requisite information relating to the behavior and activities of the inhabitant. Similarly, ANNs can be employed for automated control of daily exercises. For example, it can be used to activate reminder notes for exercise, and to regulate the air temperature of the exercise room (e.g., using a TDNN).

## 4.2 Safety and Security

One of the major aims of smart homes is to provide a secure and safe environment for their inhabitants. This may include intruder or unwanted person detection and automatic activation of, for example, fire alarm for 24 hours. With regard to the previous task, computerized technique involving face detection, person and object identification can play a vital role. Recently, many research projects have been undertaken pertaining to the use of ANNs for face detection and recognition, see for example [48] - [51]. In some research [cf. 50], it has been shown that ANNs are able to recognize face with very high success rate (82% to 100%), which suggests their suitability for application in smart home environment for intruder detection, and subsequent activation of appropriate security services such as the police or security guard.

ANNs may also be used to assess fire hazards in the home by studying smoke alarm signals from various parts in the house. In [52], the researchers have developed satellite-based remote sensing techniques for identifying smoke from forest fires. It seems that with little modification, this concept could be applied in smart homes to detect and assess fire hazards using a dedicated ANN system for intelligent decision making as to whether to activate or not the fire alarm system [52, 53].

### 4.3 Caregiver

In this category, issues are discussed to help the inhabitants of smart homes to do his or her daily routine activities, such as eating, house keeping, cleaning, etc. Already significant progress has been made in this area, especially with the help of indoor robots. In [55], the authors have employed ANNs to control a robot within the indoor environment as a personal assistant for indoor service applications such as surface cleaning, distribution of meals, etc. Such type of controlled robot has the potential to be employed in smart home environment to carry out various tasks, e.g. to deliver meal according to the daily routine of the inhabitant. ANNs have played a substantial role in many such control applications, for example, helping the robots to navigate using sensor signals taken from the surrounding environment [58, 59] or monitoring the time of taking meal [54].

Besides robots, ANNs have been valuable for doing many other household duties and tasks. For example, for automated control of bathtub water temperature within a comfortable level, both back propagation ANNs [56] and hybrid systems (neuro-fuzzy inference network) have been proposed [57]. ANNs, with the help of speech recognition techniques [61-64], could also potentially provide assistance with the online shopping activities undertaken from within the home environment.

### 4.4 Health Monitoring

Continuous health monitoring capability offers enormous benefits to individuals living in smart homes, especially for older persons and individuals with chronic diseases (heart, neurological disorders, etc) to have a better quality of life [60]. Here the idea is to have sensor devices that would constantly deliver information about the health status of the inhabitants [65-68]. ANNs or other artificial intelligence tools might be used for processing medical and physiological data, and to take intelligent decision about the overall health condition of the subject. ANNs could also facilitate information transfer to medical and health professionals in case of detected abnormality in recorded signals that would warrant urgent medical attention. Some of the examples include routine medication surveillance, falls event detection in older adults, heartbeat and ECG monitoring, blood pressure monitoring, EEG monitoring in dementia patients, etc. Already a substantial body of literature is available describing various issues related to health monitoring and using sensors placed in smart homes (e.g., bed, bath, toilet, etc) to obtain various physiological and health information data [69-71]. ANNs can play a vital role in this context for processing various biomedical signals and assisting to diagnose diseases from the acquired biosignals [72] and also, for example, to develop ANN-based medical decision support system [73].

## 5    An Integrated Framework for Smart Home

An architecture integrating the potential applications of ANNs involving the various aspects of smart homes is presented in Figure 3.

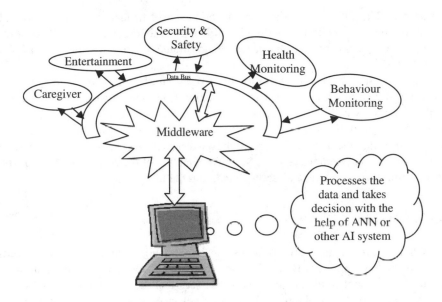

**Fig. 3.** An integrated framework for ANN-based smart home

In previous sections, we have discussed various events and devices in smart homes – we now briefly describe how these devices could be controlled centrally. In Figure 3, we have employed a central computer to operate a number of ANN models in parallel. The data bus is responsible for collecting raw data from different modules i.e., caregiver, entertainment etc. The middleware section extracts and selects the important features from the acquired data, and then passes these features on to the relevant ANNs in the computer. Therefore, essentially the middleware performs two tasks: 1) selects significant features and 2) acts like a 'postman' to deliver information to the specific ANN and vice versa. Details are described below:

In this model, each individual module connected to the data bus is self-contained, i.e., these modules have their own ANNs to take the necessary steps for the current data sequences. For example, the health-monitoring module has its own ANN to decide locally as well as its own sensor networks to acquire data from the environment. This action along with the collected data is passed to the middleware through the data bus. The middleware analyzes these data and decides whether there exits any dependencies with other module(s). For instance, there needs to be a linkage between the health-monitoring module and the behavior-monitoring module as a change in one of these modules may affect the decision-making process of the other one. One possible scenario might be that taking medication could affect the behavior of the inhabitant. This interacting information exchange could be managed via the middle-ware, however, the central server would undertake the final decision regarding any next action to be undertaken taking into consideration of all the associated data and their interdependencies. The central computer contains a number of ANNs dedicated to various specialized tasks and database relating to previous information. The middleware controls the flow of information to the relevant ANNs present in the central unit. The different modules might be designed to take care of the controls related to minor events by responding locally, and in this regard, a small IC could be built to serve the purpose as has been demonstrated in [51] for the case of face detection task.

As already stated, for major events, the overall situation has to be analyzed and should be studied in conjunction with information from other devices, and this might involve eventually calling on an appropriate emergency service. In such a situation, a central ANN could be used to analyze the overall situation and for decision-making. The proposed architecture in Figure 3 shows the overall structure of such a smart home automation system based on ANNs. The function of the central ANN is to work in the central server and thus, directly connects to the middleware.

# 6  Conclusion

Smart homes offer many benefits to its inhabitants and people with special needs. ANN technology appears to have much potential, especially in the automated monitoring and control of the smart home devices and the relevant space as well as the well being of the inhabitants. With rapid advances in technology, especially in wireless sensors and sensor networks, it is expected that it is not far when many of the dreams of the smart homes will be realized.

# References

[1] Wright, M., "Sci-fi comes home", EDN, 1999. 14(44): pp. 56-57.
[2] Brumitt, B., and JJ Cadiz, "Let There be Light! Examining interfaces homes of the future", *Proceedings of INTERACT*, 2001, pp. 375-382.
[3] Wu, H., "Supporting sensor fusion for context aware computing", Ph. D. thesis proposal, The Robotics Institute, Carnegie Millan University, 2001.
[4] Coen, M. H., "Design principles for intelligent environments", *Proceedings of 15th National Conference on Artificial Intelligence (AAAI'98)*, 1998, pp. 547-554.
[5] Seagneur, J. M., "House-Keeper, a vendor independent architecture for easy management of smart homes", Masters thesis, Trinity College, Dublin, 2001.
[6] Anderson, R. N. "Method for constructing complete annual US life tables", *National Center for Health Statistics Vital and Health Stat. Series, 2(129)*, 1999.
[7] The Australian Newspaper, Higher Education supplement, March 30, 2005.
[8] Haigh, K. Z., J. Phelps, Christopher W. Geib, "An Open Agent Architecture for Assisting Elder Independence", *Proceedings of AAMAS, Bologna,* Italy, 2002, pp. 578-586.
[9] http://www.intel.com/research/prohealth/cs-aging_in_place.htm
[10] http://www.sun.com/smi/Press/sunflash/2000-10/sunflash.20001011.3.html
[11] http://www-306.ibm.com/software/success/cssdb.nsf/CS/CGES-5W23HK?OpenDocument&Site=default
[12] www.cptech.com.tw
[13] Hagras, H., V. Callaghan, G. Clarke, M. Colley, Anthony Pounds Cornish, Arran Holmes, Hakan Duman, "Incremental Synchronous Learning for Embedded Agents Operating in Ubiquitous Computing Environments", *Soft Computing Agents-* V. Loia (Eds), IOS Press, 2002, pp. 25-55.

[14] Darnall, J. M, I. A. Essa, and M. H. Hayes ,"Exploiting Human Actions and Object Context for Recognition Tasks" *Proceedings of 7th IEEE international Conference on Computer Vision* , 1999, Vol. 1, pp. 80-86.

[15] Bobick, A. "Movement, Activity, and Action: The Role of Knowledge in the Perception of Model", *Royal Society Workshop on Knowledge based Vision in Man and Machine*, 1997.

[16] Tapia, E. M., Intille S. S. and Larson K., "Activity Recognition in the Home Using Simple and Ubiquitous Sensors", *Proceedings of Pervasive, LNCS*, 2004, pp. 158-175.

[17] Meier, A., N. Werro, Albrecht M. and Sarkinos, M., "Using a fuzzy classification query language for customer relationship management" *Proceedings of the 31st International Conference on Very Large Databases,* 2005, pp. 1089-1096.

[18] http://datamining.itsc.uah.edu/adam/tutorials/adam_tut_02_overview_05.html

[19] Tsechpenakis, G., D. Metaxxas, M. Adkins, J. Kruse, J.K. Burgoon, M.L. Jensen, T. Meservy, D. P. Twitchell, Deokar, A. and Nunamaker, J.F. "HMM based deception recognition from visual cues", *Proceedings of IEEE International Conference on Multimedia and Expo*, 2005.

[20] Haykin, S., "Neural Netwoks: A Comprehensive Foundation", Macmillan College Publishing Company Inc., 1994.

[21] Ramon y Cajal, S., "Histologie du systeme nerveux de l'homme et des vertebras" Paris: Maloine; Edition Francaise Revue: Tome I. 1952; Tome II. 1955, Madrid: Consejo Superior de Investigaciones Cientificas, 1911.

[22] Hassoun, M. H., "Fundamentals of Artificial Neural Networks" 1995.

[23] Hecht-Neilson, R. , "Neuro Computing", Addison-Wesely, Newyork.

[24] Eliasmith, C. and Charles H. Anderson, "Neural engineering Computation And Dynamics in neurobiological systems", MIT Press, 2003

[25] Haykin, S.,"Adaptive filter theory", 2nd edition, Englewood Cliffs, NJ Prentice Hall,1991.

[26] Widrow, B. and S. D. Stearns, "Adaptive Signal Processing", Englewood Cliffs, NJ: Prentice Hall, 1985.

[27] Hebb, D.O., "The Organisation of Behavior: A Neurophysiological Theory", New York: Wiley, 1949.

[28] TAKAGI, H., "Introduction to Fuzzy Systems, Neural Networks, and Genetic Algorithms" Intelligent Systems: Fuzzy Logic: Neural Networks, and Genetic Algorithms,1997, Ch. 1, pp. 1-33, edited by D. Ruan, Kluwer Academic Publishers (Norwell, Massachusets, USA).

[29] Rumelhart, D. E., J. L. McClelland, and the PDP Research Group, "Parallel distributed processing: explorations in the microstructure of cognition", 1986, Cambridge, MA: MIT Press".

[30] Chan, M., C. Hariton, P. Ringeard, E. Campo, "Smart House Automation System for the Elderly and the Disabled", *IEEE international conference on Systems, Man and Cybernetics,* 1995, Vol. 2, pp. 1586-1589.

[31] Mozer, M. C.,"The Neural Network House: An Environment that adapts to its Inhabitants", *Proceedings of the American Assocation for Artificial Intelligence*, 1998, pp. 110-114.

[32] Jorge, D. and Goncalves, V. "Ubiquitous Computing and AI Towards an Inclusive Society", *Proceedings of the 2001 EC/NSF workshop on Universal accessibility of ubiquitous computing: providing for the elderly*, 2001, pp. 37-40.

[33] Pigot, H., B. Lefebvre, J. Meunier, B. Kerherve, A. Mayers, S. Giroux,"The role of intelligent habitats in upholding elders in residence", *Proceedings of the 5th International Conference on Simulations in Biomedicine*, 2003.

[34] Rialle. V, N. Noury, T. Herve, "An experimental Health Smart Home and its distributed Internet based Information and Communication System: first steps of a research project", In V. Patel et al. (eds): *MEDINFO 2001, 10<sup>th</sup> World Congress on Medical Informatics*. Amsterdam: IOPress, pp. 1479-1483.

[35] Cook, D. J., M. Youngblood, E. O. Heierman, III , K. Gopalratnam, S., Rao, A. Litvin, and F. Khawaja, "MavHome: An Agent-Based Smart Home", *Proceedings of the first IEEE International Conference on Pervasive Computing and Communications*, 2003, pp. 521-524.

[36] Illingworth, F.R., V. Callaghan, and Hagras H., "A Neural Network Agent Based Approach to Activity Detection in AmI Environments", *Proceedings of IEE International Workshop on Intelligent Environments*, (IE05), 2005.

[37] N. Kasabov, "Evolving connectionist systems: Methods and applications in bioinformatics,brain study and intelligent machines", London: Springer, 2002.

[38] Elman, J. L. "Finding structure in time", *Cognitive Science*, vol. 14(2), 1990, pp. 179-211.

[39] Brownsell, S., G. Williams, and D. A. Bradley, "Information strategies in achieving an integrated home care environment, "*Proceedings 1<sup>st</sup> Joint BMES/EMBS Conf. Atlanta, GA*, 1999, vol.2, pp. 1224.

[40] Begg, R.K., M. R. Hassan, S. Taylor and M. Palaniswami, "Artificial Neural Network models in the diagnosis of balance impairments", *Proceedings of International Conference on Intelligent Sensing and Information Processing*, 2005, pp. 518-522.

[41] Bourhis, G., P. Pino , and A. Leal-Olmedo, "Communication and environmental control aids for people with motor disabilities: Human machine interaction optimization", *Assistive Technology- Added Value to the Quality of life*, C. Marinček, C. Bühler, H. Knops, and R. Andrich, Eds. Amsterdam, The Netharlands: IOS, 2001, pp. 139 143.

[42] Shumway-Cook A., MA Ciol,W Gruber, and C. Robinson, "Incidence of and risks factors for falls following hip fracture in community-dwelling older adults", *Physical Therapy*, Vol. 85(7), 2005, pp. 520-525.

[43] Kawarada, A., T. Tsakada, K. Sasaki, M. Ishijima, T. Tamura, T. Togawa, and K. Yamakoshi, "Automated monitoring system for home health care", *Proceedings 1<sup>st</sup> Joint BMES/EMBS conference, Atlanta, GA*, 1999, pp. 694.

[44] Hassan, R., R. Begg and S. Taylor,"Fuzzy Logic-based Recognition of Gait Changes due to Trip-related Falls",*IEEE 27<sup>th</sup> International Conference on BMES/EMBS conference, Shang Hai, China*, 2005.

[45] Blenkhorn, P. ,"Some applications of technology to give visually impaired people access to computers", *IEE Colloq. Poblems in Human Vision: How Can Technology Help?*, London, U.K., 1989, pp. 3/1-3/2.

[46] Topo, P., "Technology in everyday life and care of elderly living at home and suffering from dementia", *Gerontechnology: A Sustainable Investment of the Future*, J. Graafmans, V. Taipale, and N. Charness, Eds. Amsterdam, The Netharlands: IOS, 1997, pp. 320-323.

[47] Protas, E.J., C.Y. Wang, C. Harris, "Usefulness of an individualized balance and gait intervention programme based on the problem-oriented assessment of mobility in nursing home residents", *Disability Rehabilitation*, Vol. 23(5), 2001, pp. 192-200.

[48] Rowley, H. A., S. Baluja, and T. Kanade "Neural Network Based Face Detection", *IEEE Transactions on Pattern Analysis and Machine Intelligence*, Vol 20, No. 1,1998, pp. 23-38

[49] Feraud, R., O. J. Bernier, J. E. Viallet, and M. Collobert, "A fast and accurate face detector based on Neural Networks", *IEEE Transactions on Pattern Analysis and Machine Intelligence*, Vol 23, No. 1, 2001, pp. 42-53

[50] Reda, A., D. B. Aoued, "Artificial Neural Network Based Face Recognition", *Proceedings of 1<sup>st</sup> International Symposium on Control, Communications and Signal Processing*, 2004, pp. 439-442.

[51] Prasanna, C. S. S., N. Sudha, Kamakoti, V. "A Principal Component Neural Network based Face Recognition System and Its ASIC Implementation", *Proceedings of 18th International Conference on VLSI Design*, 2005, pp. 795-798.

[52] Zhanqing, L., A. Khannanian, R. H. Fraser, and J. Cihlar, " Automatic Detection of Fire Smoke using Artificial Neural Networks and Threshold Approaches Applied to AVHRR Imagery", *IEEE Transactions on Geosciences and Remote Sensing*, Vol. 39, No. 9, September 2001, pp. 1859-1870.

[53] Susan L. Rose-Pehrsson, S. J. Hart, T. T. Street, F. W. Williams, M. H. Hammond, D. T. Gottuk, M. T. Wright, J. T. Wong, "Early Warning Fire Detection System Using a Probabilistic Neural Network", *Fire Technology*, 2003, 39, pp. 147-171, Kluwer Academic Publishers.

[54] Kwahk, J., RC Williges, TL Smith-Jackson, "An application of neural network modeling to diagnose eating behavior of seniors in smart houses", *Human Factors and Ergonomics Society 46th Annual Meeting*, 2002 - csa.com.

[55] Hanebeck, U.D., Fischer, C. Schmidt G., "ROMAN: a mobile robotic assistant for indoor service applications", *Proceedings of International Conference on Intelligent Robots and Systems*, Vol.2, 1997, pp. 518 – 525.

[56] Khalid, M. and S. Omatu, "A Neural Network Controller for a Temperature Control System", *IEEE Control Systems Magazine*, 1992, pp. 58-64.

[57] Lin, C. T., C-F Juang, and C-P Li, "Temperature Control with a Neural Fuzzy Inference Network", *IEEE Transactions on Systems, Man and Cybernetics*, Vol.29, 1999, pp. 440-451.

[58] Kawato, M., Y. Uno, M. Isobe, and R. Suzuki "Hierarchical Neural Network Model for Voluntary Movement with Application to Robotics", *IEEE Control Systems Magazine*, Vol.8, Issue.2,1988, pp.8-15.

[59] Sanger, T. D.,"Neural Network Learning Control of Robot Manipulators Using Gradually Increasing Task Difficulty", *IEEE transactions on Robotics and Automation*, Vol. 10, No. 3, June 1994, pp. 323-333.

[60] Stefanov, D.H., Z. Bien, W-C Bang, "The Smart House for Older Persons ans Persons with Physical Disabilities: Structure, Technology arrangements, and perspectives", *IEEE Transactions on Neural Systems and Rehabilitation Engineering*, Vol. 12(2), 2004, pp. 228-250.

[61] Hassan, M. R., Nath B. and Bhuiyan, A. "Bengali Phoneme Recognition- A new Approach", *ICCIT Dhaka (www.iccit.org)*, 2003, pp. 365-369.

[62] Yang, S., M. Joo Er, and Y. Gao, "A High Performance Neural-Networks-Based Speech Recognition System", *Proceedings of International Joint Conference on Neural Networks, IJCNN* , Vol. 2, 2001, pp. 1527-1531.

[63] Obaidat, M.S. and Abu-Saymeh D.S. "Performance Comparison of Neural Networks and Pattren Recognition Techniques for Classifying Ultrasonic Transducers", *Proceedings of ACM/SIGAPP*, 1992, pp. 1234-1242.

[64] Lee, T. and P. C. Ching, "Cantonese Syllable Recognition Using Neural Networks", *IEEE Transactions on Speech and Audio processing*, Vol.7, No.4, 1999, pp.466-472.

[65] Warren, S. and Craft, R. "Designing smart health care technology into the home of the future", *Proceedings of 1st Joint BMES/EMBS Conference, Atlanta, GA*, 1999, p.677.

[66] Rhee, S., B. H. Yang, and H. Asada, "The ring sensor: A new ambulatory wearable sensor for twenty-four hour patient monitoring", *in Proceedings 20th Annual International Conference. IEEE Engineering in Medicine and Biology Soc., Hong Kong*, 1998, pp. 1906-1909.

[67] Yang, B. H., S. Rhee, and H. Asada, "A twenty four hour tele-nursing system using a ring sensor", *Proceedings of IEEE International Conference of Robotics and Automation, Leuvin, Belgium,* 1998, pp. 387-392.

[68] Handa, T., S. Shoji, S. Ike, S. Takeda, and T. Shekiguchi, "A very low-power consumption wireless ECG monitoring system using body as a signal transmission medium", *Proceedings of International Conference on Slid State Sensors and Actuators, Transducers, Chicago, IL,* 1997, pp. 1003-1006.

[69] Ogawa, M., and Togawa, T. "Attempts at monitoring health status in the home", *Invited paper 1$^{st}$ Annual International IEEE-EMBS Special Topic on Microtechnologies in Medicine and Biology, Lyon, France.* 2000, pp. 551-556.

[70] Ishijima, M., Togawa, T. "Observation of electrocardiogram through tap water," *Clin Physiol Meas,* vol. 10, 1989, pp. 171-175.

[71] Tamura, T, Togawa T., Ogawa, M. Yamakoshi K., "Fully automated health monitoring at home." *Stud Health Technol Inform.* 1998, 48, pp. 280-284.

[72] Nazeran, H. and Behbehani, K. "Neural Networks in Processing and Analysis of Biomedical Signals", *Nonlinear Biomedical Signal Processing: Fuzzy Logic, Neural Networks and New Algorithms,* Metin Akay (Eds), 2001, pp. 69-97.

[73] Silva, R. and Silva A.C.R., "Medical Diagnosis as a Neural Networks Pattern Classification Problem", *Neural Networks and Expert Systems in Medicine and Health Care,* E. C. Ifeachor, A. Sperduti & A. Starita Ed(s), World Scientific Publishing, 1998, pp. 25-33.

# A Multi-agent Approach to Controlling a Smart Environment

Diane J. Cook, Michael Youngblood, and Sajal K. Das

Department of Computer Science Engineering,
The University of Texas at Arlington
{cook, youngbld, das}@cse.uta.edu
http://mavhome.uta.edu

**Abstract.** The goal of the MavHome (**M**anaging **A**n Intelligent **V**ersatile **Home**) project is to create a home that acts as a rational agent. The agent seeks to maximize inhabitant comfort and minimize operation cost. In order to achieve these goals, the agent must be able to predict the mobility patterns and device usages of the inhabitants. Because of the size of the problem, controlling a smart environment can be effectively approached as a multi-agent task. Individual agents can address a portion of the problem but must coordinate their actions to accomplish the overall goals of the system. In this chapter, we discuss the application of multi-agent systems to the challenge of controlling a smart environment and describe its implementation in the MavHome project.

## 1   Introduction

The **MavHome** smart home project is a multi-disciplinary research project at the University of Texas at Arlington focused on the creation of an intelligent and versatile home environment. We define an intelligent environment as one that is able to acquire and apply knowledge about its inhabitants and their surroundings in order to adapt to the inhabitants and meet the goals of comfort and efficiency. Our goal is to create a home that acts as a rational agent, perceiving the state of the home through sensors and acting upon the environment through effectors (in this case, device controllers). The agent acts in a way to maximize its goal, which is a function that maximizes comfort of its inhabitants and minimizes operation cost.

With these capabilities, the home can adaptively control many aspects of the environment such as climate, water, lighting, maintenance, and multimedia entertainment. Intelligent automation of these activities can reduce the amount of interaction required by inhabitants, reduce energy consumption and other potential wastages, and provide a mechanism for ensuring the health and safety of the environment occupants [1].

In order to achieve these goals, the house must be able to reason about and adapt to its inhabitants. In particular, a smart home agent must be able to accurately predict mobility and other activities of its inhabitants. Using these

J.C. Augusto and C.D. Nugent (Eds.): Designing Smart Homes, LNAI 4008, pp. 165–182, 2006.
© Springer-Verlag Berlin Heidelberg 2006

predictions the home can accurately route messages and can automate activities that would otherwise be manually performed by the inhabitants.

MavHome operations can be characterized by the following scenario. At 6:45 am, MavHome turns up the heat because it has learned that the home needs 15 minutes to warm to optimal temperature for waking. The alarm goes off at 7:00, which signals the bedroom light to go on as well as the coffee maker in the kitchen. Bob steps into the bathroom and turns on the light. MavHome records this interaction, displays the morning news on the bathroom video screen, and turns on the shower. While Bob is shaving MavHome senses that Bob has gained two pounds over the last week. MavHome informs Bob that this has been a trend over the last two months and offers suggestions for changing his lifestyle. When Bob finishes grooming, the bathroom light turns off while the blinds in the kitchen and living room open (an energy-efficient alternative to Bob's normal approach of turning on the living room, kitchen, and hallway lights). When Bob leaves for work, MavHome secures the home, lowers the temperature, starts the robot vaccuum, and turns on the lawn sprinklers despite the fact that the Internet forecast predicts a 40% chance of rain. MavHome tracks Bob's activities while he is away from home in order to inform him of problems at home and to have the house temperature and hot tub prepared for his return at 6:00.

A number of capabilities are required for this scenario to occur. For a house to be able to record inhabitant interaction and trigger sequences of events such as the bedroom light / coffee maker sequence, advances in active database techniques are needed. Machine learning techniques are required to predict inhabitant movement patterns and typical activities, and to use that information in automating house decisions and optimizing inhabitant comfort, security, and productivity. In order for MavHome to find him away from the home, mobile computing capabilities must be present.

As can be observed from the scenario, MavHome automates the control of numerous devices within the home. To scale to this size problem, the MavHome agent needs to be decomposed into lower-level agents responsible for subtasks within the home, including robot and sensor agents, and this organization should be dynamically composable. Finally, these capabilities must be organized into a multi-agent architecture that seamlessly connects these components while allowing improvement in any of the underlying technologies.

## 2   Related Research

As the need for automating these personal environments grows, so does the number of researchers investigating this topic. Some, like the MIT AIRE group [2] and the Stanford Interactive Workspaces Project [3], design conference rooms, kiosks, and offices with seamless integration between heterogeneous devices and multiple user applications in order to facilitate collaborate work environments. The Gaia project [4] adds operating system functionality to these spaces, so that the applications do not rely upon hardware or software configurations, and ultimately so that both physical and virtual devices can seamlessly interact.

Abowd and Mynatt's work focuses on ease of interaction with a smart space [5], and work such as the Gator Tech Smart House [6] customizes devices for elder care. The problem has become so recognized that NIST has identified integration of mobile components into smart spaces as a target area for standardization [7].

Mozer's Adaptive Home uses a neural network and reinforcement learning to control lighting, HVAC, and water temperature to reduce operating cost [8], although this may occur at the sacrifice of inhabitant comfort. In contrast, the approach taken by the iDorm project [9] is to use a fuzzy expert system to learn rules that replicate inhabitant interactions with devices, but will not necessarily find an alternative control strategy that improves upon manual control for considerations such as energy expenditure. The interest of industrial labs in smart home and networked appliance technologies is evidenced by the creation of Jini, Bluetooth, and SIP (Session Initiation Protocol) standards, and by supporting technologies such as Xerox PARC's Zombie Board, Microsoft's Easy Living project, the Cisco Internet Home, and the Verizon Connected Family project.

These projects have laid a foundation for our work. However, unlike related projects, we learn a decision policy to control an environment in a way that optimizes a variety of possible criteria, including minimizing manual interactions, improving operating efficiency, and ensuring inhabitant health and safety. We also ensure that our software need not be redesigned as new devices are registered, new spaces are tested, or new inhabitants move into the environment. To accomplish this goal, our intelligent environment must harness the features of multiple heterogeneous learning algorithms in order to identify repeatable behaviors, predict inhabitant activity, and learn a control strategy for a large, complex environment.

## 3   MavHome Architecture

The MavHome architecture is a hierarchy of rational agents which cooperate to meet the goals of the overall home. Figure 1 shows the architecture of a MavHome agent. The technologies within each agent are separated into four cooperating layers. The **Decision** layer selects actions for the agent to execute based on information supplied from other layers. The **Information** layer gathers, stores, and generates knowledge useful for decision making. The **Communication** layer includes software to format and route information between agents, between users and the house, and between the house and external resources. The **Physical** layer contains the basic hardware within the house including individual devices, transducers, and network hardware. Because the architecture is hierarchical, the Physical layer may actually represent another agent in the hierarchy.

Perception is a bottom-up process. Sensors monitor the environment (e.g., lawn moisture level) and, if necessary, transmit the information to another agent through the Communication layer. The database stores this information while other information components process the raw information into more useful knowledge (e.g., patterns, predictions). New information is presented to the Decision layer upon request or by prior arrangement. Action execution information

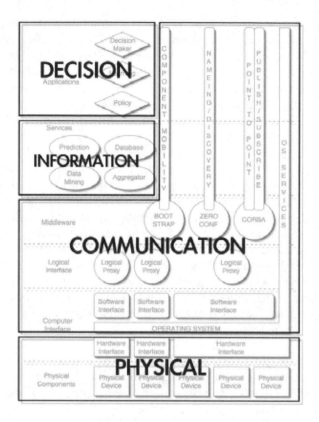

**Fig. 1.** MavHome abstract architecture

flows top down. The Decision layer selects an action (e.g., run the sprinklers) and relates the decision to the Information layer. After updating the database, the Communication layer routes the action to the appropriate effector to execute (e.g., powerline controller). If the effector is actually another agent, the agent receives the command through its effector as perceived information and must decide upon the best method of executing the desired action. A specialized interface agent provides interaction capabilities with users and with external resources such as the Internet. As shown in Figure 2, agents can communicate with parent/child agents or with other agents at the same level in the hierarchy.

The abstract layers of the MavHome architecture are realized through a set of concrete functional layers. These concrete layers are shown with some example components in Figure 3. The base layer is the *Physical Components* layer which consists of all real devices utilized in the system. These devices include powerline control interface hardware, touch screens, gesture input devices, cameras, and so forth, with the exception of the computer with which equipment is interfaced. The physical computer(s) and associated network this system resides on is considered the host of all layers above the physical. The *Computer Interface* layer contains the hardware interfaces to physical devices

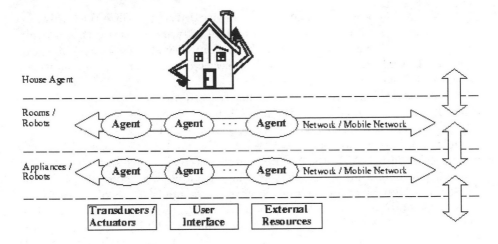

**Fig. 2.** MavHome multi-agent configuration

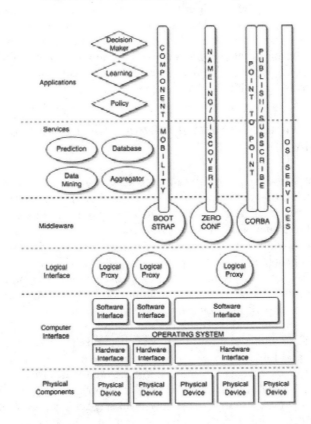

**Fig. 3.** MavHome concrete architecture

(e.g., PCI card interfaces, USB, firewire), device drivers to utilize the hardware, the operating system of the computer, and all software interfaces that provide services or APIs for hardware access. Note that since all components of above layers reside and utilize operating system services, these services are shown to extend to all layers.

In the *Logical Interface* layer, the hardware device services and APIs are utilized to create simple, light-weight programs that create a series of atomic services around each sensor and effector in the system. These *logical proxies* provide information and control via socket and shared memory based interfaces in a modular design. All of the lower layers are based on simple single application components, but in higher layers the components become more complex. The *Middleware* layer provides valuable services to the upper layers of the architecture to facilitate communication, process mobility, and service discovery. The MavHome architecture specifies middleware that provides both point-to-point and publish-subscribe types of communication, naming/service discovery provisions, and a mechanism to move system components between physical computing hardware devices. The *Services* layer utilizes the middleware layer to gather information from lower layers and provide information to system applications above. Services either store information, generate knowledge, aggregate lower level components, or provide some value-added non-decision making computational function or feature (e.g., user interfaces). The *Applications* layer is where learning and decision-making components operate.

# 4 Cooperation of Multiple Agent Components in MavHome

Automation of large, real-world, complex tasks is a pervasive goal of AI algorithms. Researchers develop innovative ideas and test them in simulation. Often, however, these researchers find that the ideas do not scale well or accurately to the larger problem that was initially targeted.

Smart environments represent one such large, real-world problem. Our approach to this problem is to combine the benefits of diverse, heterogeneous machine learning algorithms into a multi-agent system for controlling the environment. We have found that the combination of these algorithms performs better than each algorithm alone, and that the combined whole is effective for automating a complex, real-world home environment.

To automate our smart environment, we collect observations of manual inhabitant activities and interactions with the environment. We then mine sequential patterns from this data using a sequence mining algorithm. Next, we predict the inhabitant's upcoming actions using observed historical data. Finally, a hierarchical Markov model is created using low-level state information and high-level sequential patterns, and is used to learn an action policy for the environment. Figure 4 shows how these components work together to improve the overall performance of the smart environment.

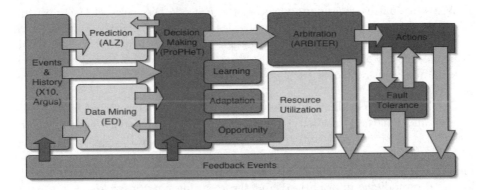

**Fig. 4.** Integration of AI techniques into MavHome architecture

Multi-agent technologies pervade artificial intelligence research [10, 11]. Their benefit to smart environments has been found primarily in unifying the diverse technologies that comprise a working smart environment [12, 13].

In order to create a cooperating multi-agent environment, we need to define a methodology for the agents to share information. MavHome uses the Common Object Request Broker Architecture (CORBA) to communicate between agents because of its clarity of interface design, ease of integration, and object-oriented design. In addition, all agent components register their presence using zero configuration (ZeroConf) technologies, which allows new agents to be dynamically introduced without redesigning the system architecture. Here we describe the learning algorithms that currently comprise the learning agents in MavHome.

### 4.1   Mining Sequential Patterns Using ED

In order to minimize resource usage, maximize comfort, and adapt to inhabitants, we rely upon machine learning techniques for automated discovery, prediction, and decision making. A smart home inhabitant typically interacts with various devices as part of his routine activities. These interactions may be considered as a sequence of events, with some inherent pattern of recurrence. Agrawal and Srikant [14] pioneered work in mining sequential patterns from time-ordered transactions, and our work is loosely modeled on this approach.

Typically, each inhabitant-home interaction event is characterized as a triple consisting of the device manipulated, the resulting change that occurred in that device, and the time of interaction. We move a window in a single pass through the history of events or inhabitant actions, looking for episodes (sequences) within the window that merit attention. Candidate episodes are collected within the window together with frequency information for each candidate. Candidate episodes are evaluated and the episodes with values above a minimum acceptable compression amount are reported. The window size can be selected automatically using the size that achieves the best compression performance over a sample of the input data.

When evaluating candidate episodes, the Episode Discovery (ED) algorithm [15] looks for patterns that minimize the description length of the input stream, $O$, using the Minimum Description Length (MDL) principle [16]. The MDL principle targets patterns that can be used to minimize the description length of a database by replacing each instance of the pattern with a pointer to the pattern definition.

Our MDL-based evaluation measure thus identifies patterns that balance frequency and length. Periodicity (daily, every other day, weekly occurrence) of episodes is detected using autocorrelation and included in the episode description. If the instances of a pattern are highly periodic (occur at predictable intervals), the exact timings do not need to be encoded (just the pattern definition with periodicity information) and the resulting pattern yields even greater compression. Although event sequences with minor deviations from the pattern definition can be included as pattern instances, the deviations need to be encoded and the result thus increases the overall description length. ED reports the patterns and encodings that yield the greatest MDL value.

Deviations from the pattern definition in terms of missing events, extra events, or changes in the regularity of the occurrence add to the description length because extra bits must be used to encode the change, thus lowering the value of the pattern. The larger the potential amount of description length compression a pattern provides, the more representative the pattern is of the history as a whole, and thus the potential impact that results from automating the pattern is greater.

In this way, ED identifies patterns of events that can be used to better understand the nature of inhabitant activity in the environment. Once the data is compressed using discovered results, ED can be run again to find an abstraction hierarchy of patterns within the event data. As the following sections show, the results can also be used to enhance performance of predictors and decision makers that automate the environment.

## 4.2   Predicting Activities Using ALZ

To predict inhabitant activities, we borrow ideas from text compression, in this case the LZ78 compression algorithm [17]. By predicting inhabitant actions, the home can automate or improve upon anticipated events that inhabitants would normally perform in the home. Well-investigated text compression methods have established that good compression algorithms also make good predictors. According to information theory, a predictor with an order (size of history used) that grows at a rate approximating the entropy rate of the source is an optimal predictor. Other approaches to prediction or inferring activities often use a fixed context size to build the model or focus on one attribute such as motion [18,19].

LZ78 incrementally processes an input string of characters, which in our case is a string representing the history of device interactions, and stores them in a trie. The algorithm parses the string $x_1, x_2, \ldots, x_i$ into substrings $w_1, w_2, w_{c(i)}$ such that for all $j > 0$, the prefix of the substring $w_j$ is equal to some $w_i$ for $1 < i < j$. Thus when parsing the sequence of symbols $aaababbbbbaabccddcbaaaa$, the substring $a$ is created, followed by $aa$, $b$, $ab$, $bb$, $bba$, and so forth.

Our Active LeZi (ALZ) algorithm enhances the LZ78 algorithm by recapturing information lost across phrase boundaries. Frequency of symbols is stored along with phrase information in a trie, and information from multiple context sizes are combined to provide the probability for each potential symbol, or inhabitant action, as being the next one to occur. In effect, ALZ gradually changes the order of the corresponding model that is used to predict the next symbol in the sequence. As a result, we gain a better convergence rate to optimal predictability as well as achieve greater predictive accuracy. Figure 5 shows the trie formed by the Active-LeZi parsing of the input sequence *aaababbbbbaabccddcbaaaa*.

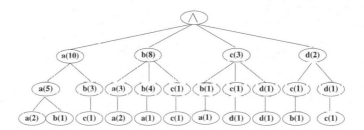

**Fig. 5.** Trie formed by ALZ parsing

To perform prediction, ALZ calculates the probability of each symbol (inhabitant action) occurring in the parsed sequence, and predicts the action with the highest probability. To achieve optimal predictability, we use a mixture of all possible higher-order models (phrase sizes) when determining the probability estimate. Specifically, we incorporate the Prediction by Partial Match strategy of *exclusion* [20] to gather information from all available context sizes in assigning the next symbol its probability value.

We initially evaluated the ability of ALZ to perform inhabitant action prediction on synthetic data based on six embedded tasks with 20% noise. In this case the predictive accuracy converges to 86%. Real data collected based on six students in the MavLab for one month was much more chaotic, and on this data ALZ reached a predictive performance of 30% (although it outperformed other methods). However, when we combine ALZ and ED by only performing predictions when the current activity is part of a sequential pattern identified by ED, ALZ performance increases by 14% [21].

### 4.3   Decision Making Using ProPHeT

In our final learning step, we employ reinforcement learning to generate an automation strategy for the intelligent environment. To apply reinforcement learning, the underlying system (i.e., the house and its inhabitants) could be modeled as a Markov Decision Process (MDP). This can be described by a four-tuple $< S, A, Pr, R >$, where $S$ is a set of system states, $A$ is the set of available actions, and $R : S \rightarrow R$ is the reward that the learning agent receives for

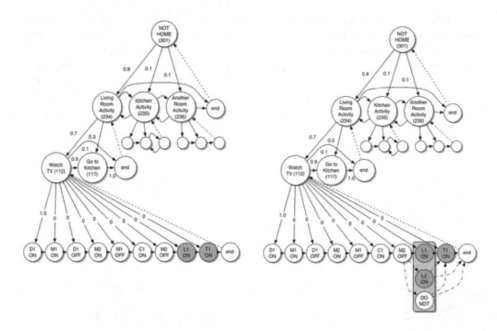

**Fig. 6.** Hierarchical model constructed from static (left) and dynamic (right) smart home data

being in a given state. The behavior of the MDP is described by the transition function, $Pr : S \times A \times S \rightarrow [0,1]$, representing the probability with which action $a_t$ executed in state $s_t$ leads to state $s_{t+1}$.

With the increasing complexity of tasks being addressed, recent work in decision making under uncertainty has popularized the use of Partially Observable Markov Decision Processes (POMDPs). Recently, there have been many published hierarchical extensions that allow for the partitioning of large domains into a tree of manageable POMDPs [22, 23]. Research has shown that strategies for new tasks can be learned faster if policies for subtasks are already available [24]. Although a Hierarchical POMDP (HPOMDP) is appropriate for an intelligent environment domain, current approaches generally require *a priori* construction of the hierarchical model. Unlike other approaches to creating a hierarchical model, our decision learner, ProPHeT, actually automates model creation by using the ED-mined sequences to represent the nodes in the higher levels of the model hierarchy.

The lowest-level nodes in our model represent a single event observed by ED. Next, ED is run multiple iterations on this data until no more patterns can be identified, and the corresponding abstract patterns comprise the higher-level nodes in the Markov model. The higher-level *task* nodes point to the first event node for each permutation of the sequence that is found in the environment history. Vertical transition values are labeled with the fraction of occurrences for the corresponding pattern permutation, and horizontal transitions are seeded using the relative frequency of transitions from one event to the next in the observed history. As a result, the $n$-tier hierarchical model is thus learned from collected data. An example hierarchical model constructed from MavHome test data is shown on the left in Figure 6.

Given the current event state and recent history, ED supplies membership probabilities of the state in each of the identified patterns. Using this information along with the ALZ-predicted next action, ProPHeT maintains a belief state and selects the highest-utility action.

To learn an automation strategy, the agent explores the effects of its decisions over time and uses this experience within a temporal-difference reinforcement learning framework [25] to form control policies which optimize the expected future reward. The current version of MavHome receives negative reinforcement (observes a negative reward) when the inhabitant immediately reverses an automation decision (e.g., turns the light back off) or an automation decision contradicts ARBITER-supplied safety and comfort constraints.

Before an action is executed it is checked against the policies in the policy engine, ARBITER. These policies contain designed safety and security knowledge and inhabitant standing rules. Through the policy engine the system is prevented from engaging in erroneous actions that may perform actions such as turning the heater to 120°F or from violating the inhabitant's stated wishes (e.g., a standing rule to never turn off the inhabitant's night light).

## 5   Initial Case Study

All of the MavHome components are implemented and are being tested in two physical environments, the MavLab workplace environment and an on-campus apartment, the MavPad (portions of the environments are shown in Figure 7. Powerline control automates all lights and appliances, as well as HVAC, fans, and miniblinds. Perception of light, humidity, temperature, smoke, gas, motion, and switch settings is performed through a sensor network developed in-house. Inhabitant localization is performed using passive infrared sensors yielding a detection rate of 95% accuracy [26].

**Fig. 7.** The MavLab (left) and MavPad (right) environments

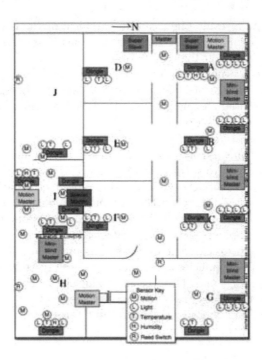

**Fig. 8.** MavLab sensor layout

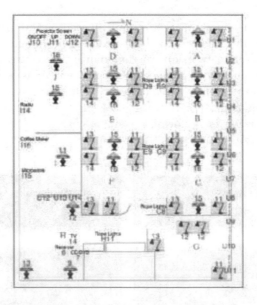

**Fig. 9.** MavLab actuator layout

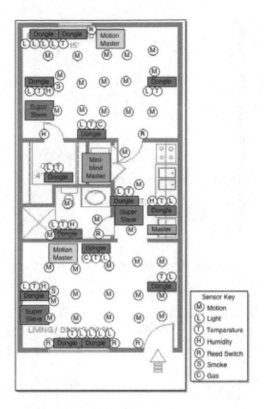

**Fig. 10.** MavPad sensor layout

The MavLab environment contains work areas, cubicles, a break area, a lounge, and a conference room. MavLab is automated using 54 X-10 controllers and the current state is determined using light, temperature, humidity, motion, and door/seat status sensors (see Figures 8 and 9). The MavPad is an on-campus apartment hosting a full-time student occupant. MavPad is automated using 25 controllers and provides sensing for light, temperature, humidity, leak detection, vent position, smoke detection, CO detection, motion, and door/window/seat status sensors. Figures 10 and 11 show the MavPad sensor and actuator layout. MavHome is designed to optimize a number of alternative functions, but for this evaluation we focus on minimization of manual interactions with devices.

As an illustration of the above techniques, we have evaluated a week in an inhabitant's life with the goal of reducing the manual interactions in the MavLab. The data was generated from a virtual inhabitant based on captured data from the MavLab and was restricted to just motion and lighting interactions which account for an average of 1400 events per day.

ALZ processed the data and converged to 99.99% accuracy after 10 iterations through the training data. When automation decisions were made using ALZ alone, interactions were reduced by 9.7% on average. Next, ED processed the data and found three episodes to use as abstract nodes in the HPOMDP. Living

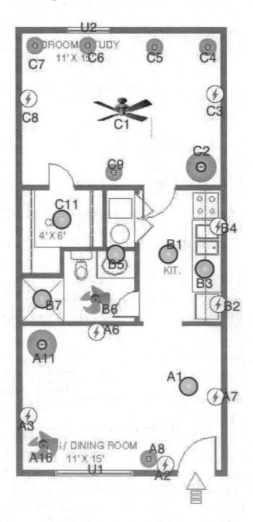

**Fig. 11.** MavPad actuator layout

room patterns consisted of lab entry and exit patterns with light interactions, and the office also reflected entry and exit patterns. The other patterns occurred over the remaining 8 areas and usually involved light interactions at desks and some equipment upkeep activity patterns. The hierarchical Markov model with no abstract nodes reduced interactions by 38.3%, and the combined-learning system (ProPHeT bootstrapped using ED and ALZ) was able to reduce interactions by 76%, as shown in Figure 12 (left).

Experimentation in the MavPad using real inhabitant data has yielded similar results. In this case, ALZ alone reduced interactions from 18 to 17 events, the HPOMDP with no abstract nodes reduced interactions by 33.3% to 12 events, while the bootstrapped HPOMDP reduced interactions by 72.2% to 5 events. These results are graphed in Figure 12 (right).

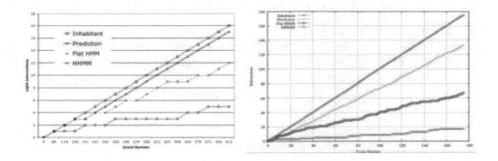

**Fig. 12.** Interaction reduction

# 6    Using a Multi-agent Smart Home to Assist Elderly and Disabled

An important application of the multi-agent technologies available in MavHome is to provide health care assistance in living environments. Specifically, models can be constructed of inhabitant activities and used to learn activity trends, detect anomalies, intelligently predict possible problems and make health care decisions, and provide automation assistance for inhabitants with special needs.

A variety of approaches have been investigated in recent years to automate caregiver services. Many of the efforts offer supporting technologies in specialized areas, such as using computer vision techniques to track inhabitants through the environment and specialized sensors to detect falls or other crises. Some special-purpose prediction algorithms have been implemented using factors such as measurement of stand-sit and sit-stand transitions and medical history [27, 28, 29], but are limited in terms of what they predict and how they use the results. Remote monitoring systems have been designed with the common motivation that learning and predicting inhabitant activities is key for health monitoring, but very little work has combined the remote monitoring capabilities with prediction for the purpose of health monitoring. Some work has also progressed toward using typical behavior patterns to provide reminders, particularly useful for the elderly and patients suffering from various types of dementia [30, 31].

Our smart environment can identify patterns indicating or predicting a change in health status and can provide inhabitants with needed automation assistance. Collected data includes movement patterns of the individual, periodic vital signs (blood pressure, pulse, body temperature), water and device usage, use of food items in the kitchen, exercise regimen, medicine intake (prescribed and actual), and sleep patterns [32, 1]. Given this data, models can be constructed of inhabitant activities and use to learn lifestyle trends, detect anomalies, and provide reminder and automation assistance.

## 6.1  Capability 1: Identify Lifestyle Trends

Our ED algorithm is designed to process data as it arrives. Because of this feature, trends in the data including increasing / decreasing pattern frequency, introduction of patterns, and change in pattern details can be automatically detected [33]. When changing patterns include health-specific events (vital signs, medication intake, or events targeted by the caregiver), a report will be given to the inhabitant and caregiver of these trends.

## 6.2  Capability 2: Detect Anomalies in Current Data

The ED data mining algorithm and ALZ predictor can work together to detect anomalies in event data. ED identifies the most significant and frequent patterns of inhabitant behavior, as well as the likelihood that the current state is a member of one of these patterns. Whenever the current state falls within one of these patterns, ALZ can determine the probability distribution of next events. As a result, when the next event has a low probability of occurrence, or when the expected next event does not occur at the expected time, the result is considered an anomaly.

When an anomaly occurs, the home will first try to contact the inhabitant (through the interactive display for a lesser critical anomaly, or through the sound system for a more critical anomaly). If the inhabitant does not respond and the criticality of the anomaly is high, the caregiver will be

## 6.3  Capability 3: Design Reminder Assistance System

Reminders can be triggered by two situations. First, if the inhabitant queries the home for his next routine activity, the activity with the highest probability will be given based on the ALZ prediction. Second, if a critical anomaly is detected, the environment will initiate contact with the inhabitant and remind him of the next typical activity. Such a reminder service will be particularly beneficial for individuals suffering from dementia.

As described in the initial MavHome design, automation assistance is always available for inhabitants, which is beneficial if some activities are difficult to perform. A useful feature of the architecture is that safety constraints are embedded in the ARBITER rule engine. If the inhabitant or the environment is about to conflict with these constraints, a preventative action is taken and the inhabitant notified. This can prevent accidents such as forgetting to turn off the water in the bathtub or leaving the house with doors unlocked.

# 7  Conclusion

The MavHome software architecture has successfully monitored and provided automation assistance for volunteers living in the MavPad site. We are currently collecting health-specific data and in the MavHome sites and will be testing in recruited residents of the C.C. Young Retirement Community in Dallas, Texas.

# Acknowledgements

This work is supported by US National Science Foundation under ITR grant IIS-0121297.

# References

1. Das, S.K., Cook, D.J.: Health monitoring in an agent-based smart home by activity predition. In Zhang, D., Mokhari, M., eds.: Toward a Human-Friendly Assistive Environment. IOS Press (2004) 3–14
2. AIRE Group: MIT Project AIRE – About Us (2004) http://www.ai.mit.edu/projects/aire.
3. Fox, A., Johanson, B., Hanrahan, P., Winograd, T.: Integrating information appliances into an interactive space. IEEE Computer Graphics and Applications 20 (2000) 54–65
4. Romn, M., Hess, C.K., Cerqueira, R., Ranganathan, A., Campbell, R.H., Nahrstedt, K.: Gaia: A middleware infrastructure to enable active spaces. IEEE Pervasive Computing (2002) 74–83
5. Abowd, G.D., Mynatt, E.D.: Designing for the human experience in smart environments. In Cook, D.J., Das, S.K., eds.: Smart Environments: Technology, Protocols, and Applications. Wiley (2005) 153–174
6. Helal, A., Mann, W., El-Zabadani, H., King, J., Kaddoura, Y., Jansen, E.: The gator tech smart house: A programmable pervasive space. IEEE Computer 38 (2005) 50–60
7. NIST: Smart space NIST laboratory. http://www.nist.gov/smartspace/ (2005)
8. Mozer, M.C.: Lessons from an adaptive home. In Cook, D.J., Das, S.K., eds.: Smart Environments: Technology, Protocols, and Applications. Wiley (2005) 273–298
9. Hagras, H., Callaghan, V., Colley, M., Clarke, G., Pounds-Cornish, A., Duman, H.: Creating an ambient-intelligence environment using embedded agents. IEEE Intelligent Systems 19 (2004)
10. Adams, J.A.: Multiagent systems: A modern approach to distributed artificial intelligence. AI Magazine 22 (2001) 105–108
11. Stone, P., Veloso, M.: Multiagent systems: A survey from a machine learning perspective. Autonomous Robots 8 (2000) 345–383
12. CSIRO: Intelligent interactive technology. http://www.cmis.csiro.au/iit/ (2005)
13. Haigh, K.Z., Phelps, J., Geib, C.W.: An open agent architecture for assisting elder independence. In: Proceedings of the First International Joint Conference on autonomous Agents and Multiagent Systems. (2002) 578–586
14. Agrawal, R., Srikant, R.: Mining Sequential Patterns. In: Proceedings of the 11th International Conference on Data Engineering. (1995) 3–14
15. Heierman, E.O., Cook, D.J.: Improving home automation by discovering regularly occurring device usage patterns. In: Proceedings of the International Conference on Data Mining. (2003)
16. Rissanen, J.: Stochastic Complexity in Statistical inquiry. World Scientific Publishing Company (1989)
17. Ziv, J., Lempel, A.: Compression of individual sequences via variable rate coding. IEEE Transactions on Information Theory IT-24 (1978) 530–536
18. Cielniak, G., Bennewitz, M., Burgard, W.: Where is ...? learning and utilizing motion patterns of persons with mobile robots. In: Proceedings of the Eighteenth International Joint Conference on Artificial Intelligence. (2003) 909–914

19. Philipose, M., Fishkin, K., Perkowitz, M., Patterson, D., Fox, D., Kautz, H., Hahnel, D.: Inferring activities from interactions with objects. Pervasive Computing **3** (2004) 50–56
20. Bell, T.C., Cleary, J.G., Witten, I.H.: Text compression. Prentice Hall (1990)
21. Gopalratnam, K., Cook, D.J.: Online sequential prediction via incremental parsing: The Active LeZi algorithm. IEEE Intelligent Systems (2005)
22. Pineau, J., Roy, N., Thrun, S.: A Hierarchical Approach to POMDP Planning and Execution (2001) Workshop on Hierarchy and Memory in Reinforcement Learning (ICML).
23. Theocharous, G., Rohanimanesh, K., Mahadevan, S.: Learning Hierarchical Partially Observable Markov Decision Processes for Robot Navigation (2001) IEEE Conference on Robotics and Automation.
24. Precup, D., Sutton, R.S.: Multi-time models for temporally abstract planning. Advances in Neural Information Processing Systems **10** (1997) 1050–1056
25. Sutton, R.S., Barto, A.G.: Reinforcement Learning: An Introduction. MIT Press, Cambridge, MA (1998)
26. Youngblood, G.M., Holder, L.B., Cook, D.J.: A learning architecture for automating the intelligent environment. In: to appear in Proceedings of the Conference on Innovative Applications of Artificial Intelligence. (2005)
27. Cameron, K., Hughes, K., Doughty, K.: Reducing fall incidence in community elders by telecare using predictive systems. In: Proceedings of the International IEEE-EMBS Conference. (1997) 1036–1039
28. Najafi, B., Aminian, K., Loew, F., Blanc, Y., Robert, P.: Measurement of stand-sit and sit-stand transitions using a miniature gyroscope and its application in fall risk evaluation in the elderly. IEEE Transactions on Biomedical Engineering **49** (2002) 843–851
29. Najafi, B., Aminian, K., Paraschiv-Ionescu, A., Loew, F., Bula, C., Robert, P.: Ambulatory system for human motion analysis using a kinematic sensor: Monitoring of daily physical activity in the elderly. IEEE Transactions on Biomedical Engineering **50** (2003) 711–723
30. Kautz, H., Arnstein, L., Borriello, G., Etzioni, O., Fox, D.: An overview of the assisted cognition project. In: Proceedings of the AAAI workshop on automation as caregiver. (2002)
31. Pollack, M.E., Brown, L., Colbry, D., McCarthy, C.E., Orosz, C., Peintner, B., Ramakrishnan, S., Tsamardinos, I.: Autoreminder: An intelligent cognitive orthotic system for people with memory impairment. Robotics and Autonomous Systems **44** (2003) 273–282
32. Das, S.K., Cook, D.J.: Health monitoring in an agent-based smart home. In: Proceedings of the International Conference on Smart Homes and Health Telematics (ICOST). (2004)
33. Heierman, E.O.: Using information-theoretic principles to discover interesting episodes in a time-ordered sequence. PhD thesis, The University of Texas at Arlington (2004)

# Author Index

# Lecture Notes in Artificial Intelligence (LNAI)

Vol. 3848: J.-F. Boulicaut, L. De Raedt, H. Mannila (Eds.), Constraint-Based Mining and Inductive Databases. X, 401 pages. 2006.

Vol. 3847: K.P. Jantke, A. Lunzer, N. Spyratos, Y. Tanaka (Eds.), Federation over the Web. X, 215 pages. 2006.

Vol. 3835: G. Sutcliffe, A. Voronkov (Eds.), Logic for Programming, Artificial Intelligence, and Reasoning. XIV, 744 pages. 2005.

Vol. 3830: D. Weyns, H. V.D. Parunak, F. Michel (Eds.), Environments for Multi-Agent Systems II. VIII, 291 pages. 2006.

Vol. 3817: M. Faundez-Zanuy, L. Janer, A. Esposito, A. Satue-Villar, J. Roure, V. Espinosa-Duro (Eds.), Nonlinear Analyses and Algorithms for Speech Processing. XII, 380 pages. 2006.

Vol. 3814: M. Maybury, O. Stock, W. Wahlster (Eds.), Intelligent Technologies for Interactive Entertainment. XV, 342 pages. 2005.

Vol. 3809: S. Zhang, R. Jarvis (Eds.), AI 2005: Advances in Artificial Intelligence. XXVII, 1344 pages. 2005.

Vol. 3808: C. Bento, A. Cardoso, G. Dias (Eds.), Progress in Artificial Intelligence. XVIII, 704 pages. 2005.

Vol. 3802: Y. Hao, J. Liu, Y.-P. Wang, Y.-m. Cheung, H. Yin, L. Jiao, J. Ma, Y.-C. Jiao (Eds.), Computational Intelligence and Security, Part II. XLII, 1166 pages. 2005.

Vol. 3801: Y. Hao, J. Liu, Y.-P. Wang, Y.-m. Cheung, H. Yin, L. Jiao, J. Ma, Y.-C. Jiao (Eds.), Computational Intelligence and Security, Part I. XLI, 1122 pages. 2005.

Vol. 3789: A. Gelbukh, Á. de Albornoz, H. Terashima-Marín (Eds.), MICAI 2005: Advances in Artificial Intelligence. XXVI, 1198 pages. 2005.

Vol. 3782: K.-D. Althoff, A. Dengel, R. Bergmann, M. Nick, T.R. Roth-Berghofer (Eds.), Professional Knowledge Management. XXIII, 739 pages. 2005.

Vol. 3763: H. Hong, D. Wang (Eds.), Automated Deduction in Geometry. X, 213 pages. 2006.

Vol. 3755: G.J. Williams, S.J. Simoff (Eds.), Data Mining. XI, 331 pages. 2006.

Vol. 3735: A. Hoffmann, H. Motoda, T. Scheffer (Eds.), Discovery Science. XVI, 400 pages. 2005.

Vol. 3734: S. Jain, H.U. Simon, E. Tomita (Eds.), Algorithmic Learning Theory. XII, 490 pages. 2005.

Vol. 3721: A.M. Jorge, L. Torgo, P.B. Brazdil, R. Camacho, J. Gama (Eds.), Knowledge Discovery in Databases: PKDD 2005. XXIII, 719 pages. 2005.

Vol. 3720: J. Gama, R. Camacho, P.B. Brazdil, A.M. Jorge, L. Torgo (Eds.), Machine Learning: ECML 2005. XXIII, 769 pages. 2005.

Vol. 3717: B. Gramlich (Ed.), Frontiers of Combining Systems. X, 321 pages. 2005.

Vol. 3702: B. Beckert (Ed.), Automated Reasoning with Analytic Tableaux and Related Methods. XIII, 343 pages. 2005.

Vol. 3698: U. Furbach (Ed.), KI 2005: Advances in Artificial Intelligence. XIII, 409 pages. 2005.

Vol. 3690: M. Pěchouček, P. Petta, L.Z. Varga (Eds.), Multi-Agent Systems and Applications IV. XVII, 667 pages. 2005.

Vol. 3684: R. Khosla, R.J. Howlett, L.C. Jain (Eds.), Knowledge-Based Intelligent Information and Engineering Systems, Part IV. LXXIX, 933 pages. 2005.

Vol. 3683: R. Khosla, R.J. Howlett, L.C. Jain (Eds.), Knowledge-Based Intelligent Information and Engineering Systems, Part III. LXXX, 1397 pages. 2005.

Vol. 3682: R. Khosla, R.J. Howlett, L.C. Jain (Eds.), Knowledge-Based Intelligent Information and Engineering Systems, Part II. LXXIX, 1371 pages. 2005.

Vol. 3681: R. Khosla, R.J. Howlett, L.C. Jain (Eds.), Knowledge-Based Intelligent Information and Engineering Systems, Part I. LXXX, 1319 pages. 2005.

Vol. 3673: S. Bandini, S. Manzoni (Eds.), AI*IA 2005: Advances in Artificial Intelligence. XIV, 614 pages. 2005.

Vol. 3662: C. Baral, G. Greco, N. Leone, G. Terracina (Eds.), Logic Programming and Nonmonotonic Reasoning. XIII, 454 pages. 2005.

Vol. 3661: T. Panayiotopoulos, J. Gratch, R. Aylett, D. Ballin, P. Olivier, T. Rist (Eds.), Intelligent Virtual Agents. XIII, 506 pages. 2005.

Vol. 3658: V. Matoušek, P. Mautner, T. Pavelka (Eds.), Text, Speech and Dialogue. XV, 460 pages. 2005.

Vol. 3651: R. Dale, K.-F. Wong, J. Su, O.Y. Kwong (Eds.), Natural Language Processing – IJCNLP 2005. XXI, 1031 pages. 2005.

Vol. 3642: D. Ślęzak, J. Yao, J.F. Peters, W. Ziarko, X. Hu (Eds.), Rough Sets, Fuzzy Sets, Data Mining, and Granular Computing, Part II. XXIII, 738 pages. 2005.

Vol. 3641: D. Ślęzak, G. Wang, M. Szczuka, I. Düntsch, Y. Yao (Eds.), Rough Sets, Fuzzy Sets, Data Mining, and Granular Computing, Part I. XXIV, 742 pages. 2005.

Vol. 3635: J.R. Winkler, M. Niranjan, N.D. Lawrence (Eds.), Deterministic and Statistical Methods in Machine Learning. VIII, 341 pages. 2005.

Vol. 3632: R. Nieuwenhuis (Ed.), Automated Deduction – CADE-20. XIII, 459 pages. 2005.

Vol. 3630: M.S. Capcarrère, A.A. Freitas, P.J. Bentley, C.G. Johnson, J. Timmis (Eds.), Advances in Artificial Life. XIX, 949 pages. 2005.

Vol. 3626: B. Ganter, G. Stumme, R. Wille (Eds.), Formal Concept Analysis. X, 349 pages. 2005.

Vol. 3625: S. Kramer, B. Pfahringer (Eds.), Inductive Logic Programming. XIII, 427 pages. 2005.

Vol. 3620: H. Muñoz-Ávila, F. Ricci (Eds.), Case-Based Reasoning Research and Development. XV, 654 pages. 2005.

Vol. 3614: L. Wang, Y. Jin (Eds.), Fuzzy Systems and Knowledge Discovery, Part II. XLI, 1314 pages. 2005.

Vol. 3613: L. Wang, Y. Jin (Eds.), Fuzzy Systems and Knowledge Discovery, Part I. XLI, 1334 pages. 2005.

Vol. 3607: J.-D. Zucker, L. Saitta (Eds.), Abstraction, Reformulation and Approximation. XII, 376 pages. 2005.

Vol. 3601: G. Moro, S. Bergamaschi, K. Aberer (Eds.), Agents and Peer-to-Peer Computing. XII, 245 pages. 2005.

Vol. 3600: F. Wiedijk (Ed.), The Seventeen Provers of the World. XVI, 159 pages. 2006.